Journey To The River

The political and engineering challenges endured to build the Tennessee-Tombigbee Waterway

Donald G. Waldon

Journey to the River © copyright, 2025, Donald G. Waldon. All rights reserved. No part of this book may be reproduced without the express, written consent of the publisher except in the case of a brief quotations embodied in critical articles or reviews.

Cover design by Nautilus Publishing
For information, contact Nautilus Publishing, 155 CR 418, Oxford, MS 38655
ISBN: 978-1-949455-71-7
First Edition
Printed in the United States of America

This book is dedicated to those individuals throughout the long history of the Tennessee-Tombigbee Waterway whose influence, leadership, and stewardship helped make it a reality. Some of those waterway champions are noted in this memoir; but others were likely not recognized for their important contributions. I apologize for such unintentional oversights.

CONTENTS

Preface 7

Acknowledgements 11

CHAPTER I
First Introduction to Tenn-Tom 13

CHAPTER II
"Mr. Smith" Goes to Washington 27

CHAPTER III
Genesis of the Tenn-Tom Compact...................................... 41

CHAPTER IV
Johnson Endorses Tenn-Tom 55

CHAPTER V
My First Budget Season 57

CHAPTER VI
Nukes To Build Tenn-Tom? 61

CHAPTER VII
Times of Uncertainty 65

CHAPTER VIII
The Nixon Years 69

CHAPTER IX
Tenn-Tom Goes To Court 81

CHAPTER X
Learning on the Job 87

CHAPTER XI
Time to Move On 99

CHAPTER XII
From the Pan into the Fire 105

CONTENTS

CHAPTER XIII
Time Again To Move On 123

CHAPTER XIV
A Behemoth Endeavor 129

CHAPTER XV
Construction's Local Benefits 145

CHAPTER XVI
Bridges Too Far? 151

CHAPTER XVII
Carter's Hit List 159

CHAPTER XVIII
Back In The Courts 175

CHAPTER XIX
The Last Battle 191

CHAPTER XX
Changing of the Guard 221

CHAPTER XXI
Mother of All Celebrations 233

CHAPTER XXII
Setting New, Higher Standards 249

CHAPTER XXIII
If You Build It, Will They Come? 275

CHAPTER XXIV
The Authority, One of a Kind 303

Epilogue 311

Appendices 319

Index 337

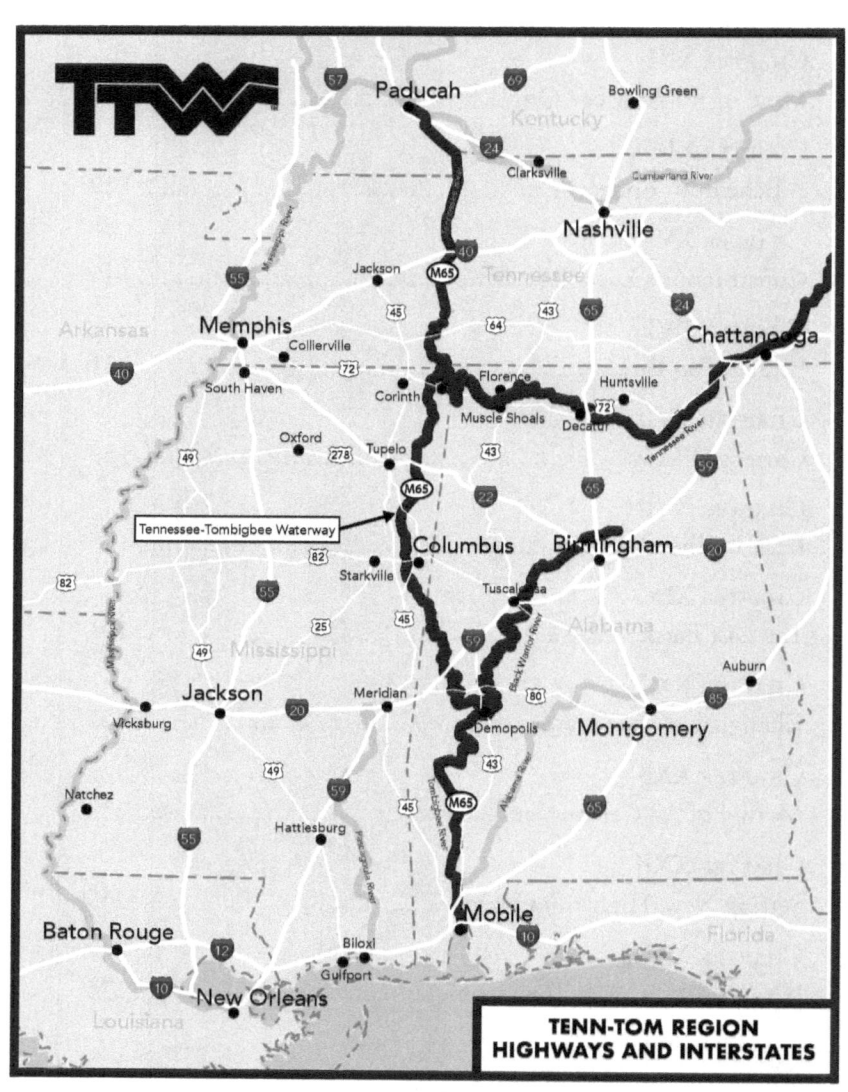

It Had More Champions Than Enemies

Preface

It was warm and sunny in Mobile, Alabama, on that Christmas Eve in 1949 when an adventurous 12-year-old boy and his friends rigged up a new "ride" at the neighborhood park. The industrious boys lashed one end of a long steel cable to the base of a pine tree and tied the other end around a sprawling live oak that stood some 30 feet tall. Onto the cable, they threaded a hollow pipe so that a rider would have something to hang from as he sped down the cable.

With pride, my friends and I surveyed our contraption, a crude forerunner of a modern-day zip line.

Since building the thing had been my idea, I insisted on taking the inaugural ride. With not an ounce of fear, I climbed the live oak, and my friends slung the pipe up to me. Taking a deep breath, I leapt from the tree like a fledgling bird leaving its nest. My flight, though, was short-lived. Just a few feet from the tree, the pipe hit a kink in the cable, and it suddenly stopped, causing me to lose my grip. I made a swan dive headfirst from near the top of the tree. I threw my arms in front of me to help break my fall. Luckily, I just missed landing in an empty cement wading pool.

When I regained consciousness, my friends were hovering over me. Both my arms had bones protruding through the skin near my wrists, and I bled from my nose and mouth. I asked my friends to help me home, which was only a couple of blocks away. Apparently in a state of shock, they said they'd have to take the ride down first, before someone got hurt!

Trying to hold one broken arm with the other, I managed to get within sight of my house before I passed out again. My next memory was of being jarred to consciousness when my father crossed a bumpy railroad track as he rushed me to the hospital. To make matters worse, the emergency room doctor and attendants apparently had been imbibing, because their work had to be redone. Some weeks later, I had to have both arms reset with new casts that encased both forearms and hands to the tips of my fingers.

With both hands useless, I could not dress or feed myself and needed help to use the bathroom. My younger brother, Dan, served as my "hands" for all my needs. Whenever I'd call from the bathroom for his help, I would hear the back screened door slamming as he rushed outside to avoid the unpleasant chore of tending to me. After my pleading, he would eventually come back to help.

Attending school was especially challenging. Classmates would help carry my books, but at lunch in the cafeteria, I refused to lap up my food like a dog or ask someone to feed me. Instead, I would sneak across the street to a mom-and-pop store where I could buy a snack that I could manage to eat without help. I knew it was against the rules to leave the school grounds, but other students routinely went to the store during lunch, including those who smoked — yes, even at that young age — where they could buy a cigarette for two cents.

One day I was there trying to hold and eat a candy bar when the school principal walked in. All the students, including me, rushed out the back door, trying to avoid getting caught. It was dumb of me to think I might go unnoticed. How many kids at school had two broken arms? When I returned to class, the principal was there waiting for me. I pleaded my case, telling him that I did not smoke and was there only to get something to eat, but still, he suspended me for two days — my first and only time to incur such punishment.

Three months passed before doctors removed my casts, and I could once again use my arms and hands. My doctor told me not to play any contact sports for at least three years so that my arms could fully heal and so I could avoid the risk of another fracture, which could result my losing a limb. As much as I loved sports, including football, I complied with the doctor's advice until my junior year in high school.

This nearly fatal mishap on a homemade zip line would play a role in connecting me to the Tennessee-Tombigbee Waterway and a career with the waterway that would span the better part of six decades.

The Tennessee-Tombigbee Waterway (Tenn-Tom) has a long and storied history. The concept of connecting these two rivers for transporting commerce dates back to the mid-1700s. Folklore credits the French explorer, the Marquis De Montcalm, for recommending to King Louis XV the need for such a canal to help expand French settlements in the territory now called the state of Tennessee. At about that same time, another Frenchman, Jean-Baptiste Le Moyne, Sieur-de Bienville, who had established settlements in New Orleans, Biloxi, and Mobile during the early 1700s, was exploring the lands along the Tombigbee River as far north as today's Northeast Mississippi. During these ventures, his troops built Fort Tombecbe on the bank of the Tombigbee some 270 miles upriver from Mobile in what is now Sumter County, Alabama, near the town of Epes. The stockade/trading post helped the French lay claim to that part of the new world before the English could, while also facilitating trade with the Choctaw Indians.

Before the advent of railroads, rivers and streams were the primary means of transporting goods. Shortly after Tennessee became a state in 1796, early settlers recognized the need for a waterway route connecting the Tennessee River to the Tombigbee River to help generate more commerce and trade opportunities with the more populated areas along the eastern Gulf Coast. In 1810, the citizens of Knox County, Tennessee, were the first to formally petition the U.S. Congress to build such a connection. However, more than 50 years lapsed, and it was during President Ulysses S. Grant's administration that the Corps of Engineers would conduct its first study of the proposed waterway. Numerous studies would follow to investigate possible routes for the waterway, including a connection with the

Tennessee River via the Black Warrior River and the Bear Creek watershed in north Alabama and another route that would utilize the Coosa-Alabama River watershed in Northeast Alabama and Georgia to connect with the Tennessee River near Chattanooga.

None of these studies were optimistic about the economic feasibility of undertaking such a herculean engineering feat. Finally, in the late 1930s, the Corps recommended construction of a waterway to follow the present route of the Tombigbee River. The work of the Tennessee Valley Authority (TVA) to develop commercial navigation on the Tennessee River at that time was a major contributing factor in strengthening the economic worth of connecting the Tombigbee River with the Tennessee.

Then came a war. Most water resources development, including the Tenn-Tom, was shelved during World War II. In 1946 the U.S. Congress finally authorized construction of the Tenn-Tom. Another generation passed before President Richard Nixon included funds in his 1972 fiscal year budget to start construction of the waterway. Still, the project continued to face myriad obstacles and challenges. A railroad group and a group of environmentalists filed landmark lawsuits. Additionally, a cadre of members of Congress where hell-bent on stopping the funding. The waterway, despite that opposition, was completed in December 1984 at a cost of nearly $2 billion.

Over the past 60 years, I was involved in and was a witness to the planning and construction of the waterway, which has become an integral part of the nation's inland water transportation system. Regrettably, the details of some of the Tenn-Tom's more important milestones and the names of the people involved were not recorded because of the sensitive nature of deliberations that occurred at the highest levels of government. Friends and waterway associates have asked me to share my recollections of my many years associated with the waterway. This is my attempt to do so.

Acknowledgements

The accounts that I have described herein are based mainly on personal recollections, since I was intimately involved in so many of them or was a witness to them. At times, I have checked or verified dates and other details of events by referencing other primary sources. For example, I relied heavily on the publication, "The Tennessee-Tombigbee Waterway: A Case Study in the Politics of Water Transportation," by W.B. Stewart, Jr., in describing the early years of the Tennessee-Tombigbee Waterway Development Authority, as well as the minutes of the compact's business meetings during those formative years. Stewart's book is an excellent resource about the history of the waterway prior to its construction.

I also referenced *Mixing the Waters*, by Jeffrey K. Stine, 1993 first edition, which provides an account of the political, engineering, and environmental challenges the waterway and its supporters faced. My primary resources, though, were my own personal files and the extensive archives of the Tenn-Tom Waterway Development Authority. In that regard, I thank Mitch Mays, the authority's administrator; and staff members Hope Oakes, Emily Oakes, and Ireland McDowell for their cooperation and assistance. I am also indebted to N.D. "Skeeter" McClure, Bill Satterfield, Wynne Fuller, and Al Wise for their comments and input concerning waterway-related matters that involved them. Their knowledge was invaluable. Without the aid of Al Wise, Skeeter McClure, Wynne Fuller, Tom Cayce, and Mike Wilson, I never would have been able to recognize so many Corps employees, in both the Mobile and Nashville Districts, who helped plan, design, and build the waterway.

I am indebted to the Tennessee-Tombigbee Waterway Council for financing my part of the costs to publish the book and most grateful for the support of Mike Williams, Will Sanders, Mitch Mays, and the organization's other leaders. Frank McCormack's suggestions and advice, as well as his editing of the manuscript, were invaluable.

Finally, I want to thank my wife, Jackie, for her encouragement and for undertaking the unenviable chore of reviewing the first draft of the manuscript and for her comments and suggestions that helped improve the narrative.

While I believe the substance of these accounts is correct and credible, this publication is not intended to be used as an academic reference for researchers. However, I trust that it will be informative and interesting to the general reader who wants to learn more about one of the nation's largest and most important public works projects. I believe it also provides insights, based on my personal experience, into the political landscape in the South and in Washington during the last quarter of the 20th century, including the growth of the environmental movement.

The Tennessee-Tombigbee Waterway had to overcome a litany of political, legal, and environmental roadblocks, any one of which could have killed the project. Fortunately, many individuals from all walks of life made timely and critically important contributions to overcome the myriad impediments that threatened the waterway's future and helped ensure its eventual success. While writing this memoir about my many years of involvement with the building of the waterway and its development, I especially wanted to memorialize and shed deserved light on some of those individuals who were involved and whose contributions otherwise might never have received any accolades. Just as I have inadvertently failed to mention some who helped me in writing my memoirs, I have undoubtedly failed to recognize others who made important contributions during the evolution of the waterway. I sincerely apologize for both oversights.

CHAPTER I
First Introduction to Tenn-Tom

Like most teenagers, I had little if any idea about what career I wanted to pursue. Initially, I mused about being a doctor and investigated the prospects of attending Tulane University in New Orleans to study pre-medicine. During the summer after finishing high school and before enrolling at Tulane, I began to seriously ponder those commitments, both the finances and the decade or longer I'd have to invest to become a doctor. I concluded that I'd best pursue another career path. It was one of the most regrettable professional decisions that I ever made, although both my life and career have been fulfilling.

I graduated from Murphy High in Mobile, Alabama, one of the largest public schools in the South. As I recall, there were nearly 700 in my class and a total of about 3,000 students in four grades on a campus that resembled a small college. Most all my friends who planned to attend college intended to attend Auburn; the University of Alabama; or Mississippi Southern College (now called the University of Southern Mississippi) in Hattiesburg, Mississippi, which at the time had a reputation as *the* place to go to play and have fun. I had visited all three schools and for various reasons was not interested in attending any of these colleges. I was so unsure that I decided to bypass college and start working with my father, who was a boilermaker. As the name implies, boilermakers erected large boilers and appurtenant facilities at electric power-generating plants and other large plants, such as paper mills and chemical manufacturers. The work was dangerous, but the pay was at the top of the wage scale for craftsmen.

Without my knowledge, my mother, working with my high school counselor, began exploring what scholarships might be available and what might be a suitable major for me. Both my parents worked and had never shown much interest in my schooling, and her taking these steps of her own volition was not typical of her. Mother and Dad were both great parents and providers. Mother had finished high school, while my father, like many men during the Depression, went to about the eighth grade. He was self-educated and knew as much about building boilers for large power plants as a graduate engineer knew. No one, either in my father's or my mother's family, had ever attended college. That was why having Mother so involved in getting me enrolled somewhere in college was such a surprise. It might have been that she had dreamed about getting a degree but never had the opportunity.

After some last-minute rushes to submit enrollment applications and with a small scholarship in hand, I enrolled at Mississippi State University. None of my high school classmates joined me at Mississippi State. Going from Mobile to a small college town like Starkville where I did not know anyone was like being in the French Foreign Legion.

The burgeoning economy of the 1950s after World War II created nearly unlimited opportunities for engineers, including new careers in the nuclear and chemical industries. I cannot remember what prompted me to study civil engineering, but engineering was the "hot" career field, and civil engineering appealed to me more than the other fields. It was common knowledge that State (and most likely other engineering schools) tried to winnow out want-to-be engineering students, especially during the students' first two years of classes. Many who enrolled in engineering chose to drop that major. Some of those switched to industrial management or other similar business majors. At State, that important life-changing decision was usually made after the first semester of inorganic chemistry, taught by the infamous Dr. Clyde Q. Sheely, who held several patents and was one of the founders of Mississippi Chemical Corporation. He didn't need the income, so students believed he taught for the sheer pleasure of terrorizing them. His classes were huge, with at least 100 or more students. About half or more of those would fail the course. Sheely was one of those professors a student never forgot.

I stuck it out, and in the spring of 1961, during my senior year, I began interviewing for jobs. Several of the companies that conducted interviews on campus were engineering and construction firms. While in college, I had worked at Mitchell Engineering, Inc. (later CECO, Inc.) in Columbus, Mississippi, as a draftsman and in the shop fabricating steel buildings. Sitting at a drafting table for eight hours every day did not appeal to me, so I felt I would not be content working as a design engineer. The best job opportunity regarding salary and benefits was with Martin-Marietta, an aerospace company. Its facility in Georgia needed structural engineers to help design and build a huge cargo plane called the C-5A. I also had contemplated joining the U.S. Navy to become a pilot. Another employment opportunity was with the U.S. Bureau of Reclamation to design and build the huge Glen Canyon Dam on the Colorado River and other major water projects in the Western states. While the Vicksburg, Mississippi, District of the Corps of Engineers recruited graduates from MSU, the Mobile District recruited mainly from Auburn. This posed a problem for me since I had no interest in living in Vicksburg but had a strong desire to return to Mobile.

I applied to the Mobile District, even though it had no openings for engineers. I had nearly given up hope of working in Mobile and had narrowed my options to working for a construction firm in Memphis, helping build the C-5A in Georgia, or joining the Navy either as a pilot or with the Seabees. Much to my surprise and delight, Mr. Fred Lewter, a supervisor with the Corps in Mobile, was able to get me an interview. Mr. Lewter was a neighbor while I was in high school and had always shown an interest in me.

It was that fall I had taken from the homemade zip line when I was 12 that paved the way for me to develop a kinship with Mr. Lewter. Because I couldn't play any contact sports before my junior year of high school, I was free during football season when I was a sophomore. That year, Mr. Lewter asked me to help him coach football for the sixth and seventh graders at Oakdale Elementary, where his son was a student. The school had not had a team for several years because no one had volunteered to be the coach. During the 1950s, as the country began to recover from World War II, most parents, especially fathers, were too busy making a living to be involved in their children's activities. Mr. Lewter offered to volunteer as the coach if I agreed to help him. While I am sure he had intended to be actively involved, he seldom made it to practice and mainly just attended the games. I had played football throughout elementary and junior high and was familiar with the game, but I was concerned that the players, who were only a few years my junior, would not respect me as their coach. That, however, proved not to be a problem. The students, able to play football for the first time in years, were most agreeable to accepting me as their coach. It was only a one-year stint of coaching, but it was memorable. My association with Mr. Lewter during that football season led him to later become one of my champions and a mentor. I credit his influence on my behalf that led to the opportunity for me to return to Mobile, my hometown, and work for the U.S. Army Corps of Engineers.

The interview with the Corps in the Mobile District went well, and the Corps offered me a position in the hydraulics and hydrology branch. My work there mainly entailed developing weekly schedules for regulating the operations of all the federal dams and reservoirs in the district, mostly in Alabama and Georgia. The operations of these projects varied depending on the time of the year, hydrologic conditions, and the amount of electricity generated at projects that had hydropower facilities. After about six months of my working there, the district offered an engineering training program for new hires that allowed participants to spend time in all the various departments or functions of the Corps. I leaped at the opportunity and spent the next nine months learning more about the Corps and its mission. This was an excellent learning experience, and I especially enjoyed the time I spent traveling and working on projects under construction or in operation.

Mobile had a very robust construction program in the 1960s, both for water resource development and military projects. The Mobile District's civil works jurisdiction encompassed a large part of Mississippi, all of Alabama except the Tennessee River Valley area, the western part of Georgia, and the Florida Panhandle. The district was also responsible for the design and construction of facilities at all the military installations, including NASA, in those states, as well as supporting ventures in Central and South America.

I had the opportunity to spend a couple of months working on construction of the Walter F. George Lock and Dam on the Chattahoochee River at Ft. Gaines, Georgia. While most of my responsibilities were menial, helping to build such a massive project was an unforgettable experience. One day I was checking the grade on the landfilled earthen dam when a bulldozer that was compacting soil began to sink. The huge machine was sinking out of sight when the operator cut the engine and jumped off just before it sank below grade. Although the Corps had investigated subsurface conditions during the design of the project, it failed to find a honeycomb of limestone caverns underneath the dam site. No one had considered this potential disastrous failure of the dam until the weight of the bulldozer caused a cave-in. To remedy the problem, workers injected thousands of cubic yards of grout material into these subterranean voids. Some local farmers several miles from the dam complained that the grout had found its way into their water wells, cutting off their source of groundwater.

My immediate supervisor was Freddy Jones, who later became head of construction for the Mobile District portion of the Tenn-Tom. Although only a few years older than I was, he was a great mentor for a young engineer, and he gave me a variety of responsibilities.

This experience, albeit brief, taught me much about management of a large public works project and the working relationships among the private contractors and the Corps.

One of my responsibilities was to inspect the construction of the control room for the dam's powerhouse. The work entailed a maze of conduits that housed an intricate system of electrical wiring needed to operate the powerhouse. It was my job to check and verify that the conduits were correctly installed before they were covered with concrete for the floor of the control room. Much to everyone's horror, especially the contractor's foreman, I discovered that all the conduits had been installed incorrectly. To speed up the installation, a worker, instead of following the blueprints, had measured the locations of all the conduits using measurements from the first one he had installed. As a result, all had to be torn out and replaced. It was a toss-up whether the contractor was more irritated by my catching the error or by the actions of the poor electrician, who had made the grievous mistake of not double-checking his work. The contractor must have sent him packing; I never saw him again on the job.

Another job assigned to me was inspecting the fill of some limestone caves that would be inundated as part of the reservoir. My job was to keep count of all the loads of dirt that were being hauled some distance in large, motorized scrapers from a borrow pit, then dumped into the holes. These scrapers carried as much as 25 to 40 cubic yards of material and traveled very fast, creating a lot of dust along the haul road. I told the contractor to water the road, or I would have to shut down the hauling for safety reasons. He kept giving me excuses about why he could not water the road, and he likely felt he could intimidate me, since I was a junior engineer. Later, visibility got to nearly zero along the road, and a scraper came very close to colliding with me in my truck. It made me so livid that I immediately told the contractor I was shutting down work. He snarled, saying that I did not have the authority to stop work. Hoping my superiors would back me, I snarled back, telling the contractor that he would not get credit for any more loads until the haul road was watered and the dust kept under control. I never had any more difficulties with the contractor.

My first exposure to a waterway was in the summer of 1962 when worked as a Corps of Engineers' engineer trainee during the construction of Walter F. George Lock and Dam on the Chattahoochee River in Georgia. The 85-foot-tall lock is the third highest in the nation.

Those kinds of interpersonal experiences were most helpful in helping me deal with conflicts and issues later during my career. The short time I spent working on the construction of the Walter F. George Lock and Dam was certainly beneficial later when I became involved with the Tenn-Tom construction.

Most large public works projects are built in rural areas with limited accommodation, so finding a place to stay can be a worker's most daunting challenge. When I worked on the Walter F. George Lock and Dam project, I was fortunate to find a room at a boarding house in Blakely, Georgia, about 30 miles from the project. I heard that the dwelling was the former family home of the famous actress and wife of Paul Newman, Joanne Woodward, and that I was staying in her bedroom. I enjoyed telling everyone that I had slept in her bed.

The days working on the lock and dam were hot and dusty. The highlight at the end of each day was stopping off at an old-fashioned icehouse in Ft. Gaines for a cold beer. To be able to walk inside the icehouse where large blocks of ice were stored was heaven after spending the day in Georgia's blazing summer heat. When I entered the icehouse, I did not want to leave to go to my car or even to the boarding house, neither of which had air conditioning.

I also enjoyed my time at Altoona Lake in Northwest Georgia and at Jim Woodruff Lock and Dam on the lower Chattahoochee River on the Florida state line. I spent about two months there working with those responsible for the operation and maintenance of these two large multiple-purpose projects. Later, I spent a couple of weeks with a safety engineer as he inspected facilities being built at Redstone Arsenal in Huntsville, Alabama, as part of the country's new space program. Huntsville was exploding with growth in the early 1960s after Dr. Werner Von Braun and his fellow German scientists had chosen this small city as the location for the space program. That part of North Alabama reminded Von Braun of his native Bavaria. It was strange to see new houses being built in cotton fields that had been planted but not yet harvested. It was the epitome of a boomtown. Less than 60 years later, Huntsville is now projected to become the state's largest city.

I spent the rest of my training working in the other offices in the district and with the different engineering disciplines, including structures and hydraulics. One of my more memorable stints was with the stream gauge section. The Corps had gauges installed on most all the rivers to measure stream flow and river stages. Periodically, the gauges had to be serviced to remove the charts that had recorded the hydrologic data, and new gauges had to be installed. Another trainee and I were traveling with one of the men who took care of these gauges. It was somewhat boring work, but it was enjoyable since it involved traveling throughout the district. One trip took us to the Florida Panhandle. We learned later that the Corps employee we were traveling with was a serious alcoholic, but we had not seen any indication of that. We stopped one morning in Blountstown, Florida, for gas. The other trainee and I went inside the service station to buy some snacks, and when we returned, the truck was gone. We impatiently waited for an hour or longer, assuming the guy would eventually return, but he never did. There were no cell phones then, and neither of us had a credit card, so we were stranded and at the mercy of the world. I found a pay phone and called the office in Mobile and reported to the supervisor that the employee had disappeared with the truck. The supervisor did not appear to be too concerned and assured me that the man would soon return. We waited the entire afternoon and finally walked about two miles to a small motel, where we stayed for two days before anyone. I was so upset and felt so helpless. All our personal items were in the truck. I was exasperated that no one from the district office had come to get us. Finally, late in the afternoon on the second day after his disappearance, the guy showed up at the motel, behaving as if nothing had happened. It was evident that he had been drinking and was hung over. We told him to immediately drive to Mobile. I was never so glad to get home. I found out later that everyone knew about his drinking problem but covered for him by looking the other way. When I left the district three years later, the employee was still working there and driving a government truck.

While the Corps made no commitments, it tried to place those completing the training program in their field of choice. I enjoyed construction, and it was certainly my preference. However, that line of work required frequent relocation, and I felt that way of life would pose an inconvenience to my family. After much thought, I chose a position that was available in the navigation branch of the planning division in the district office. I based my decision on several factors. First, planning was what I referred to as "soft engineering." It involved formulating projects, working with local sponsors, and being involved in a project from its inception to undertaking the steps needed to determine whether the project was economically feasible and warranted congressional authorization. I also liked those who worked in the branch, including its supervisor, Bill Dolive.

The district office was in the Loop neighborhood of west Mobile. The buildings were two-story, temporary, WWII wooden buildings. They were connected with covered catwalks, which gave the appearance of a small college campus setting. There was not a better venue or a better group of people for someone beginning his career. Mobile was and still is the Corps' largest district office in terms of employees and workload. As I recall, the district at that time had about 1,000 employees, including those who worked at project sites away from the district office. The district had its individual bowling and golf leagues as well as a softball team that helped foster camaraderie among employees and opportunities to meet and develop friendships. It was certainly one of the most pleasant times I experienced during my entire working career.

I shared an office with Joe Hutton, who became a close friend and mentor. Joe was a World War II veteran and had received his engineering degree from Ole Miss on the GI program. He was a tail gunner on B-17s, flying bombing missions from England to targets in Europe, one of the most dangerous assignments one could have. Although he was older, we were very compatible, and I could not have had a better office mate and friend.

Hutton and I worked together on several proposed port projects. One time we were returning from meetings in Apalachicola, Florida, and stopped for gas. We learned then that President Kennedy had been assassinated earlier that day. There were no radios or air conditioning in the government vehicles, and we were both shocked to learn that the President had been dead for several hours. Not knowing who or what was behind the assassination, I became concerned that it might have been the result of the Cuban missile crisis. Living in Mobile, which was within the range of the armed Russian missiles in Cuba, had kept me and others on edge during the crisis. Those concerns were heightened by what seemed like endless trainloads of military equipment passing through Mobile destined for Southern Florida in anticipation of a possible invasion of Cuba. For me, it was a scary time. Growing up in Mobile during the Cold War in the 1950s, all students wore "dog tags," I assume for identification in case we were killed in a nuclear blast. We frequently had to participate in drills at school by crouching under our desks, as if that would save us from a nuclear bomb blast. It was a scary time for a youngster, and I am sure these lingering memories made me more troubled by the President's assassination. I continue to believe that we don't know the motives behind or those involved in this American tragedy, and we might never know them.

The early 1960s was a busy time for my new employer, the navigation branch, with a number of studies for waterway and port improvements. One such study was a reanalysis of the Tennessee-Tombigbee Waterway. The waterway had been studied during the late 1930s, but war delayed its congressional authorization until 1946. The Alabama and Mississippi congressional delegations had worked tirelessly to secure funding to start its construction, but their efforts were always stymied, mainly because of opposition by Congressman Clarence Cannon of Missouri. Cannon, the namesake of one of the House office buildings, ruled the appropriations process in the House with an iron fist and had vowed to kill any funding for the Tenn-Tom because of his hatred for Congressman John Rankin of Mississippi, the most vocal champion of the waterway in those days. Instead of providing construction funds, Cannon would continue to delay the project by offering some funds to once again study the project's merits.

There was considerable political pressure to complete this most recent restudy, and it was the top priority of the navigation branch. The study included a review of the waterway's design, an update of its cost estimate, and a reevaluation of its navigation benefits. At the time, it was the largest, most costly, and most complex water resources project ever proposed by the Corps of Engineers, rivaling the Panama Canal. The complexity of the study required nearly an all-hands staff effort. Although I had other projects and assignments, I joined in the effort by helping to identify potential shippers and commodities that could utilize the waterway. Once we identified these potential users, we needed to compute their savings in transportation costs by comparing the barge rate to that of the most likely alternative mode of transportation, which was likely rail. I, of course, did not have a clue how the Tenn-Tom would become such an important part of my career.

There had been a series of devastating hurricanes during the 1950s, which caused widespread damage and loss of life along both the Gulf and Atlantic coasts. These storms prompted Congress to authorize studies to determine the feasibility of hurricane protection works. Most colleges did not offer coastal engineering courses, and no one in the district had an inkling of knowledge about this unique field. The Corps assigned the navigation branch to study the district's coastline, including the Florida Panhandle, Alabama, and Mississippi coasts to the state line with Louisiana. Although I had been in the branch for only a short time and was "the new kid on the block," the branch assigned the project to me.

This was an awesome if not scary challenge for me since I had little experience working for the Corps and no knowledge of coastal engineering. I researched where I could quickly study oceanography and hydrodynamics and concluded that two of the best schools in this field were Massachusetts Institute of Technology and Texas A&M. MIT has an international reputation as an engineering and technical school. So, it was not surprising that institution was renowned in these fields, but Texas A&M's acclaim was because of one professor. I cannot recall his name, but he was responsible for planning and determining the best beach locations for allied troops to invade the

Pacific islands, such as Iwo Jima and Okinawa, during World War II. Each island had different offshore characteristics, and to make things even more complex, little information concerning these factors existed for these remote islands.

I attended MIT during the summer of 1963 and the following summer at Texas A&M. What I learned there along with "home schooling" allowed me to approach my assignment with some measure of confidence. It likely helped that my meager knowledge was far more extensive than that of my colleagues with the Corps. The time I spent at MIT and in Boston was an unforgettable experience that included trips to MIT's Woods Hole laboratory and its research ship at Martha's Vineyard on Cape Cod. There were students at MIT from all over the world, all very intelligent.

I had assumed that Texas A&M was located somewhere along the Texas Gulf coast since it was renowned for oceanography. When I arrived in Bryan or College Station, I found a hot, muggy college town located between Houston and Dallas. Once people learned I was from Alabama, they wanted to ask me about Bear Bryant, who had recently left A&M to coach the Crimson Tide. Bryant was a legend at A&M long before becoming such an icon at Bama.

One of the key factors in designing hurricane barriers and other coastal structures was to determine the design storm and its effects, especially storm surge. To do so required knowledge of past storms, including anecdotal information about measured tidal surges and the extent of flooding caused by hurricanes of record. I spent many hours in local libraries researching old newspapers, some as early as the 1800s. Being a history buff, I was easily drawn to other stories in these old publications. Storm surges depend largely on wind direction and velocity, as well as wave refraction and the slope of the continental shelf at a specific location. The relatively flat or gradual slope of the offshore waters along the Mississippi coast is a main reason it has had record tides and storm surges during past hurricanes, as opposed to the Pensacola-Ft. Walton area, where there is a narrow continental shelf with less distance for the surge to "pile up."

Determining the record storm or the design criteria for different locations was a very timely and tedious task. Had today's data processing capabilities been available, this repetitious process would have been much simpler and faster. I believe the only projects that involved these coastal engineering techniques were for the design and configuration of the jetties at Destin, Florida, and those at Perdido Bay in Orange Beach, Alabama. The congressional study produced few if any hurricane-protection projects, mainly because of lack of public support. Property owners, tourists, and other beach enthusiasts opposed any obtrusive structures, including artificially built sand dunes that might block or hinder the scenic view of the beach and the ocean. While damage and losses continue to escalate each year, that attitude has now been bolstered by the federal government and insurance companies that cover most of the financial damages to both private and public properties. As a result, more and more developments are being exposed to these devastating storms.

CHAPTER II
"Mr. Smith" Goes to Washington

In the fall of 1965, Hurricane Betsy, after pounding the Bahamas and Florida, built up steam as it entered the Gulf of Mexico and came inland at Grand Isle, Louisiana, packing wind gusts of 145 mph. Betsy was the most destructive storm to have hit the USA at that time, causing $1.2 billion in damage. While the storm passed west of Mississippi, it nevertheless caused extensive damage along the western end of the Mississippi coast. Still, it was nothing like the devastation wrought by Camille in 1969 and Katrina in 2005.

Until FEMA was established in 1979, the Corps was the lead federal agency responsible for aiding in recovery and reconstruction after a presidentially declared national disaster. I was part of a team from the Mobile District that was detailed to Mississippi to coordinate the cleanup and recovery from Hurricane Betsy. We were there for several weeks, working 10 or 12 hours each day, seven days a week. I worked mostly in Hancock County, the most westward part of the Mississippi coast that had been damaged. At that time, the movie, *This Property is Condemned*, starring Robert Redford, Natalie Wood, and Charles Bronson, was being filmed in the small coastal town of Bay St. Louis. It was impossible not to play hooky from my work and watch the scenes that were being shot there. The stars and film crew were staying at the Broadwater Beach Hotel in Biloxi, and I learned that Natalie Wood hung out in one of the local taverns when she was not on set. Needless to say, I became a regular there. She was the most beautiful creature I had ever seen and was friendly to everyone to boot. I never saw Bronson or Redford off the set, but who cared? Natalie's strange and questionable death several years later felt like a personal loss.

I would return to Mobile about once or twice during the week and go by my office after hours to check my inbox before going home for the night and returning to Mississippi the following morning. On one of those trips, I found a note from my boss, Dolive, telling me not to return to Mississippi the next day. The note said I had a meeting with someone from the Bureau of the Budget (BOB) in Washington D.C. To my knowledge no one from BOB had ever visited the Mobile District, and I wondered why I was to meet with this important visitor. With no one around to tell me more, I concluded it likely concerned a study that I had helped prepare that had wound its way through the chain of command of the Corps and Army to BOB for review and approval. So, I dismissed the importance of the meeting, went home, and got a good night's sleep.

The next morning when I reached my office, the Mobile District was awash with excitement about the visitor from Washington; everyone speculated about why he was there. I learned later the official had arrived the day before and had asked to review the personnel files at the district office. Based on those reviews he had scheduled interviews with about six employees, including me. I learned that all of us were about the same age, had about the same years of government service, and all were civil engineers. The others had at least a 24-hour notice that the meeting was likely an interview for a possible position, while I had no idea what to expect until I arrived at the office that morning. The others were all decked out in coats and ties. I was wearing my casual clothes for the beach cleanup work in Mississippi. I certainly had no time to get nervous about the interview, which was likely an advantage. There was also little pressure on me to do "good" during the interview, because I was happy with my current job and enjoyed living in Mobile. I had little interest in leaving, especially for a job in Washington.

I met with John "Jack" Roose, who was the principal budget examiner for water resource programs in the Bureau of the Budget. He explained that BOB was part of the Executive Office of the President, composed of about 100 budget examiners who were the core of the staff for the White House. BOB helped prepare the President's annual budgets and was responsible for reviewing legislation, regulations, policies, and congressional testimonies proposed by the federal agencies. In 1973, the organization and mission of BOB were expanded to include oversight and direction of the Executive Branch to administer management principles applicable to government. BOB later became the Office of Management and Budget, or OMB.

Roose said that a staff of about four examiners was responsible for all federal water resource agencies like the Corps of Engineers, Department of the Interior, TVA, etc. The program employed a larger number of examiners because of the heavy workload of reviewing and approving project feasibility studies and approving individual projects before they were sent to Congress for authorization. Roose had been to several other districts before coming to Mobile. He was searching for someone with a background and knowledge about the Corps' planning process and its civil works program, and who was willing to relocate to Washington.

After about an hour of discussing the subjects typical for a job interview, we said our goodbyes. As I was leaving, I mentioned that I was happy in my present position and that it provided some opportunity for further promotion but that I was certainly not averse to leaving Mobile and the Corps for new adventures. I left and went back to Mississippi to work on storm recovery and never gave much further thought to the interview.

A couple of weeks passed, Joe Tofani, the top civilian at the Corps' headquarters in Washington, called me. He was a legend within the Corps, and receiving a call from him made me more nervous than the BOB interview had made me. He said he was calling on behalf of

BOB to see whether I would be interested in coming to Washington for further interviews. If so, he would issue travel orders and make the necessary arrangements. Before I had a chance to tell him why I was reluctant to do so, he said that he could not believe that anyone with the Corps would not leap at the opportunity to work at this level of government. I realized that if I turned down the offer for the interviews, I would likely upset the hierarchy within the Corps. It was obvious that Tofani and others felt it would be in the best interest of the Corps to have a former Corps employee working in BOB. With some hesitation, I told him to make the arrangements. "What the heck?" I thought. I had never been to Washington, and if nothing else resulted, I would at least get a free trip to D.C.

The Corps booked me into a hotel that was certainly no five-star establishment, but it was conveniently located about six blocks from the White House. When I woke up on the morning of my interview, I saw that it had snowed during the night. Being from Mobile, I rarely saw snow, and I wasn't prepared for that kind of weather. My suit was lightweight, and I did not have a topcoat or overshoes since I never needed them back home. Getting a taxi during bad weather in D.C., especially for a short ride, is nearly impossible, so I felt I had no choice but to walk to my interview. Not being familiar with the route, I wandered to the mall entrance side of the White House complex instead of to the main entrance on Pennsylvania Avenue. Not knowing any better, I walked past the guardhouse along with others who were going to work. The only difference between them and me was they were all wearing Executive Office badges. After entering the compound, I asked for directions to BOB, which was in the Executive Office building. Located next door to the White House and part of that compound, it is one of the more unique, ornate buildings in Washington. Built during the Grant Administration, the building was once occupied by the departments of the Army, Navy, and State. The offices had 16-foot ceilings and massive doors with brass doorknobs depicting the seal or insignia of the department that originally occupied that space. Most offices had fireplaces. The building's exterior walls are massive marble slabs that were cut to size on site and stacked atop each other. One of its more impressive rooms is the Indian Treaty Room, where most all the treaties with the American Indian tribes were signed. The vice president's office is also located there. Later, after I joined BOB, my out-of-town visitors were always most impressed that my office was only two doors from Vice President Hubert Humphrey's office.

After asking for more directions, I finally found the main entrance. The guard at the front desk was most upset that I had gained access without proper clearance and began to quiz me about how I had gotten into the secure building. I told him it was my first time there, and I did not have a clue about how I got into the building. He finally called someone to retrieve me. Years later, some of my old BOB colleagues still kid me about the stir I caused by breaching White House security that day. How could anyone get off to a worse start?

There were four of us Corps of Engineers who had been invited for interviews. The BOB interviewers purposely kept us separated, and I never knew anything about the other three candidates. For two days interviewers subjected me to the most intensive sessions possible. I believe everyone in the building except President Lyndon Johnson and the security guard who was upset with me talked to or questioned (if not grilled) me. It was not as much an interview as it was an interrogation. When I left to come home, I was completely mentally drained and couldn't have cared less whether I got the job.

A couple of weeks went by, and everybody at work would ask me daily whether I had heard anything from Washington. I learned later that the position required top-secret clearance, and the BOB was conducting preliminary investigations into my background before offering me the job. In mid-February of 1966, Roose finally called me to offer me the position. I was dumbstruck. I did not believe BOB would offer me the job, and, therefore, I had not thought about the pros and cons of accepting the job. That nonchalance changed immediately because BOB wanted an answer within one week or two at most, and I'd have to relocate and be on the job by mid-March.

Earlier that year, long before the BOB interview, my supervisor, Bill Dolive, had submitted papers for me to be promoted to the GS-12 level, only to have to withdraw them. The military was closing Brookley Air Force Base, the largest employer in Mobile, and all these government employees, including some engineers, were being transferred to other bases or about to be unemployed. Government regulations gave them priority for any advertised positions, regardless of whether they had any experience or qualifications for the jobs. When one of these engineers applied for the position that was being established for me, my boss had no choice but to close or withdraw the announcement. So, it did not look like I would be getting a raise in grade in the district any time soon. My family had just settled into a new home, and with the Brookley closure placing so many homes on the market, the prospect of selling my house would be bleak. My friends and family were not much help in making an important decision. Some encouraged me to go, while others emphasized the negative aspects of my going to Washington.

Dolive was very supportive of whatever decision I'd make. I told him I was reluctant to leave him in a lurch by not having someone to take over the coastal engineering studies since he had invested so much in me, personally, by sending me to MIT and A&M. He said, "If you leave, we will train someone else, so don't let that be a factor." He also told me that if I decided to go, and it did not work out, I could always come back to Mobile and work for the Corps.

"What the heck? If it does not work out, I can always come home," I thought. That convinced me to accept the position. Once the movers and shakers in the district knew that I would likely accept the BOB offer, they pulled a rabbit out of the hat and said they would reward me with a GS-12 grade increase if I stayed. That upset me more than pleased me. I felt if there had been a way to overcome the issues caused by the Brookley Field closure, then why had the Corps not done so already? Their not going to the mat for my raise until I was about to depart was a factor in my decision to leave.

I knew a quick sale of my home wasn't likely, but fortunately, a friend agreed to rent it with an option to buy. Like the Okies who left for California during the Dust Bowl years, I loaded the car to the top and left with my wife, a 5-year-old son, and a 2-year-old daughter, destined for Washington, hoping to beat the moving van there since we had no place to live and needed to find an apartment before our furniture and belongings arrived. Certainly, many unknown challenges as well as new opportunities lay ahead.

We found a garden-type apartment to rent in Fairfax, Virginia, before the moving van arrived. It was nice but certainly a step down from our new dwelling in Mobile. I was not financially able to buy another home until I sold our house in Mobile. I also accepted the new job without a promotion. It was standard BOB policy to hire government employees only at their present salaries and to not offer a raise until after a trial period. With the cost of living being much higher in Washington and with considerably more expenses related to work, I knew that times were going to be financially tight for the foreseeable future.

When I arrived at BOB in mid-March of 1966, I learned that Jack Roose, who had interviewed me in Mobile, had been promoted to principal examiner, or the supervisor, for water resources. The other three examiners working on these programs had announced they were leaving or considering other positions outside of BOB. I assumed they were in contention for the supervisor's job or felt they were under consideration and that it was time for them to seek other opportunities. I learned later that federal agencies were always trying to hire BOB employees for their knowledge of the budget process and to capitalize on any trade secrets they might have about workings of the Executive Office of the President. At that time, the average tenure for a budget examiner was less than three years; that time was even shorter for the director and political appointees, mainly because of the job's demands. It is a high-pressure, time-demanding workplace and is the only agency in the federal government that allows those in charge to fire someone or ask someone to leave with or without cause.

Greeting me on my desk on that first workday was a tall stack of feasibility reports on five major waterway improvements. I was surprised to find in the stack of reports the restudy of the Tennessee-Tombigbee that I had briefly worked on in Mobile. It had gone through the review process within the Corps and had just recently been forwarded to BOB for review and approval. The other proposed projects were an extension of commercial navigation on the Columbia River in Washington; the Red River Waterway in Louisiana; the Trinity River in Texas, which would extend navigation from Houston to Dallas, a project strongly supported by President Johnson; and a very ambitious project to build a connecting navigation route between Lake Erie and the Ohio River (LEOR). Jack Roose told me with a smile that they had saved them for me since I was now their expert on the Corps' planning process.

As was typical, the Corps had tipped off the political interests for these projects, and all were contacting the White House to pressure BOB to clear the proposed waterway projects so the Corps could send them to the Congress for approval and funding. All that pressure was eventually directed at me to complete my work and recommend whether the Johnson Administration should support or oppose each project. Not knowing where to start such an impossible task, I took the report that was on top of the pile, which was the Columbia River project.

The Corps of Engineers, being part of the U.S. Army, is under the command of the secretary of the Army, who delegated the Corps' civil works functions to Army's general counsel. Later in 1970, the Congress created a new position of assistant secretary of the Army-Civil Works as the office responsible for the Corps' civil functions. A fellow Alabamian, Robert K. Dawson, served in this important position from 1985 to 1987 during the Reagan Administration. Working for the general counsel was Jim Tozzi, a young Army captain with a PhD in economics. When Robert McNamara, a former automobile executive, became secretary of defense, he brought with him several young, highly skilled program analysts like Tozzi to help him gain better control of this large agency. They were called McNamara's Whiz Kids, and all made their mark on the government. I often say there are a lot of smart people in Washington and that brains are a dime a dozen there, but those who are the most successful are the overachievers who also have superb organizational and people skills to get things accomplished. Tozzi is one of the smartest, most capable professional people I ever met, and he went on to have an outstanding career in government and as a lobbyist.

Tozzi had reviewed the waterway studies before the Army sent them to BOB, and he was most willing to share with me his findings and concerns. He knew I was under a lot of pressure to complete my review and was willing to help me. We became silent partners, and having him as an ally with his skills proved to be invaluable. He had taken a special interest in the Trinity River Project and offered to spend more time delving into the economic justification of the Texas project, which allowed me to concentrate on the other four waterway projects. I reminded him that the Trinity River was a high priority for the Texas mafia in the White House, including the President. His response was a mere chuckle.

BOB has an institutional bias against new programs and projects, especially those that have significant budget impacts. Therefore, my job was to find reasons why these projects were not sound federal investments since all, including the Tenn-Tom, had marginal benefit-to-cost ratios. A waterway project must generate enough national economic benefits, measured primarily in savings in commercial transportation costs, to exceed its costs, including both capital and annual operating expenses, which are annualized over a 50-year economic life. Benefits and costs for other water resource projects, such as flood control, are amortized at 100 years. Regional economic development impacts, measured in terms of new jobs and increases in personal income, are not included as a project's economic benefit. Any such economic gain a region might enjoy as a result of the federal project would be offset by the same losses somewhere else, resulting in a net gain of zero for the nation. That said, most all political as well as grassroots support for these kinds of public works projects can be attributed to their potential for stimulating the local and regional economies and are viewed as economic engines. It seemed that Senator John Stennis' office was calling the White House daily urging that the Tenn-Tom be cleared so the restudy could be sent to Congress for consideration for funding in that fiscal year's appropriation bill. The

White House was sensitive to the Mississippi senator's needs since he was a ranking member on both Appropriations and Armed Services committees. This was at a time when the Johnson Administration was escalating the nation's involvement in Vietnam, which called for more defense spending. Other powerful members of Congress were also lobbying the White House for the other projects. Some of these project champions included Senators Russell Long and Carl Ellender for the Red River; Congressman Mike Kirwin of Ohio for LEOR; and last but certainly not the least, the pressure coming from the White House itself to clear the Trinity River project. All those inquiries initially came to Carl Swartz, the highest non-political or career official in BOB. He had spent many years there and was unflappable. He would stroll into my office and inform me of the latest inquiries the White House had received from Capitol Hill, but he never told me to curtail my review or succumb to the outside pressure. However, I was not making many friends with the President's congressionnel liaison staff.

All five projects were finally released later that spring with advice to the secretary of the Army that all were marginally justified, and funding for their construction would not be consistent with the President's program. A project, regulation, or legislation proposed by a federal agency required that the BOB determine whether the proposal was or was not consistent with the President's program. My superiors and I made such determinations many times without ever checking with the White House on most routine matters. However, using such discretion could backfire because of unforeseen political ramifications. The memorandum I wrote to the BOB director summarizing the results of my review of the Tenn-Tom restudy surfaced years later during the trial of the second lawsuit filed to stop the waterway. The plaintiffs' attorneys had found a copy during discovery and were quick to point out that I, now an employee of the waterway authority and a strong advocate of the waterway, was once advising decision makers that the project was marginally justified.

It is interesting to reflect on the outcomes of these projects, which were the last efforts to significantly expand the scope or reach of the nation's inland waterway system. Even with President Johnson's strong support and that of many influential Texans in the Dallas and Houston area (we called them the Big Mules), the Trinity River was killed by the state's voters. The state as the non-federal sponsor of the project was responsible for the construction of all the highway bridges that would span the waterway. The Legislature asked the voters to approve a referendum to issue the bonds to finance bridge replacements. Much to the surprise if not utter shock of the Trinity River waterway's backers, the referendum failed by a wide margin, effectively killing the project. In the early days of promoting the waterway, some of its sponsors took Will Rogers to see the Trinity River in Dallas. At that time of year, the river was not much more than a creek with little water in it. They asked the acclaimed humorist what he thought about the river, expecting that he would endorse the waterway project. Much to their disappointment, he responded: "If it was me, I would pave it!" The Tenn-Tom would face a similar challenge when Alabama and Mississippi were required to pay for 13 highway bridges across the waterway.

The Lake Erie-Ohio River or LEOR was an ambitious project that would utilize the Mahoning and Beaver rivers to build a barge canal from Lake Erie at Ashtabula, Ohio, to the Ohio River at Rochester, Pennsylvania. While most of the proposed project was in Ohio, where it enjoyed strong support, especially in the Youngstown area, a small part would flow through Southwest Pennsylvania. Much to everyone's surprise, Pennsylvania's governor announced that he would not support the waterway, allegedly a position influenced by the railroad industry. The Corps and Congress have a long-standing rule that a water project must be supported by the affected states if it is to be eligible for federal funding. Although there were efforts to revive the project, Pennsylvania's opposition meant the end of LEOR. The extension of navigation on the upper Columbia River between Richland and Wenatchee, Washington, suffered the same fate because of public opposition. Any political support that could have gone to that proposed project was redirected toward another project in the state: the expedited completion of the Columbia-Snake Waterway, which would provide a barge route from the mouth of the Columbia River to Lewiston, Idaho, on the Snake River. Although it has been a viable commercial artery for more than 50 years, it now faces a growing threat from environmentalists and American Native tribes, who want to remove the locks for the benefit of annual salmon migration. I'm not optimistic that it will survive this latest threat.

While the projects faced many challenges, only the Tenn-Tom and the Red River projects would eventually move forward. The lesson here is that a water project, regardless of its benefits and political support in the Congress, cannot become a reality unless it has unwavering local support and the support of the state or states where it is located.

I quickly learned that I had to change some working habits and improve my skills if I were to succeed at BOB. When in Mobile, I never attended or participated in a meeting with the district engineer. Those meetings in the front office were always attended by my supervisor, Bill Dolive, or his boss, and never by a junior staff member like me. At BOB, I was expected to call or contact whoever could be helpful in addressing the matter at hand in the most expeditious manner, whether it was a general at Corps headquarters or some high-level official in another agency. I was uncomfortable for a while not following the protocol ingrained in me in Mobile, but I soon learned to work with whoever offered the most help to address the matter in question.

The job entailed a voluminous amount of written material, such as reports, issue or policy papers, and other kinds of data. I generally left for home every evening with a briefcase full of bedtime reading, but I still found it difficult to keep on track with all the reading material. The average person reads about 250 to 300 words per minute. As a rule, engineers and scientists are notoriously slow readers, sacrificing speed for comprehension. Those majoring in humanities or similar pursuits are generally faster readers. I learned that a speed-reading course based on Evelyn Wood's concepts was available at another federal agency, and I immediately applied. My first bad habit to break was to stop sub-vocalizing or mentally repeating the individual words while I read. Most readers subvocalize, and since a person can speak only about 300 words per minute, the speed of reading is limited to this level. Using Evelyn Wood's techniques, I increased my speed to about 1,000 words per minute and maintained my comprehension to about 90 percent. Some in the class read as much as 1,500 words per minute. The reading techniques required total concentration and constant practice.

Engineers typically lack a strong education in economics. I concluded that to be effective, I needed to acquire at least a rudimentary knowledge of economics. I certainly did not need anything else to occupy my time, but I enrolled in a night class of Economics 101 taught by the University of Maryland at the U.S. Department of Agriculture's headquarters. You can learn only so much from an elementary course, but I was no longer a complete ignoramus when it came to discussing basic economic theories.

Chapter III
Genesis of the Tenn-Tom Compact

After BOB cleared the restudy and sent the project to Congress, the supporters of the Tenn-Tom began a concerted effort to secure funding. Since the project's authorization in 1946, that fight had been waged mainly by one congressman, John Rankin of Northeast Mississippi. Later in the 1960s, the project began to acquire a growing number of champions in both the House and Senate, largely as a result of a promotional campaign led by the Tennessee-Tombigbee Waterway Development Authority.

Rankin was one of the strongest supporters of President Roosevelt's New Deal and co-authored legislation that created the Tennessee Valley Authority. However, his colleagues in the House held him in low esteem because of his outspoken views on racial segregation, which hindered him from accomplishing much for his district, including his persistent campaign to fund the Tenn-Tom. He was defeated in 1952 by Congressman Thomas Abernathy, another Democrat, when their two districts were combined through redistricting. After Rankin's defeat, other members of the Mississippi delegation, like Senator John Stennis and Congressmen Tom Abernathy and Jamie Whitten, assumed the leadership role for the waterway. They were joined by Senator Lister Hill and Representatives Carl Elliott, Frank Boykin, and Bob Jones from Alabama as important advocates of the waterway. This growing support was still not successful in getting congressional approval to begin planning or designing the waterway, which was necessary to make it eligible for construction funds. It became evident that a more formal organization or association was needed to coordinate these efforts in Congress and increase broader grassroots support for the project in its region.

Alabama Takes the Initiative

Lieutenant General Lewis Pick, a former commander of the Corps of Engineers, was one of the first to promote a multi-state organization. At that time, the general was serving as Governor Jim Folsom's director of the Alabama State Planning and Industrial Development Board. He believed the time was ripe for building the waterway, but a strong and effective regional promotional organization was needed to help achieve it. General Pick was instrumental in reaching a historic agreement between the Corps of Engineers and the Bureau of Reclamation on relative institutional responsibilities for establishing a basin-wide plan to develop the Missouri River watershed, which would involve as many as 100 dams. That plan was called the Pick-Sloan Project. Regrettably, the general died shortly after joining the Folsom Administration and before his leadership could help advance the Tenn-Tom project. However, his enthusiasm for the waterway made Governor Folsom one of its most dedicated champions. The governor initiated the needed steps in the state Legislature to begin forming a compact. He also traveled to Mississippi and met with Governor J.P. Coleman, which led to Mississippi's support to form a two-state compact.

Alabama State Senator Neil Metcalf from Geneva County is given credit for crafting compact legislation. The compact has withstood the test of time, from the early days when the waterway was nothing more than a dream, to the need to address the myriad challenges during its construction, to today when it is still effective to ensure the waterway's operation and development. The compact has never been amended or revised since it was enacted over 60 years ago. Senator Metcalf was the legislation's principal supporter in the Alabama state senate and was instrumental in getting that legislative body's approval by a 33-0 vote. The Senate-passed bill, S.56, was later approved by the Alabama House of Representatives, with the full support of the speaker, Rankin Fite of Hamilton, by an overwhelming vote of 73-3. The bill was quickly signed by Governor Folsom on August 13, 1957.

Some influential leaders in Alabama showed considerable interest in not building the congressionally authorized project that basically followed the Tombigbee River and connected with the Tennessee River in Northeast Mississippi. Instead, they wanted to build an Alabama route. This plan would follow the Warrior River to Mulberry Fork and from there construct a man-made canal that would connect with Tennessee River via the Bear Creek tributary in North Alabama. Governor Folsom's and the Corps' opposition to that plan led to everyone eventually backing the authorized plan. The all-Alabama route would have cost more and had a lesser benefit-to-cost ratio.

Mississippi Responds

With the backing of Governor Coleman, the Mississippi State Legislature initially considered a bill identical to the compact legislation that the Alabama State Legislature passed in 1957. The bill's chief sponsor was Senator Bill Burgin of Columbus, Mississippi. Other senators from the Northeastern part of the state supported the proposed legislation. The bill was referred to the finance committee, which Burgin chaired, where it was favorably reported out of committee. It passed the Senate 39-2. One of the dissenters was W.B. Lucas of Macon, who lived in a county along the Tombigbee. He objected to the compact because he felt the waterway would adversely affect the railroad industry. Railroad lobbyists had been building opposition to the waterway within Congress for several years, but the senator from Noxubee County, Mississippi, was the first local voice of opposition from the railroads. It would not be the last. Later, the railroads helped finance two landmark lawsuits aimed at killing the project.

William Jolly, Cline Gilliam, and Luther Sims, all of Columbus, introduced in the bill in the Mississippi House of Representatives. The legislation got bogged down in committee mainly because of objections by Representative Thompson McClellan of West Point, a waterway supporter. He was using his delay tactics as leverage to get a commitment to build a highway bridge across the Tombigbee between his county and the adjoining Lowndes County. The Columbus Chamber of Commerce, led by Glover Wilkins, who later would head the compact, joined forces with McClellan's city chamber of commerce (West Point), and they were able to convince McClellan to withdraw his hold on the bill in committee with no promises to build the bridge. McClellan later would see his bridge come to fruition as one of the dozen or so new bridges built during the waterway's construction. That bridge replaced Waverly Ferry. The bill finally passed the House by a vote of 122-2, and Governor Coleman signed it on May 3, 1958, nearly one year after Alabama had approved the compact.

Congress Approves the Compact

When it became evident the two states would approve the compact, congressional supporters of the Tenn-Tom began taking steps to have the Congress ratify the Tennessee-Tombigbee Waterway Development Authority as an interstate compact. In the U.S. Senate, Senators Jim Eastland and John Stennis of Mississippi and John Sparkman of Alabama co-sponsored legislation "granting the consent and approval of the Congress" to the Tenn-Tom compact. The Alabama delegation, including Bob Jones, Frank Boykin, George Grant, George Andrews, Carl Elliott, Kenneth Huddleston, and Armstead Seldon, introduced similar bills in the House. Tom Abernathy and Frank Smith of Mississippi also sponsored the legislation. Their support occurred only after the two governors assured them the states had no intention of using the compact as a vehicle to build the waterway if the federal government continued to delay its construction. Governor Folsom had made such a threat, which was ludicrous, given the cost of the waterway, which far exceeded the states' financial capabilities.

With the assurance that the compact was a promoter, not a builder, and with the Corps' blessing, the Senate approved the legislation with no debate and on a voice vote on July 15, 1958. The House followed suit and passed a similar bill on August 4, 1958. Ten days later, on August 14, 1958, President Eisenhower signed the bill.

Governors Folsom and Coleman met in Columbus, Mississippi, on September 15, 1958, to make the decisions needed to initiate the authority. Folsom brought with him a check for $50,000 and was bodacious enough to suggest that Mississippi match the amount. The two also agreed that Mississippi could select the location for the compact's headquarters and that Alabama would name its administrator. Mississippi chose Columbus as its headquarters, and Alabama named W. H. Drinkard, a member of Folsom's administration, as the charter administrator. Glover Wilkins, the executive director of the Columbus Chamber of Commerce, was hired as the assistant administrator. Less than four years later, Wilkins became the administrator, and Drinkard resigned to return to Alabama. Folsom was in his last year in office and would be succeeded by John Patterson. Although from the Eastern part of the state, Patterson became as much an advocate for the waterway as his predecessor, and his leadership was instrumental in expanding the authority's influence. That could not be said about Ross Barnett, who succeeded Coleman as Mississippi governor in 1960. He showed little interest in the authority or the waterway and became more embroiled in the state's racial issues.

Folsom's first appointments to represent Alabama were State Senator Neil Metcalf; the Speaker of the House Rankin Fite of Hamilton; Barrett Shelton of Decatur; Louis Eckles of Florence; and E.N. Merriweather of Mobile. Both Shelton and Eckles were publishers of daily newspapers and used these publications to promote the compact. Shelton was known as Mr. Tennessee Valley for his success in attracting economic development to that part of the state. He would later serve again as an authority member during Governor George Wallace's last administration.

Governor Coleman also appointed some outstanding civic leaders to serve as Mississippi's charter members. They were Louis Wise of

Columbus; George McLean, a Tupelo newspaper publisher; Phillip Sheffield, a junior college president in Fulton; R.C. Liddon, a bank president in Corinth; and Sam Coker, a Yazoo City businessman. Wise, general manager of Four-County Electric Power Association, a TVA distributor, was a close friend of Governor Coleman and was instrumental in garnering the governor's support for the Tenn-Tom and the compact. He continued to serve for many years and was one of the authority's most dedicated and influential members.

The first meeting of the Tennessee-Tombigbee Waterway Development Authority was held on September 15, 1958, in Columbus, Mississippi. Representing the states of Alabama and Mississippi at this historic event included, from left: State Senator Bill Burgin (Mississippi); Gov. J.P. Coleman (Mississippi); Lt. Gov. Carroll Gartin (Mississippi); Gov. "Big Jim" Folsom (Alabama); and State Senator Neil Metcalf (Alabama). Tennessee joined the compact the following year, followed by Kentucky in 1962 and Florida in 1967.

Tennessee Joins the Authority

The compact law included a provision that other states could become a member, subject to the approval of the member states. Early in the first year of Tennessee Governor Buford Ellington's administration, a delegation from the authority traveled to Nashville to meet with the governor and ask for his support to have Tennessee join the compact. Those attending were Wilkins and Drinkard of the authority staff; Louis Wise of Columbus, the compact's first chairman; and Neil Metcalf, the author of the compact legislation and a member representing Alabama. The governor said he was a strong supporter of the waterway, but he would take a neutral stance on joining the compact since he felt that was a matter best addressed by the General Assembly.

State Representative James Bell of Savannah, Tennessee, a close associate of Governor Ellington, introduced a bill to authorize Tennessee to join the compact. The bill would also authorize an appropriation of $100,000 for the state's participation. The funding measure drew stiff opposition from Bell's colleagues as well as negative editorials by the *Nashville Banner*, one of the state's leading newspapers. Faced with the prospect of the bill's failure, Bell withdrew the funding proposal, and the modified bill passed the House on February 10, 1959, by a vote of 87-4. Bell asked Senator Ottis Knippers of Lawrenceburg to manage the bill in the State Senate. With the elimination of the funding provision, the legislation had smooth sailing in the Senate and passed without a dissenting vote, 30-0. Two groups, Citizens for TVA and the Tennessee Municipal League, were especially effective in lobbying the members of the General Assembly to support the legislation. Governor Ellington signed the bill making Tennessee a member on February 26, 1959.

The original members appointed by Governor Ellington as Tennessee's representatives were Kenneth Woods of Henderson, former head of the state's Democrat party; Colonel Gilbert Dorland of Nashville and a former commander of the Nashville District of the Army Corps of Engineers; Homer Snodgrass, an educator from Savannah; and George Clark, a banker; and Pat Charles, a real estate developer, both from Chattanooga. Colonel Dorland's experience with the Corps of Engineers and his technical expertise were invaluable to the authority's efforts to advance the waterway's progress. Woods' influence in the Democrat party helped foster unwavering political support in the state for the waterway and the compact's activities.

Kentucky Follows Suit

With Tennessee now a member of the compact, Wilkins and the authority began to test the waters of Kentucky joining the fold. Kentucky, especially the western part of the state, had been strongly supportive of the waterway's authorization. An officer of the Paducah Chamber of Commerce had appeared at a congressional public hearing in 1945 in support of the waterway's authorization and construction. U.S. Senator Alben Barkley, the Senate majority leader, had been instrumental in getting the Senate to authorize the project. The authority contacted Governor A.B. "Happy" Chandler shortly before he left office in 1959, and a news article later quoted the governor as saying he favored the goals of the compact. However, it would be more than two years before the Kentucky Legislature would consider the measure.

In January 1962, State Representative Milton Ashby of Sebree, Kentucky, which is near Henderson, introduced a resolution calling for Kentucky to join the compact. It seems his brother-in-law in Florence, Alabama, sold him on the importance of the Tenn-Tom and the compact. Ashby was a highly respected legislator, but he was going to need help. Wilkins met with the new Kentucky governor, Bert Combs, who agreed to support the compact, and had a bill drafted. Many members of the Legislature believed the governor and his running mate, the lieutenant governor, were opposed to everything the previous governor's administration had accomplished. That anti-Chandler reputation virtually guaranteed that any proposed legislation that Governor Combs offered would be dead on arrival in the Legislature. A strong allegiance to the railroad industry within the Legislature, especially by members from the Eastern part of the state, made it even more difficult to secure enabling legislation. These legislators believed the waterway would hurt the state's railroads. The Louisville and Nashville, or L&N Railroad, headquartered in Louisville, Kentucky, would later become one of the waterway's most formidable opponents.

With a few exceptions, the delegation from the western part of the state was solidly in support of the compact. The Ashby Bill passed the House on February 21, 1962, with 46 representatives voting in favor and 22 opposed. In the closing hours of the legislative session, the Senate took up the Ashby Bill, and it passed with a 21-11 vote. The West Kentucky senators were united, with only two opposing the compact. Senator George Overby of Murray, Kentucky, opposed the measure because he felt the waterway/compact would enable coal and rock industries in Alabama to unfairly compete with those interests in his state. It was widely reported that Reed Crushed Stone Company was opposed to the compact and probably influenced Overby's vote. His strongest objection, however, was likely his revulsion to any legislation that the Combs administration offered. Governor Combs approved the legislation on March 22, 1962.

Unlike the other compact governors, Governor Combs chose to appoint members mostly from his administration to the authority. Those appointments were Phillip Swift, the Aeronautics commissioner; J.O. Matlick, Conservation commissioner; and Robert Diehl, chairman of the Flood Control and Water Usage Board of Kentucky. The governor's other appointments were Representative Milton Ashby of Sebree, the sponsor of the compact legislation; and Edwin Paxton, Jr., a newspaper publisher in Paducah who had been a strong advocate for the waterway since the 1930s, before it was authorized by the Congress. Paxton served for many years as a member of the authority and was later succeeded by his son, Jack Paxton.

Florida Makes It a Fivesome

One of the obvious benefits of increasing the number of states in the compact was that it helped broaden the political presence and influence in Washington and within the member states themselves. When the authority approached the state of Florida, interest in the

Tenn-Tom was mixed. Earlier, when the Tenn-Tom was being considered for authorization, some in the Florida Panhandle felt the waterway, while benefiting Mobile, would put the port at Pensacola at a great disadvantage. Some even suggested the mouth of the waterway be moved to Perdido Bay so that it would be of greater benefit to Florida. However, interest in the waterway began to change in the 1960s.

Florida had its own major waterway project being built, the Cross-Florida Barge Canal, which would link shipping on the eastern Gulf Intracoastal Waterway at Yankeetown, Florida, with the Atlantic coast in Jacksonville via a canal built across the upper peninsula of the state. Like the Tenn-Tom, the barge canal had a long history, with Philip II of Spain first proposing the project in 1567. The canal was even part of the Gulf Intracoastal Waterway project, constructed during World War II to protect coastal shipping from German U Boats. Nearly 1,100 miles of the intracoastal canal had been built from Brownsville, Texas, to Carrabelle, Florida, in Apalachee Bay, when the war ended. The rest of the project, including the Cross Florida Barge Canal, was mothballed. President Kennedy resurrected the Barge Canal in 1963, and later Lyndon Johnson threw his support behind the project. However, it became a clarion for the fledging environmental movement and politicians in south Florida who represented the larger population centers of the state. They were concerned that construction of the canal would harm the ground water aquifers that their part of the state depended on for its water supply. The project was eventually abandoned altogether. More on that story later.

The Tenn-Tom Authority began working with Governor Farris Bryant in 1964. That led to an agreement "of a mutual assistance pact," i.e., both parties would help each other to advance their respective waterway projects. Politics had also improved in West Florida for the Tenn-Tom with the election of Congressman Robert Sikes, who informed the Congress that Pensacola and the Florida Panhandle now supported the waterway and looked forward to its completion. When legislation to approve Florida's joining the compact was introduced in the Florida Legislature in 1967 during Governor Claude

Kirk's administration, it passed unanimously both in the House and in the Senate, with no dissenting votes. The legislation included authorization for an annual appropriation of $15,000. Governor Kirk, who had attended high school in Alabama and earned a law degree there, signed the bill into law on June 26, 1967. In approving the legislation, he stated that he "was delighted for the state of Florida to join hands with her four sister states in pushing for this great project, which will mean so much to the economic development of this broad region."

Although Florida was less affected by the waterway, some of its members were some of the most influential to serve on the compact. State legislation stipulated that the governor's five appointees include two members of the state conservation board, designated by that board. One was Doyle Connor, an elected commissioner of agriculture and one of the most powerful politicians in the state at that time. He served for nearly the entire time the state was a member of the compact. Other notable members included Tom McKenzie, Sr., and later his son, who owned a large tanker trucking company; James Loudermilk, a Pensacola businessman; and Steve Richards, who was affiliated with the Port of Tampa.

Much credit for expanding the compact to cover such a broad region of five states goes to the leadership of the authority, especially to Chairman Governor John Patterson, Vice Chairman Louis Wise, and its other charter members. However, the person who deserves the lion's share of the credit for accomplishing such a feat of political alliance and governmental relations was Glover Wilkins. His exceptional abilities to engender cooperation, if not friendships, with important and influential interests would be even more evident during his service to the waterway in the years to come.

Now with five member states, the authority's membership was composed of the five governors and five additional members from each compact state for a total of 30 members. The Alabama and Mississippi governors had unfettered discretion to appoint their members. Tennessee's law specified that the membership be made up of a member representing each of the western, central, and eastern sections of the state, along with two at-large members. Kentucky's law specified that one of the five members be the lieutenant governor and the other four appointed by the governor. Florida's membership was also different. While the governor had the discretion to appoint three members to four-year terms, the state board of conservation named the remaining two members. In those early years before Congress approved construction of the waterway, the compact devoted all its energies and resources to promoting and nurturing grassroots support within the five-state region for the project and increasing needed bipartisan political support at the state capitols and in the U.S. Congress.

Appendix A lists all the authority members who have served as chairman and vice chairman each year since the compact's inception, as well as those who were appointed administrator/secretary, including their terms of service.

Tenn-Tom congressional supporters, led by Alabama Senators John Sparkman and Lister Hill, met with President Lyndon Johnson in December 1966. Johnson agreed to include funds in his FY 1968 budget to start the project's engineering and design work, which was a step needed before construction could begin. Coincidentally, it was the first President's budget I helped prepare for the Corps of Engineers. Tennessee Governor Buford Ellington's friendship with the President helped influence this important budget decision.

CHAPTER IV
Johnson Endorses Tenn-Tom

Governor Patterson and Barrett Shelton, a newspaper publisher from Decatur, Alabama, and a civic leader in the Tennessee Valley, were two of a handful of influential Southerners who publicly supported John Kennedy for President. The authority heard that the President had decided to include funds for the Tenn-Tom in his next budget. There was no firm evidence that he planned to do so, but regardless, his tragic death squashed any plans he might have had. He had made a similar commitment to fund the Cross Florida Barge Canal, and President Johnson, after succeeding Kennedy, followed with his support of the Florida project. Patterson and the authority wanted such an endorsement for the Tenn-Tom and began taking steps to secure such a commitment. Unfortunately, the compact and the waterway lost Patterson's leadership in 1963, since the Alabama Constitution prevented a governor from serving a second term. George Wallace succeeded Patterson, but his reputation as a staunch segregationist distracted his influence in Washington, as it did for Ross Barnett in Mississippi. Both were embroiled in racial issues. Patterson's political effectiveness at the national level had also been diminished because of the violence suffered by the Freedom Riders while in Alabama during his administration. The baton to lead the compact was passed to Governor Buford Ellington of Tennessee, who served two terms during the 1960s. He was a friend and confidant of President Johnson and served in his administration during the time between his two governorships. The waterway certainly benefited from that close relationship.

At the request of the authority, U.S. Senator John Sparkman of Alabama, also a friend and a close colleague of Johnson when he served in the Senate, met with Johnson in December 1967 to discuss funding for the Tenn-Tom. Joining him were several other waterway supporters from both the U.S. House of Representatives and the U.S. Senate. The delegation requested the President to start funding the waterway's engineering and design (E&D), which was needed to advance the project to the next stage, construction. Before the meeting, BOB prepared briefing papers that recommended that the President not agree to fund the waterway. The project was viewed as lacking economic justification and would pose a major commitment for federal funding if constructed. Nevertheless, Johnson included $600,000 in his FY 1968 budget request to congress to start the E&D of the waterway. This was a major milestone for the Tenn-Tom, as well as one for me. By coincidence, the funds were included in the first budget I helped prepare for the Corps of Engineers. Congress later approved the President's budget request with little fanfare, and funds needed to continue the preconstruction planning and design of the project were included in subsequent fiscal years. Well-deserved credit should go to the waterway's congressional supporters, who helped the project accomplish this important step. However, Governor Ellington's influence on Johnson had much to do with getting this presidential commitment. The next challenge and the most difficult one would be getting the waterway approved as a new construction start, something its promoters had been trying to accomplish for 20 years — since its authorization.

CHAPTER V
My First Budget Season

A budget examiner's job evaluation at BOB is largely based on the quality of work required to develop the President's annual budget. That laborious process starts in mid-September and is generally wrapped up by the end of December, except for addressing agency appeals of BOB's funding decisions and other final preparations of the budget documents for transmittal to Congress by early February. The fiscal year began on July 1, which was later changed to October 1 to give the Congress an additional three months to pass the 13 appropriation bills that fund the federal government. The additional time has been of little help in recent years since the Congress has been unable to fulfill this important constitutional duty and pass the appropriation bills, causing the federal agencies to operate on continuing resolutions, which greatly diminishes any flexibility in funding the affected agencies and their programs.

Except for my boss, Jack Roose, we, the other three examiners for water resources, were all greenhorns in 1966 and were about to be initiated into the budget review and formulation process for the first time. The federal budget process began each year in mid-September when the federal agencies submitted their requests to BOB. Requests included reams of detailed information to justify any proposed new projects, programs, or increases in funding for current programs. In addition to the Corps, the other water resource programs included TVA, three power marketing agencies, the Bureau of Reclamation (BuRec), and several smaller agencies like the International Boundary Water Commission (IBWC), which was part of the State Department. Specific agencies were assigned to each of the three examiners. I was assigned responsibility for TVA and would share the construction account of the Corps with another examiner. I also had responsibility for a couple of other smaller agencies.

Most of the discretionary funding for water programs was in the construction accounts for the Corps and BuRec. We were given a detailed schedule of all the various contracts for each project under construction. The project schedules included both the contracts underway as well as those scheduled for award during the coming fiscal year. They also included the proposed date of the award and the contract's anticipated quarterly earnings or expenditures. The budget needs for the individual projects could be reduced by manipulating or postponing the anticipated contract awards. While stretching out construction in this manner would reduce the budget needs for a project, it could postpone its completion and delay its expected benefits. These delays could also increase the total costs of the project. All these negative impacts had to be weighed against a lower budget amount for the specific project, and ultimately, for the agency.

Most all the Corps and Reclamation projects had their congressional supporters as well as active stakeholders. We examiners were expected to know the identities of these project champions and be cognizant of any specific requests they might have made for funding. There were only a few projects that did not have active political interests. We spent a lot of time meeting with Corps officials. We also met with the so-called project stakeholders, especially concerning those projects eligible to be new construction starts, such as the Tenn-Tom. My first opportunity to meet Glover Wilkins and members of the authority was in the fall of 1966 when they called on BOB to request funding for the waterway. Most of the meetings with the project sponsors were with small groups, but not the authority's meetings. Its meetings were more like formal hearings that several people attended. The meetings usually featured a presentation that addressed some issue related to the waterway, such as its economics. Wilkins would also follow up with a more informal visit in the spring after the details of the budget were known. Most all the other project stakeholders came calling only in the fall. Not Wilkins. He, with his Southern gentlemen's charm, used the spring visits to become more acquainted with the BOB staff.

The two months of intensive budget reviews and meetings culminated in a meeting with the director in mid- to late-November. This director's review was also attended by other key officials from BOB, as well as the White House congressional liaison. We first-timers had heard how important it was to perform well at that meeting. Stephen Aldrich, a fellow examiner and also a newcomer, and I were responsible for reviewing the Corps' request for its construction program. To do so, we had to analyze each project under construction and the estimated earnings of the scores of individual contracts. Aldrich and I once worked 36 hours straight with no sleep and without leaving the office during the week leading up to the director's review. We understood that the director and others attending would focus most of their attention on the projects under construction. Not knowing what to expect, we had over-prepared to the extreme.

The BOB director was Dr. Charles Schultze, a former PhD economist from the University of Maryland. He was there for my first two years and was my favorite of the six directors I worked for during my nine years at BOB. Schultze was a laid-back, Camel-smoking, gregarious individual who made everyone feel at ease. He did not impose his intelligence on anyone, and I never felt uncomfortable in his presence. The director's position has always attracted some of the most capable people to serve in government. During my time there, I had the honor of working for Cap Weinberger, who later served as secretary of defense in the Reagan Administration; and George Schultz, who would serve in other cabinet posts for Nixon and later as Reagan's secretary of state. I also worked for Charles Zwick and Robert Mayo, who had very successful careers in the private sector; as well as Roy Ash, a former CEO of Litton Industries.

The assistant directors I worked for were an impressive list of "who's who" in government. One such assistant director was Dr. Jim

Schlesinger, a brilliant but serious and opinionated former professor at Harvard, who would later become head of the Atomic Energy Commission, director of CIA, and defense secretary during the Nixon/Ford years. Later, Carter picked him to be the first secretary of the Department of Energy. Other notable individuals serving as BOB assistant director included Don Rice, who was about my age and later became head of the Rand Corporation and secretary of the Air Force; John Sawhill, later administrator of the Federal Energy Administration and president of Nature Conservancy; and Frank Carlucci, who held several top governmental positions, including deputy director of the CIA for Carter and defense secretary for Reagan. There were others equally as talented. It seemed the front office of BOB always attracted some of the most intelligent and capable people serving in government, which certainly raised the bar for the budget examiners, including me, and for their level of performance.

The budget hearing with Director Schultze was a pressure-filled, three-hour session. None of us were fired after the meeting, so we assumed we had passed the test, and our bosses were satisfied with our work. I learned later that several examiners were asked to leave after the end of the budget season. That kind of news puts even more pressure on one to survive in that work environment. After the review, the agencies were notified of the director's decisions. The agency heads could appeal any of the decisions. We reviewed any appeals and sent recommendations back to the director. If the agency was still not satisfied with its budget, it could make a final appeal to the White House, but that avenue was only for major issues. The appeal process could last well into the Christmas holidays. During some of the early years, I was frantically shopping for gifts at the downtown department stores on the afternoon of Christmas Eve.

The budget season was hectic, stressful, and all-consuming for four months. These work conditions were likely the reasons why most all the examiners were in their late 20s or 30s and why most of the appointees, like the director and assistant directors, stayed only a couple of years, at most. However, most went on to even higher-level positions in government.

Chapter VI
Nukes To Build Tenn-Tom?

The Atomic Energy Commission (AEC), later to become part of the Department of Energy, initiated a program in 1961 to investigate and test the use of nuclear devices for non-military or peaceful purposes. The program, called Plowshare, involved as many as 23 nuclear explosions, mostly at the Nevada Test Site (NTS) north of Las Vegas. These detonations tested the feasibility of using this method to accomplish major excavations of soil and rock materials for highway construction, canals, and harbors. Detonations also tested the method's use for oil and gas production. The method was similar to today's concept of fracturing shale oil.

In 1964, an Atlantic-Pacific Interoceanic Canal Commission was established to determine the feasibility of using nuclear explosives or conventional methods to build a sea-level canal in Panama or Columbia. A sea-level canal with no locks would be able to accommodate ships with much deeper drafts and handle more commerce than the present Panama Canal. The Corps of Engineers was designated as the engineering agent, coordinating with AEC and the other members of the commission. I had the responsibility of overseeing the Corps' involvement in the canal study and other public works projects included in the Plowshare program.

To work in the Executive Office of the President, a budget examiner must acquire a top-secret clearance and must handle certain sensitive documents. I quickly learned that even that high level of clearance, which I held, would not suffice to be involved in AEC's nuclear program. During most meetings, I was asked to leave the room and wait in the hall until highly sensitive matters were discussed. I told Mr. Carl Swartz, the head of the Natural Resources Programs Division, that I needed a Q clearance, the highest security given by the government, if I were to be involved in Plowshare. He politely told me to try to make it work with my current clearance. I found out later that if I got a Q clearance, Swartz would also have to be cleared at that level, since he was my top supervisor, and he had the safe where such classified documents were kept. I persisted, though, and he finally relented. With the higher clearance, I was exposed to the most fascinating aspects of this highly secret program. I was able to tour the Lawrence Livermore Laboratory in California where nuclear energy research was conducted for the government. To enter the lab, one had to clear three or four checkpoints. It reminded me of something from a James Bond movie.

I visited the NTS a couple of times and saw firsthand the results of some of the nuclear tests. The Limited Test Ban Treaty at that time banned any nuclear tests in space, in the atmosphere, or underwater. All the tests at NTS were underground, and the nuclear devices, generally a one- to three-kiloton bomb, exploded at a depth that was determined by the type of soil or rock surrounding the bomb. The goal was to prevent any debris or radioactive material from escaping into the air. The bomb vaporized the subsurface material near the device, causing the earth above it to cave in, creating a perfect cone, the size of which varied according to the size of the bomb blast. After I'd walked in and around a crater that a detonation created, the technicians would run a Geiger counter over my coveralls and shoes, and it always sounded off. "This probably means the end of me fathering any more children," I would think. I am sure it was safe, as they would not have a visitor like me exposed to any unreasonable danger. However, a National Cancer Benefits Center was established in 1995 to monitor any health-related issues for former employees at NTS.

Those who had contracted some forms of cancer were awarded cash payments of as much as $400,000, tax free. Fortunately, I have had no reason to try to qualify for such largesse.

I went to NTS once to witness an actual blast, but the shot was postponed for several days because of concerns that prevailing winds would carry radioactive emissions into Canada. While I was disappointed to miss seeing an actual detonation, the trip was not a total loss. AEC made arrangements with the Sahara, one of the nicer casinos in Vegas at that time, for government employees to stay for $9 per night. Its expansive buffets with a variety of delicious entrees were less than $2 for dinner. Gamblers got most of their meals free. The best treat was to be entertained in the lounge, for the mere price of a drink, by Don Rickles and other celebrities.

Dr. Edward Teller, a brilliant nuclear physicist and a key member of the Manhattan Project, along with his rival, J. Robert Oppenheimer, designed and built the first nuclear bomb that was dropped on Hiroshima, Japan, to end World War II. Sadly, Teller's long-held jealousies of and insecurities about Dr. Oppenheimer's fame would later tarnish, if not destroy, the reputations of both men. Teller was an advocate of non-military uses of nuclear energy and was instrumental in getting AEC to implement the Plowshare program. While it was before I was associated with the program, Plowshare in 1964 conducted studies and tests to determine the feasibility of using nuclear bombs to excavate about three miles of the deepest excavation of the so-called Divide Cut section of the Tenn-Tom. I was told it was Teller's brainchild. Three routes for excavation were studied, and the Bear Creek route was deemed the best for using nuclear explosives. The proposal was to use a series of devices, ranging from 10 to 50 kilotons, for or a total of 1.9 megatons. By comparison, the bombs that devastated Hiroshima and Nagasaka to end the Second World War were 16 kilotons and 21 kilotons, respectively. For the Tenn-Tom, the nuclear option was dropped because of collateral damage to nearby communities, which included exposing the public to harmful fallout and likely contaminating groundwater. Surprisingly, it was also found to be more expensive than the conventional means of excavating the

Divide Cut section via the Yellow Creek route.

Years later, during a speech I gave at the University of Tennessee, I mentioned this proposal to use nuclear devices. The theme of the conference was multimodal transportation and attracted attendees from throughout the state. I just happened to give my speech on April Fool's Day. In jest, I told the audience that I had a very important announcement I wanted to make concerning the use of nuclear energy to help build the waterway. I went into elaborate details about the Corps of Engineers gaining approval from the Department of Energy to use a series of nuclear devices to excavate the Divide Cut section of Tenn-Tom. I explained that the obvious advantage was that it would accomplish the excavation in a manner of seconds, but there were some disadvantages that had to be dealt with. For example, the entire population of Iuka, Mississippi, would have to be evacuated and relocated. The detonation would also permanently change the course of the Tennessee River to flow south down the Tombigbee, instead of its current northern route to the Mississippi River. Everybody was laughing and knew I was joking — except for two people, a reporter from the Knoxville newspaper and an engineering professor who was moderating the conference. Amazingly, the professor had worked with Dr. Teller on the Plowshare study in 1964. At first, he was elated to hear that his work was about to bear fruit. But when he realized he'd been duped, he became embarrassed and noticeably upset. The newspaper reporter, believing he had the biggest news scoop of a lifetime, dashed out of the auditorium without asking me any follow-up questions and hurriedly wrote his news flash for that afternoon's edition. Fortunately, the newspaper editor questioned the veracity of the story. The editor did include a story about my lame joke, which was later reprinted in *USA Today*.

While the Plowshare program proved the technical feasibility of using nuclear energy for heavy construction projects, such as a sea-level ship canal and/or something like the Tenn-Tom, the AEC did not, because of environmental and political objections and potential international treaty violations, pursue any of the proposed projects.

Chapter VII
Times of Uncertainty

The last half of the 1960s was a tumultuous time of conflicts, protests, and anarchy for the nation, especially for those of us living in Washington, D.C. The Vietnam War continued to escalate with more deaths and casualties, as well as more protesters, especially college students, some who took to the streets to not only protest the nation's involvement in that conflict but also to promote Marxism in our government and way of life. One of the leading groups that helped incite others was the Students for a Democratic Society or SDS. The violence and demonstrations peaked in the summer of 1967 when over 100,000 protesters intent on disrupting the affairs of the government descended on Washington. They tried to literally invade the Pentagon and clashed with policemen and soldiers, resulting in injuries and numerous arrests. The students encircled the Executive Office Building where I worked, and we had to shove and negotiate through a mob of protesters to get inside the building. One night they confiscated trash cans throughout that part of the city and stacked them on the two main bridges across the Potomac River. It must have required a lot of work because it created an impassable log jam of cans that completely blocked any vehicles from driving into the district from Virginia.

The following year was particularly tumultuous. In April 1968,

Dr. Martin Luther King, Jr., was assassinated in Memphis. Rioting broke out in Chicago, Baltimore, and Washington. Rioters burned and looted buildings and stores within about six blocks of the White House. That first afternoon of the rioting, the President dismissed all government workers early for their safety. This was before the Metro or the subway was built, and commuter traffic was so heavy that office hours were staggered. Work hours at some agencies started as early as 7 a.m., others as late as 9 a.m., which was BOB's official arrival time. I knew traffic would be chaotic with everyone leaving at the same time, so I decided to wait until later that evening to head for home in Virginia. Once I was outside and saw all the smoke from the burning buildings and the chaos, I realized how serious the riots were and became very concerned about my own safety.

My route to catch the bus took me along Pennsylvania Avenue next to the iron fence fronting the White House. I glanced in that direction and was shocked to see soldiers installing powerful spotlights to shine into the street. They were setting up machine guns on tripods in case the rioters attacked the White House. I was dumbfounded by such a scene. "Surely, this could only take place in a banana republic and not in the United States," I thought to myself. I remembered thinking my friends and family in Alabama would likely not believe me when I told them what I had just witnessed.

I made it to Virginia without much difficulty, unlike some of my co-workers who left earlier. The rioters attacked some of their buses, knocking out windows and trying to turn over the buses, but fortunately, no one was seriously injured. About a dozen people were killed in the district, and 8,000 were arrested during the four days of rioting before police and federalized troops quelled the looting and burning. The government was completely shut down during that period.

In June 1968, Robert Kennedy was struck down by an assassin's bullet in Los Angeles while he was campaigning for the Democrat presidential nomination. Johnson had decided not to run for another term, mainly because of his growing unpopularity that stemmed from our country's involvement in the Vietnam War. Some expected that Robert Kennedy's death might spark another series of riots, and the White House made preparations just in case, but none occurred. Later that summer, some 10,000 protesters, led by SDS, invaded Chicago to create havoc for the Democrat Convention, but they were met by 23,000 policemen and national guardsmen. The disruptive and chaotic convention eventually nominated Hubert Humphrey to run against Richard Nixon. No one was killed on the streets during the demonstrations, but there were a lot of broken bones and injuries on both sides. While all this turmoil was happening on the home front, more and more Americans were being killed and maimed in Vietnam as that conflict continued to expand.

The next year, 1969, was an even more eventful year for me personally. Nixon had been elected President, and we in the Bureau of the Budget had to adjust and make the transition from working for a Democrat President to serving a new Republican administration. We were expected to immediately accommodate the new administration's policies and program priorities. To make matters even more difficult for me, my boss, Jack Roose, who had recruited me, announced that year that he had accepted a position with another agency and that he would be leaving BOB. While I was pleased with his career advancement, his leaving was a mixed blessing for me.

Much to my surprise, I was promoted to succeed Roose as principal examiner. All my hard work was paying off with more responsibilities and more pay. The downside was that two of my colleagues, who also had been in contention for the position, felt it was time for them to explore other opportunities. Other agencies offered them attractive positions, so my next chore was to hire three examiners, including someone for my former position. I was fortunate to find three very intelligent and aggressive young men, one of whom I recruited from the Philadelphia District of the Corps. They all did an outstanding job while at BOB and later had impressive careers, one becoming a corporate senior vice president for State Farm Insurance.

Chapter VIII
The Nixon Years

The election of Richard M. Nixon in 1968 brought some major changes in government, such as "New Federalism," a concept in which, as Nixon said, "Power, funds, and responsibility will flow from Washington to the states and to the people." He wanted to centralize more power and influence within the White House. To do so, he created the Domestic Council within the White House, which was tasked with formulating and coordinating domestic policy. To help bring an end to the war in Vietnam and foster better international relations, including dialogues with China, Nixon strengthened the National Security Council and put Henry Kissinger in charge.

Another Nixon initiative that affected me personally was the expansion of the mission and responsibilities of BOB. The bureau's new role was to direct federal agencies to implement better management practices needed to help improve an agency's performance in carrying out its programs. We worked with several different analytical methods, including a process called the Planning, Programing, and Budgeting System and another called Management by Objectives. We budget examiners had the burden of introducing these systems to the agencies and compelling them to implement them as part of the federal budget process. We spent many hours getting these systems implemented. Looking back on that, I doubt whether any of these efforts led to better decisions on federal spending. With its new management moniker, the Bureau of the Budget (BOB) was renamed the Office of Management and Budget, or OMB. These new responsibilities, along with requests for assistance from the new Domestic Council, just added more demands on the already overworked budget examiners.

By consolidating more power within the White House and attracting so many talented people to join his administration, Nixon began to have considerable influence on the governance of the federal establishment. Had it not been for a preoccupation with ending the Vietnam War and later the Watergate scandal, which led to his downfall, Nixon likely would have been one of our most successful presidents, certainly during that century. His administration began taking steps to reform the welfare programs, strengthen federal energy programs, and initiate policies and measures to protect and improve the environment. Watergate sidetracked these and other policy initiatives.

The Congress had no institutional abilities to establish budget priorities or develop fiscal and economic information independent of what the executive branch produced. Nixon was running roughshod over the Congress by impounding appropriations for programs that he believed were not consistent with his administration's priorities. The Congress, in turn, rebelled from this domineering treatment and abrogation of its constitutional responsibilities by passing the Congressional Budget and Impoundment Control Act in 1974. Included in the legislation was the establishment of budget committees in both houses of Congress, which eroded the more overarching funding prerogatives long held by the appropriations committees as well as by OMB. The legislation also established an independent and nonpartisan Congressional Budget Office to serve the Congress similar to the way OMB served the executive branch. Another important change was revising the federal fiscal year to begin on October 1 instead of July 1.

Nixon was the first "green" President and was unequaled in advancing the burgeoning environmental movement, which began in the 1960s. Americans, including politicians, became increasingly more concerned about the environment and its effects on health and quality of life. Rachel Carson's widely read book, *Silent Spring*, focused attention on the effects of DDT on many bird species, including America's symbol, the bald eagle. Nixon later abolished the use of DDT insecticide. In 1969, a river in Cleveland, Ohio, caught fire and burned from the dumping of industrial waste. The quality of air in many large urban areas had become nearly unbreathable. These deteriorating conditions led to the first Earth Day in 1970, which was billed as a national holiday, of sorts.

Nixon's biographies do not describe him as having any innate feelings or concerns about nature or conservation while he was growing up in southern California in a middle-class setting, or later as a struggling lawyer. I suspect he became interested in the environmental movement because he foresaw the political advantages of embracing it. He also had some influential advisors in his administration in that regard, like Nat Reed, a conservationist from Florida who was appointed by the President as the assistant secretary of interior for National Parks, Fish, and Wildlife. He and other environmentalists in the administration, like John Whitaker, had considerable sway with the President.

One of the President's early actions was to establish by executive order the Environmental Protection Agency (EPA), a move that was later ratified by Congress. He approved the National Environmental Policy Act (NEPA) of 1969 and a follow-up bill in 1970, arguably the most important and far-reaching legislation concerning environmental quality. The Council on Environmental Quality was also created and installed as a functioning component of the Executive Office of the President. Nixon later approved the Air Quality Act, the Water Quality Act, and the Endangered Species Act. These laws, along with NEPA, are the framework for most of the federal programs and regulations concerning the environment.

Nixon Nixes a Waterway

With the endorsements of both Presidents Kennedy and Johnson, construction of the Cross Florida Barge Canal was progressing well when Nixon took office, despite growing local and national environmental opposition. In 1969, the Environmental Defense Fund (EDF) filed a suit in the Federal District Court in the District of Columbia to stop construction of the canal, arguing that the Corps was in violation of NEPA, among other allegations. In NEPA, Congress requires all federal agencies to prepare an environmental impact statement (EIS) for projects. The Congress did not grandfather Corps projects already under construction. By not grandfathering those projects, the Corps was in violation of NEPA on the day the law was signed and was subject to litigation until it could complete the EIS process for its construction projects. Environmental groups were having a field day filing suits throughout the nation against projects that were under construction and not in compliance with NEPA.

On January 15, 1971, the D.C. federal district judge granted a preliminary injunction stopping construction of the canal until the outcome of the environmental litigation. At the time, about $75 million had been spent on the project, with work nearly completed on two locks. Four days later, much to my surprise and dismay, the President issued an executive order suspending further work on the project. My boss, Wes Sasaki, and I were called to the White House, where we learned of the decision to stop the project. White House staff were concerned that the Corps might not comply with the President's directive to stop work on the canal until the Congress had the opportunity to overturn the President's decision. I was directed to immediately travel to Florida to make sure the Corps complied. I had no doubts the Corps would act as the President directed, and when I arrived at the project site, all work had been halted.

One morning, the project engineer and I went to a local cafe for coffee. I cannot recall the name of the town, but I believe it was Palatka, Florida. As soon as we were seated, a man came to our table and introduced himself as the city's mayor. I knew immediately that I had been set up by the Corps. The mayor asked me to join him because he had something for me to see and to take back to Washington. He showed me the early stages of a port the city was building in anticipation of the barge canal being completed. With tears in his eyes, the mayor asked me, "What am I going to do with this now that you've stopped the canal? We've wasted scarce public funds." I responded, "I didn't stop the work on the project. The President did. If you want my advice, join with the other project supporters to lobby the Congress to intercede on behalf of the project's continued construction." While I tried to appear firm and resolute, I felt a lot of empathy for the mayor, since the federal government was no longer fulfilling its commitments to complete the project. Proponents of the project did lobby Congress, but no further work was ever accomplished, and in 1990, Congress deauthorized the project. The part of the canal that was already completed is now called the Margorie Harris Carr Cross Florida Greenway, named after an environmentalist who successfully fought construction of the barge canal. Years later, there were serious efforts by some in Congress to stop construction of Tenn-Tom, even though it was nearly halfway completed. Some waterway supporters said the Congress would never be so irresponsible as to abandon that much of an investment. I reminded them what had happened with the Cross Florida Barge Canal.

Nixon and Tenn-Tom

Nixon lost his first presidential race to John Kennedy in 1960, although he won 26 states compared to 22 states for Kennedy. The popular vote was nearly a tie. With a total of 68 million voters, Kennedy garnered a mere 100,000 more than Nixon. Although Nixon won the race against Hubert Humphrey in 1968, winning 32 states with 302 electoral votes and narrowly winning the popular vote, that race was, nevertheless, too close for comfort for the Nixon camp. In that election, George Wallace, governor of Alabama, had run on the American Independent Party ticket. He and the 10 million people who voted for him nearly played the spoiler in the election by forcing the decision to name the winner away from the Electoral College and placing the decision into the hands of the U.S. House of Representatives. Wallace had won five states in the Deep South and attracted a lot of supporters from the industrialized areas in the Northern and Midwestern states. Having narrowly lost in 1960 and winning much too closely in 1968, the Nixon campaign staff immediately began preparing for the 1972 campaign. An important part of that plan was to capture the states Wallace had won, as well as other states in the South. The Tennessee-Tombigbee Waterway became an important part of this so-called "Southern Strategy."

With pre-construction planning, or engineering and design, now funded each year, thanks to President Johnson's initiative, the Tenn-Tom Waterway Development Authority had begun an all-out campaign to secure funds to start construction of the waterway. It solicited prominent Republicans from the compact states to use their influence to persuade the Nixon Administration to fund the waterway. Jack Edwards, an Alabama congressman who represented the southern part of the state, including Mobile; and Louie Nunn, governor of Kentucky, were especially effective in that regard. The congressional delegation, led by U.S. Senator John Stennis of Mississippi and Representatives Joe Evins of Tennessee and Jamie Whitten of Mississippi, had worked in unison to keep the waterway's pre-construction planning funded each year. By doing so, the project had progressed to the stage of being eligible for funding as a new construction start.

Jack Edwards was one of several Republicans from the South who rode Republican presidential candidate Barry Goldwater's coattails into Congress in 1964. Goldwater was a popular conservative U.S. Senator from Arizona. Edwards worked tirelessly to persuade the White House to include $1 million in the President's budget to start the waterway's construction. The campaign and political staff were intrigued with the proposal because of the waterway's popularity in the region, and it fit perfectly into the President's Southern Strategy for reelection. However, OMB and the White House's Domestic Council were adamantly opposed to funding the project. To them, the waterway's economics were marginally justified, at best, and the $1 million startup funding would commit the federal government to an eventual obligation far exceeding $1 billion. In the fall of 1969, the waterway authority met with Director Robert Mayo and other representatives from the White House and OMB, including me, to formally request $1 million be included in the President's 1971 budget. The meeting included a presentation by the waterway compact's economics consultant, Dr. Joseph Hartley of Indiana University, in an attempt to allay skeptics' concerns about the project's economic justification.

There were some, including the railroad industry, who did not believe it made political sense for the President to endorse the Tenn-Tom just after he had stopped construction of the Cross Florida Barge Canal. Local and national environmental organizations, as well as the railroad lobby, had joined forces for the first time to fight the Florida project and were basking in their victory. There were some major differences between the Tenn-Tom and the Florida project. The waterway authority's promotional campaign had unified a broad-based regional grassroots support for Tenn-Tom, and as a result, it enjoyed strong bipartisan political support in the Congress and in the state capitols. The Cross Florida Barge Canal never had that. The Florida project faced strong opposition from both local and national environmental groups, while the Tenn-Tom had no organized opposition. However, that would soon change.

Nixon listened to his political advisors instead of his "bean counters" in OMB and included $1 million in his FY 1971 budget to start construction of the waterway. The dreams and hopes of many generations of Tenn-Tom supporters were now one big step closer to becoming a reality. Having the funds in the President's budget made it easier for those waterway supporters who served on the House and Senate appropriations committees to merely concur with the President's recommendation. With little fanfare, the Congress approved the start-up funds as part of the Corps' appropriations bill. The President signed the FY 1971 public works appropriations bill, including the Tenn-Tom's funds, in October 1970, another momentous milestone for the project.

The Corps of Engineers had faced a nearly impossible task since January 1, 1970, when Nixon signed the National Environmental

Policy Act. The law stipulated that a sponsoring agency must prepare an environmental impact statement (EIS) for any project or action that might affect the environment. As stated earlier, NEPA did not exempt or grandfather those projects or actions that were already underway when the law was signed. That presented a dilemma for the Corps. Every Corps project under construction that had not gone through the EIS process was in violation of NEPA. Environmental groups were quick to recognize this violation of the law and began filing lawsuits against some of these projects, expecting the courts to at least grant a temporary injunction that would halt construction or any further progress until the projects met NEPA's requirements. The Corps, like others, were caught by surprise when Nixon included funding for the Tenn-Tom. Once that decision was known, Corps headquarters directed the Mobile District to immediately begin its environmental review of the waterway. Preparation of the EIS was given the highest priority. An EIS can be time-consuming and complex, especially for a project like the Tenn-Tom, which would be the largest and most costly project ever undertaken by the Corps. Even the Corps' expeditious work to comply with NEPA would not keep the waterway out of the crosshairs of the environmentalists and L&N (CSX) Railroad.

Tenn-Tom's Groundbreaking

The Tennessee-Tombigbee Waterway Development Authority recognized the importance of getting the President to attend a groundbreaking ceremony or some other waterway-related event. Such a personal relationship or involvement by the President could be viewed politically as his now "owning the project," and that association could solidify his continued support for the project. That presidential exposure would prove to be a difficult undertaking. Many in the White House and in OMB strongly advised the President against attending any waterway event. Even the newly constituted Council on Environmental Quality joined the naysayers by pointing out that the waterway's environmental impacts were unknown since the NEPA process had not been completed. Its potential impacts could be profound since the project included construction of ten locks and dams, millions of cubic yards of excavation, and other improvements along the 234-mile project. Others argued the project was not economically justified and not worthy of such a large public investment.

The authority, which recognized the importance of having a Republican lead the compact, elected Governor Louie Nunn of Kentucky as its chairman. Nunn became a very vocal advocate for the waterway. He wrote President Nixon and advised him that his affiliation with the Tenn-Tom, because of its broad regional popularity, would not only be beneficial to his Southern Strategy, but the waterway would also be an economic generator once it was completed. Some in the White House were concerned that Governor Wallace might use such an event to try to upstage the President or embarrass him. Congressman Edwards assured them the governor would never do such a thing. When the President's schedulers said the President couldn't commit to a date because of his busy schedule, the authority responded by telling the White House to pick any date and place during April or May and it would guarantee a big turnout.

This open-ended invitation and the President's political operatives' intent to win the South in the next election convinced the White House that the President should dedicate the waterway at a time and place to be determined. A ceremony was held in Mobile, Alabama, on May 25, 1971, to commemorate the Tenn-Tom's start of construction. The President was the featured speaker. The state docks where the ceremony was held estimated that some 75,000 waterway supporters and politicians of every stripe were there to give the President a rousing welcome. The event was great for Nixon's campaign and was a momentous occasion for the waterway and its future. Governor Wallace was one of the many dignitaries who attended, and as expected, he welcomed his former political opponent to Alabama. Wallace could not have been a more congenial host. Given the significance of this milestone event for the waterway, all of the compact governors attended, including Governor Reuben Askew of Florida, who attended his first waterway event; and Kentucky Governor Louie Nunn, who was instrumental in persuading the Nixon White House to endorse the waterway. When the President announced he would be traveling to Mobile for the waterway's ribbon cutting, I fantasized about how nice it would be if I could accompany the President to my hometown on Air Force One and see my friends there, but I immediately returned to reality and thought: "It ain't gonna happen."

The Nixon campaign staff had hoped the President's endorsement of the Tenn-Tom might dissuade Wallace from running again. However, he did run this time for the Democrat nomination. He ran a strong campaign for the blue-collar vote and won several states, including Michigan and Maryland. However, that all ended when he was shot five times at a campaign stop in Maryland, leaving him paralyzed from the waist down. He still was the third-highest vote getter of the 17 candidates, but his injuries forced him to withdraw from the race before the Democrat Convention. Nixon went on to win the 1972 race in a landslide victory against George McGovern, winning all the states except one and amassing some 520 electoral votes to only 17 for McGovern. That resounding victory would be short-lived as the Watergate scandal grew into one of the biggest constitutional crises the nation had ever faced.

President Richard Nixon traveled to Mobile, Alabama, on May 25, 1971, to dedicate the start of construction of Tenn-Tom. As part of his "Southern Strategy" campaign to win reelection, he included $1 million in his 1972 budget to initiate construction of this long-awaited project. An estimated 75,000 waterway supporters greeted the President and other dignitaries, including all five governors of the waterway compact as well as members of Congress from those states. Greeting the President here were Governor George Wallace and Mrs. Cornelia Wallace and on the right, Governor Windfield Dunn (Tennessee).

Chapter IX
Tenn-Tom Goes To Court

About the time President Nixon was in Mobile dedicating the Tenn-Tom, environmental groups were conspiring about how they could use legal means to stop construction of the waterway. The Environmental Defense Fund (EDF), a nonprofit environmental advocacy organization, and the Committee for Leaving the Environment Natural, or CLEAN, joined forces to stop the waterway. EDF had a successful track record of challenging Corps projects in the courts and was a major player in the successful campaign to kill the Cross Florida Barge Canal. EDF also later helped finance a lawsuit to stop the construction of Gillham Dam in Arkansas. Gillham Dam was the first fully litigated case challenging the Corps' compliance with the provisions of NEPA. The New York City-based group felt confident that it would enjoy similar success challenging the Tenn-Tom.

CLEAN was a shell of an organization established by two professors at Mississippi State University (MSU). The organization attracted only a handful of students as members. However, its involvement in any ligation against the waterway was important because it addressed the question of standing. CLEAN could argue that its members who lived near the proposed waterway would be affected and harmed by any adverse environmental impacts that the construction caused.

CLEAN and EDF were not strangers. They had formed a partnership in 1970 and filed a lawsuit in the U.S. District Court of D.C. to stop the use of a new product that was developed at MSU to kill or control fire ants. The litigation was never adjudicated because one of the participating states working with the U.S. Department of Agriculture withdrew its support for using this product because of its similarity to DDT, which had just been banned. However, they felt the lawsuit helped publicize an awareness of the dangers of the biocide, leading to its ban, and believed the same could have a similar effect on the public support of Tenn-Tom. The coalition filed a lawsuit against the Corps of Engineers and Tenn-Tom in the D.C. district court on July 14, 1971, less than two months after Nixon's ribbon-cutting event in Mobile. To help give the lawsuit more standing for the plaintiffs, a professor at Mississippi University for Women, located in Columbus, Mississippi, joined as the third plaintiff in the case. To litigate the case, the group hired Richard Arnold, who had gained experience in Corps practices, including its adoption of regulations concerning NEPA, during his successful involvement in the Gillham Dam case. He would prove to be a formidable foe for the waterway. After hearing arguments from witnesses on both sides, the judge issued a temporary injunction to postpone the start of construction until a court hearing could be held to consider a permanent injunction as requested by the plaintiffs. The Tenn-Tom Authority and other waterway supporters realized the outcome of this fight would determine whether the project would proceed or suffer the same fate of the Cross Florida Barge Canal.

The authority had three immediate issues to address in addition to coordinating a legal defense of the waterway. Wilkins and the authority's in-house attorneys, Bill Burgin and Hunter Gholson of Columbus, Mississippi, immediately proposed that the waterway compact represent the member states and other interests as a defendant-intervenor. The states approved the proposal, which allowed the authority to take an active role in the defense of the waterway. Such involvement in the litigation would be a financial burden for this small agency, but as Wilkins told the authority members, "We might as well go out of business if the waterway is not victorious in the courts."

The Tombigbee River Valley Water Management District, the Mississippi-designated agency for fulfilling that state's local cooperation obligations to the project, also became a defendant-intervenor. The district was a productive partner with the authority to address the myriad issues and threats the waterway would face before its completion. Jimmie Mills, a former fellow engineering student at MSU and later a colleague with the Corps, served as the district's chief engineer for many years. He later served as its executive director.

Wilkins learned that the senior attorneys with more trial experience in the Justice Department were in its Civil Division and not in its Land and Natural Resources Division, where cases like the Tenn-Tom were normally assigned. U.S. Senator James O. Eastland of Mississippi chaired the Judiciary Committee, and his leadership and influence in that position would pay great dividends for the waterway's case. He requested the attorney general (AG) to move the case to the Civil Division, and the AG agreed. It was an important accomplishment for the defense. The Justice attorneys who defended the Corps and the waterway were outstanding and could take much credit for the eventual outcome of the case.

The next task would be much more difficult to accomplish. The defense felt that it was crucial for the case to be moved to a federal district court closer to the waterway. The Justice Department attorneys believed the district court in North Mississippi was the best venue, but the two defendants-intervenors, the waterway authority and the water management district, instead wanted the case moved to the south Alabama district. They were likely swayed by the Corps, since that venue would have been more convenient for accessing records and data ensconced in the Mobile District office. For fear that such a request would upset the presiding judge, the Justice Department initially chose not to request a change in venue but later argued to have the case transferred to North Mississippi. However, the two defendant-intervenors continued to argue for transferring the case to the federal court in Mobile. Much to everyone's surprise, the presiding judge in D.C., in January 1972, agreed to transfer the case to North Mississippi, where it would be tried by that district court's chief judge, William Keady. The rumor was that Senator Eastland persuaded the judge to grant the change of venue.

The Judiciary Chairman had publicly berated the judge who issued the temporary injunction. U.S. Senator John Sparkman of Alabama had also weighed in by issuing a press release that strongly recommended transferring the case from the D.C. court. The change of venue and the assignment of the case to justice's Civil Division greatly improved the chances for the defendants to win the case.

Judge Keady immediately took charge and scheduled the trial to begin in June 1972 with a pretrial hearing in April of that year. He ruled at the pretrial hearing that the plaintiffs' arguments about the soundness of the waterway's economic justification was not germane. Such questions were best heard and decided by Congress and not the courts. The judge further ruled that the trial would consider only those arguments related to the plaintiffs' main complaint that the Corps had not followed the procedural requirements of NEPA. The Corps had hurriedly completed the project's EIS, which concluded that studies and research would continue during construction to address any mitigative or enhancement measures that might be needed concerning the project's effects on the environment. The judge's ruling to narrow the scope of the trial was devastating to the plaintiffs. They had marshaled an army of expert witnesses to address the economic, ecological, and biological aspects of the project's potential impacts, only to learn that many of these issues would not be litigated.

The trial lasted eight days. The authority encouraged supporters to attend the trial, which was held in Aberdeen, Mississippi. There was never an empty seat in the courtroom. In August 1972, Judge Keady ruled in favor of the defendants. He dissolved the preliminary injunction and dismissed the plaintiffs' case with prejudice, which barred those complaints from future litigation. The plaintiffs immediately appealed the decision to the Fifth Circuit Court of Appeals and filed a flurry of motions to stall any work on the waterway. The Fifth Circuit concurred with Keady on lifting the injunction, which meant construction could commence, pending the decision on the merits of the plaintiffs' appeal. The Appeals Court finally ruled in April 1974, nearly three years after the lawsuit was first filed, and found that the Corps had complied with the provisions of NEPA.

On December 12, 1972, at the site of the Gainesville Lock and Dam (later to be named after Howell Heflin of Alabama), the authority held a second groundbreaking to officially begin construction on the waterway, Ultimately, the litigation had delayed construction by 18 months. That delay not only increased the total cost of the project, but it also deferred its economic benefits for that many months. Costs to litigate a case of this kind can be astronomical, not only for attorney fees and court costs, but for the cost of research and preparation of expert witness testimonies and other exhibits. In this case and many others, it was all for naught.

CHAPTER X
Learning on the Job

We examiners at OMB were encouraged to work with our respective agencies to learn more about their programs, priorities, and issues. I took full advantage of the less demanding spring and summer months at OMB to see firsthand some program activities, including projects, and to learn more about issues with those agencies for which I was responsible. These field trips took me to distant places throughout the United States. One of the more memorable trips included a three-day ride in a small, fast helicopter normally used by the Bureau of Reclamation to inspect high voltage transmission lines. We left Phoenix, Arizona, and flew along the Gila River to Yuma, where I ate for the first and maybe the last time truly authentic Mexican food. From there we flew south along the Colorado River into Mexico to where it empties into the Gulf of California. Little did I know one of the most difficult and complex issues I would face at OMB would involve the Colorado River. The next day we headed north along the Colorado River to Lake Havasu and saw the London Bridge, the same bridge that spanned the River Thames in London from 1831 until its disassembly and transport to Arizona in 1968. This is also where a series of water conveyance works divert water for more than 300 miles from the Colorado River to supply the Phoenix and Tucson areas. The project, which I was heavily involved in later during my time at the Interior Department, was called the Central Arizona Project, or CAP, and took some 20 years to complete at a cost of $4 billion.

Somewhere north of Blythe, California, the pilot showed me something I never knew existed in North America: ground drawings or geoglyphs similar to those in Peru. About 200 of these drawings, depicting birds, snakes, geometric shapes, and human forms, are scattered throughout the desert. The California geoglyphs are distinguishable only from the air, which raises the obvious question: How were the Indians able to draw these shapes and forms in such proper scale without the benefit of an above or overhead perspective? Could they have had some extraterrestrial assistance? There is a question about their dates of origin, but some estimate they were drawn sometime between 900 BC and 1200 BC. When I was there 50 years ago, their existence was purposely concealed to discourage public visitation. I understand they are well known now, and I hope this unique national treasure is being protected from harm by off-road vehicles and other intrusions.

I left that spectacular creation of man to see another testament of human ingenuity: the Hoover Dam in Nevada. We approached the dam through the Black Canyon, flying about midway from the top of the canyon's cliffs. The pilot was obviously showing me his skills. Flying through the canyon, I saw at eye level bighorn sheep perched on ledges that seemed to be only a few inches wide. We hovered over the dam before landing, which gave me an ideal perspective and appreciation of this engineering marvel. The dam is about 700 feet high and forms Lake Mead, the largest man-made reservoir in the world. The dam was started in 1931 as a "make work" project by the Bureau of Reclamation during the height of the Great Depression. Amazingly, it was completed in four years at a cost of less than $50 million, a pittance compared to current building costs. During peak construction, the project employed over 5,000 workers, who lived in makeshift quarters in this desolate location. More than 100 people were killed toiling in some of the most hazardous working conditions of any kind of heavy construction work.

During my tour of the dam and powerhouse, one of the dam's 17 generators was idle for repairs. This gave me a rare opportunity to go inside the giant turbine. The turbine rotates from the force of water, which spins the generator and produces electricity. Standing inside the turbine was unsettling. The only thing separating me from a 700-foot wall of water were the gates on a penstock, and anyone could've opened them by merely flipping a switch. "I hope no one working there has a grudge against someone from Washington," I said in jest before walking into the turbine. For an engineer, touring Hoover Dam was like visiting the Taj Mahal. The huge dam, along with Lake Mead, provides electricity for 1.3 million homes, supplies 18 million people with fresh water, and irrigates 2 million acres of farmland. This tour of the Colorado River proved very helpful just a few months later when I became involved in an international issue regarding Mexico's rights to water from the river.

I was fortunate to see a lot of this wonderful country during these kinds of field trips while I worked at OMB and later at the Interior Department. My bucket list includes traveling to Hawaii, the only state I have never visited. My trips when I was at the Interior Department also took me to Puerto Rico and the Virgin Islands. There were many other memorable trips, but none compared to the Colorado River trip.

My friend who had rented our home in Mobile eventually was able to purchase it, which allowed me to buy a home in Virginia. I purchased a townhouse in Centreville in a new development called London Towne. The population in Northern Virginia was exploding in the 1970s, and real estate was certainly a seller's market. Fearing some other buyer would beat me to the purchase, I bought the property with only the foundation finished and sealed the deal based on a tour of a model home. The development included a new elementary school within walking distance. Centreville was considered the outer limits of Washington's suburbia, but the quality of living there far outweighed the inconvenience of commuting 25 miles to work.

Living in North Virginia offered a lot of opportunities for day trips on the weekends, and I took full advantage of those diversions from my high-pressure and ever-demanding job. Those trips provided much-needed therapy, both physically and mentally. North Virginia was convenient to Chesapeake Bay and the beaches along the eastern shore and the Blue Ridge mountains, and all the natural attractions that were even closer. Virginia is part of the cradle of American history, with many historic places like Williamsburg and Civil War battlefields. We lived only a mile or so from the Manassas Battlefield, which was my family's favorite place to sled after a snow. Once during a hike with my son and his Cub Scout den members, we discovered the remains of an old grist mill on Cub Run near our home. After checking with the county historical organization, I learned there was no record of the mill. After more research, the historical group concluded the mill was likely built in the 1750s before the Revolutionary War. Nearby was Bull Run, which was a prominent location in two important Civil War battles, the First and Second Battles of Manassas. Fitzhugh Lee Thomas, a namesake of two famous Confederate generals and a colleague at OMB, lived on a large farm that joined the Manassas Battlefield. The King of England granted the land to his family in the 1660s.

Unlike today, Washington in those days also offered attractions and events to enjoy without any fear of crime or risk to personal safety. During the summer, the city offered free concerts held on a floating band shell along the Potomac River. This was a great place for a picnic in the early evening while listening to the Washington Symphony or one of the excellent military bands. The National Geographic Society frequently held public presentations about its expeditions or travels. There were other diversions that helped break the drudgery and pressure of working at OMB, like the bureau's fast-pitch softball and football teams that were part of a D.C. government agency league. Our games were played on the Washington Mall, the open space between the Washington and Lincoln monuments, near our office. One Saturday morning in the fall, we interrupted our budget review work to play a game of flag football against the Smithsonian Institution. Flag football is normally not a rough game, but I remember this game well. We were not that good, but we felt we could beat a bunch of archeologists and historians. Unfortunately, the Smithsonian team consisted of 11 big bruisers who no doubt spent all their time moving filing cabinets and dinosaur bones. They beat us unmercifully, and by the end of the game I was covered in claw marks, bloody lips, and contusions, but I still had to go back to work. One of my teammates suggested I go see the White House medical staff. I was reluctant, but my colleague was insistent, and he led me away to the infirmary. The Navy doctor was delighted to have a patient, since his patients are usually limited to the President and, in emergencies, those working in the White House. He eagerly cleaned my scratches and applied Band-Aids and bandages. I thanked him and went back to work, wondering if anyone at OMB other than me had ever been treated by the President's doctor.

I have always enjoyed coffee and found it very inconvenient to leave my desk and go down two flights of stairs to the cafeteria or snack bar in the basement of the Executive Office Building for just a cup of coffee. I decided to buy a coffee pot for the office, a Mr. Coffee, which had just come on the market. My office started selling a cup for a dime, and whoever drank the last cup had to make a fresh pot. The arrangement was a hit, and we began selling coffee to everyone on the floor. Unfortunately, one of the busybodies on the floor informed me I was in violation of General Services Administration (GSA) regulations that forbid electrical appliances in offices. GSA is the landlord for all federal buildings. I told him that I planned to keep making coffee until GSA shut me down, and if that happened, he was the number one suspect for "ratting" on our operation. As far as I know, Mr. Coffee pot is still there making coffee.

I was amazed by how much money the coffee pot was generating — enough to open an account at the local credit union. We would declare dividends two or three times each year and use the proceeds to fund office parties. For one of the parties I hosted at my home, I bought lobsters for each of the 20 or so coworkers and their spouses who came. Now, I'm a Southern guy, and I had been told a lobster must be kept alive until it's steamed or boiled. Not knowing any better, I dumped the lobsters in an upstairs bathtub — full of tap water

— until I boiled them for dinner. Later, I heard a lot of commotion upstairs, and when I went to check it out, I found my son and one of his friends attacking the lobsters with sticks. By the time the party started, I was sure all the lobsters were dead, but there was no way that I was going to buy replacements, given the expense. Fortunately, no one got sick, as far as I know. Turnover at OMB was frequent, and the coffee fund helped subsidize some legendary farewell luncheons. Those luncheons, held at local eateries and bars, would last for hours. These kinds of diversions helped those of us working in such a stressful environment to maintain some perspective, if not sanity. We worked hard, but we played hard too, sometimes.

Colorado River Controversy

One of the most difficult and complex issues I dealt with at OMB involved international treaty violations with Mexico concerning water from the Colorado River. The Colorado River is one of the most extensively developed, heavily regulated, and litigated rivers in the world. The Colorado flows 1,450 miles through parts of seven Western states and eventually empties into Mexico's Gulf of California. The states came together to form an interstate compact in 1920 to apportion the water yielded by the river basin among the compact states. Nevertheless, those same states have fought over these allocations, which has led to myriad lawsuits, including a 1963 case decided by the U.S. Supreme Court, which settled a long-standing dispute between Arizona and California concerning the amount of water they were entitled to from the Colorado River. Since that 1963 case, populations have greatly increased in the basin states, which has created even greater demand for water — more water than the river basin can accommodate. There's an old saying that goes, "In the West, whiskey is for drinking, and water is for fighting!"

To complicate matters, under the terms of a 1944 treaty, Mexico is entitled to a share of the Colorado's water. The treaty stipulates that Mexico is entitled to 1.5 million acre-feet per year of water from the Colorado. Beginning in the 1960s, though, the water Mexico was receiving was so salty it was unusable for drinking or irrigating crops.

The river is naturally salty, and as more water was used to leach salt from irrigated soils, the return flows from those irrigated croplands were making their way back into the river and actually exacerbating the salinity problem for Mexico. This became the most serious issue between the two countries, and the president of Mexico had threatened to sue the United States in the International Court of Justice over its perceived treaty violation. The experts felt Mexico would likely prevail in the courts.

President Nixon and his national security advisor, Dr. Henry Kissinger, were heavily involved in trying to bring the Vietnam War to an end, and Kissinger had told his staff he was not to be distracted by other international issues until the war was settled. To begin addressing the problem with Mexico in Kissinger's absence, the President appointed Herbert Brownell, Eisenhower's attorney general and a member of Nixon's brain trust during his first campaign. My staff and I were assigned to Brownell and charged with helping find a solution that would appease Mexico without alienating the basin states. I soon realized that it would be a hard nut to crack.

We spent the next several weeks analyzing an exhaustive number of alternatives, but none was ideal. The Bureau of Reclamation and the states were not cooperative. They believed Mexico was already getting much more water under the treaty than it deserved. The states that depended on water from the Colorado River, especially Arizona, Nevada, and Southern California, were exploding in population. These increased demands were beginning to compete for water used for irrigation and other domestic uses, like golf courses. The states were unwilling to give up one additional drop of water to Mexico.

We finally arrived at what we believed was the most cost-effective and viable solution. Our recommended solution included adopting some conservation measures and eliminating some low-priority, if not wasteful, uses of water from the river. Lining the All-American and Coachella canals with concrete would save nearly 100,000 acre-feet of water annually that was otherwise seeping into the ground. An irrigation district near Yuma, Arizona, was so laden with salt that the district was dumping 10 feet of water on each acre of irrigated land just to grow low-quality oranges suitable only for making juice. Such wasteful use of a scarce commodity was possible only because the district owned the water rights to that amount of water. What's more, the irrigation district had to pay only a small amount for the water, which the federal government and U.S. taxpayers heavily subsidized. We recommended that the government purchase the irrigation district's water rights and those of other marginal operations along the lower Colorado. These acquired water rights, plus the water saved by lining the irrigation canals with concrete, could then be credited to Mexico and used to improve the quality of the water it was entitled to under the terms of the treaty.

As expected, the basin states were adamantly opposed to our solution. Instead, they proposed that a series of desalting plants be built, some costing as much as $250 million and all with high operating costs. Interior had an Office of Saline Water (OSW) that had been conducting research on different types of desalting technology. OSW primarily concentrated on reverse osmosis and distillation technologies. The distillation process worked similar to that of a whiskey still, and several commercial prototypes were already in operation in some Middle Eastern countries, Australia, and other arid regions of the world. Distillation also supplied potable water on our naval vessels. Reverse osmosis was a newer technology that removed salt and other impurities from feedstocks by forcing saline water through a system of membranes that removed the salt compounds. Dupont was developing the technology with federal funding. As is the case for most federally funded research for commercial applications, the private company involved usually acquires the patent and reaps the profits at the expense of the taxpayer. I once accompanied OSW officials to Puerto Rico to meet some Saudi officials to sell them on the reverse osmosis technology. We also visited a distillation plant at St. Croix in the Virgin Islands. At that time, Orange County in Southern California was the only place to use this technology by treating sewage effluents and recycling the treated water for non-human uses.

We were obviously at an impasse with the basin states, and further negotiations were fruitless. The issue would have to be decided by the President. I have never professed to be an excellent writer, but one skill I had to master while working in OMB was preparing a memorandum for the President. No matter what the subject was or how complex and involved it was, the memo could not be more than one page long. That might not sound like a difficult task, but it takes a lot of practice and some skill to distill all the salient points of a major issue worthy of the President's attention down to just a page (pun intended).

I prepared the memo, got OMB to sign off, and hand carried it to Kissinger's office for review and recommendation. My boss, Don Crabill, who was associate director for natural resources, was concerned that Kissinger would choose the states' option, which was the most politically expedient solution but also the most expensive for the government. Crabill was especially concerned that Kissinger's staff would remove the OMB recommendation from the memorandum when it was finally sent to the President. He learned the final version of the memo was in the office of Egil Kroh, who controlled the paper flow to the President. Crabill instructed me to go to Kroh's office and review the memo to make sure our recommendation was still there. While walking to Kroh's office, which was next to the Oval Office, I began to agonize about how I was going to explain, without revealing the real reason, why I needed to see the memorandum. When I arrived, Kroh's secretary told me he was in a meeting but would return shortly. I explained I did not need to see him but wanted to do a quick review of the memorandum for the President. Much to my surprise, she let me see the memorandum, which was in the inbox on Kroh's desk. I went into his office and began rummaging through a stack of papers on his desk, fearful that he might walk in at any minute. I hurriedly read the memo and found it had not been changed, except for Kissinger's recommendations. I was disappointed to see Kissinger had chosen to support the basin states' position, despite the cost. I thanked the secretary and immediately left. I reported to Crabill what I'd learned and admonished him to never again give me an assignment like that.

The Watergate investigations later disclosed that John Ehrlichman, the deputy to H.R. Haldeman, Nixon's chief of staff, had directed Kroh to establish a special investigations unit inside the White House. The group, which was called "the Plumbers" and attracted the likes of J. Gordon Liddy, was responsible for several burglaries and other illegal violations. Kroh, along with Ehrlichman, Haldeman, Liddy, and others, would later be indicted, convicted, and serve time in prison for their crimes.

In the end, the President approved Kissinger's and the states' positions. Later, in 1974, the Congress enacted a Colorado River Basin Salinity Control project, which authorized several measures to decrease the salt content in the river, including building desalting plants. Since then, millions of dollars have been spent on these kinds of projects, with mixed results, and the U.S. continues to be in non-compliance with the treaty obligations to Mexico. In the 1990s, the All-American and Coachella canals were finally lined with concrete, just as we'd recommended more than two decades earlier.

The only thing I enjoyed about being involved in this issue was getting to know Mr. Brownell. He was such a pleasure to work for and appreciated our hard work. I had no proof, but I always felt he supported our position. Still, all of us together could not overcome the influence Kissinger had with the President, particularly concerning international relations. I was invited to a reception President Nixon and the First Lady hosted for His Excellency Luis Echeverría Álvarez, president of the United Mexican States, and Mrs. Echeverria at the White House on June 15, 1972. I still have that invitation, since Alvarez was there to discuss the Colorado River issues that had caused me so much grief. Later, when more Watergate allegations surfaced, and President Nixon's popularity plummeted, we in OMB were drafted to attend more White House functions, including receptions for foreign dignitaries. The political atmosphere was so toxic that even members of the administration were reluctant to visit the White House, and we were told to go to fill empty seats. It was a very sad time for a President who could have been one of this country's greatest leaders had he not been so paranoid and distrustful of everyone.

One of the most difficult issues I faced during my time in Washington had nothing to do with the Tenn-Tom. In 1972, President Nixon appointed Henry Brownell, President Eisenhower's attorney general, to resolve an international crisis with Mexico. Mexico was threatening to sue the United States in the International Court of Justice (World Court) for violating its treaty rights to water from the Colorado River. My team of budget examiners was assigned as the ambassador's ad hoc staff. A practical solution was developed to enable the U.S. to meet its treaty obligations, but, as is typical in Washington, politics trumped good government decisions. The ambassador is shown here with me and members of my team at a reception held in his honor at the State Department.

CHAPTER XI
Time to Move On

Working at OMB is not where one plans to spend a long career. I stayed much longer than most budget examiners did. While I sometimes felt burned out, I still enjoyed my work there and felt comfortable that I could handle my responsibilities as well as anyone else handled theirs. A person gains that level of confidence after drinking from a fire hose for a long time. I had several opportunities to leave, but for different reasons turned down the offers. My immediate boss and mentor, Wes Sasaki, who was one of a few who had made OMB a career, always reminded me that a budget examiner can use his or her experience only once as leverage into higher position. Sasaki was an American Japanese, born and raised in California, where he and his family were forced to live in internment camps after Japan bombed Pearl Harbor. He was able to join the Army as a way of not being interned. His Asian American regiment fought in some of the bloodiest battles against the Germans in Europe. When he returned after the war, he got his degrees at Syracuse University and eventually became a senior official in OMB. He was mainly responsible for my being promoted to the principal examiner's position. He probably had more influence on my career than anyone else, and during my time at OMB we became close friends. He was not only very intelligent and would share with me his experience and knowledge about the workings of OMB, but he also was unflappable. Regardless of the crises or pressures, he was always the calmest and coolest person in the room. I like to think that some of that demeanor rubbed off on me. I never had to be concerned that he would not back me, regardless of the circumstances, especially in political scrapes with White House staff. He introduced me to the corn cob pipe. I seldom ever saw him when the pipe was not in his mouth. I threw away all my brier pipes and smoked corn cobs for many years. He and I frequented a small Italian restaurant that was close to the office and was where we usually ate mussels heavily laced with garlic. When we'd return to the office and meet someone in the elevator or in close quarters, the person would say, "I noticed that you two have been to the Trieste again, eating mussels." It is still one of my favorite dishes. Sasaki is the only person I have ever known who loved boiled or steamed shrimp but ate them with the shells on. He would discard the tails, saying that it was too much trouble to peel the shrimp. I saw him only a couple of times after I left OMB, which I regret, but I still often think of him.

Following Sasaki's advice to leverage my time in OMB to land an ideal job, I turned down some jobs that, in hindsight, I see that I probably should have accepted, but I believed an even more attractive offer might be forthcoming. Nixon appointed John Sawhill, one of OMB's assistant directors, to start a new agency called the Federal Energy Administration, which was the forerunner to the U.S. Department of Energy. Sawhill asked a couple of us examiners to join him, but I declined the offer because the position dealt mainly with administrative or human resource matters. A few months after Sawhill arrived there, Gerald Ford, who became President after Nixon resigned, fired Sawhill. I might have survived Sawhill's abrupt departure, and if I had, I would have been in an excellent position for one of the higher positions with the new Department of Energy, but I have never had second thoughts about not taking Sawhill's offer. There were other chances to leave OMB, but the one that appealed to me the most was a position in the Office of the Secretary at the U.S. Department of the Interior.

John Whitaker was the person in the White House responsible

for matters related to natural resources and the environment. He is credited for influencing Nixon regarding environmental initiatives, such as establishing EPA, approving NEPA, and establishing other landmark programs such as the Water and Air Quality Acts. He was very close to Nixon, and after working on Nixon's presidential campaign, he joined the White House as secretary of the cabinet. I got to know him well when he became John Ehrlichman's deputy with the Domestic Council. Unlike Ehrlichman, he had not become involved in Watergate, which would eventually end the political careers of the President and many of his closer advisors in the White House. Whitaker left The White House in early 1973 to become the under secretary of Interior, the number-two position in the department. In the past, the leadership of Interior had been westerners. That changed under Nixon when Rogers Morton from Kentucky was appointed secretary, and Whitaker, another easterner, was picked as Morton's deputy. They had accepted these positions to institute reforms or changes in some of the department's policies and programs like grazing fees for ranchers, its heavily subsidized irrigation program, and antiquated mineral leasing policies. Whitaker asked me if I would join him and help accomplish some of these much-needed changes. With no specific job mentioned, I told him that I would certainly like to discuss the prospects further. The Bureau of Reclamation and the power marketing programs of Interior like Bonneville Power were part of my OMB responsibilities, and I was certainly knowledgeable about these agencies and programs, including some of the warts that Whitaker had highlighted. As a budget examiner, I had tried to eliminate some of these government give-a-ways to corporate farmers and ranchers, but I had had little or no success.

Whitaker called me again after several weeks and said he had the ideal job for me, given my background and experience. He wanted me to be the deputy to the assistant secretary of Land and Water. It was a position that Jim Watt had held during Nixon's first years in office. Later, during Reagan's first term, Watt would become the department's secretary. I told Whitaker I was interested in the position, having worked closely with that part of Interior. He said, "Great! I'll arrange for you to meet with Jack Horton."

Having butted heads with Horton on some water projects, I knew him. He also represented Interior, and I represented OMB when he and I were members of the Water Resources Council, a federal interagency organization established to prepare new principles and standards for evaluating multiple objectives for water projects. My first meeting with Horton, which I had assumed was an interview, was anything but that. We chatted about a litany of subjects but did not discuss the deputy's job. I left with the impression that he was not that enthusiastic about my being his deputy. A few weeks went by without any word from Horton or the department until I received a call from Whitaker. I noticed immediately that he was upset with me. Not one to mince words, he blurted out, "I thought you said you wanted to come to Interior, so why haven't you done so? I needed you here yesterday!"

I told him that it is hard to accept a job that has not been offered. He abruptly ended our conversation, and it was only a few minutes later that Horton's secretary called to schedule another meeting. Horton was from Saddle String in eastern Wyoming between Buffalo and Sheridan, where his family was one of the first to settle that part of the state. Saddle String was essentially his ranch with its own post office, which abutted the beautiful Bighorn National Forest. He had attended Princeton University, where he had been an all-American lacrosse player. He earned a master's degree in economics from Oxford University in England while on a Rhodes scholarship and later flew 175 missions as a Navy pilot in Vietnam. With all these impressive credentials and being one of Washington's most eligible bachelors, he came across has being "just an ol' Wyoming cowboy."

When we met again, I began the meeting by saying that I was interested in working for him but only if there could be mutual trust. If he felt that I would be more loyal to Whitaker than to him, he needed to say so. Finally, I told him if he had any doubts about me serving as his deputy, he needed to tell me right then, and I would report back to Whitaker that I was not interested in the position. That would end any discussion about the job, and Whitaker would never know about his reservations. Apparently, my frankness impressed him, and he offered me the position during the meeting. After a couple of days of thought and consideration, I accepted his offer. By coincidence and nothing more than that, President Nixon resigned the presidency and in disgrace flew to California on August 9, 1974. Two days later I left OMB for new adventures at the headquarters of the Department of Interior, only five blocks away.

Chapter XII
From the Pan into the Fire

Before leaving OMB and joining the Interior Department, I negotiated some conditions about the position that I felt were important. I had never belonged to or been involved with a particular political party. I had worked for both Democrat and Republican parties and never concerned myself with their respective political philosophies or ideology. When I worked for the Johnson Administration and later for Nixon, I viewed my role as that of a hired gun by doing my best to help carry out each administration's programs and directives.

The deputy assistant secretary's position was classified as a GS-17, Schedule C, or a political appointment; it was not a civil service classification. Those holding a Schedule C position worked at the pleasure of the President and his administration. I had been offered the job in Interior not because of political connections but for my experience and skills. I realized that at that level of government, my new boss, Jack Horton, or later his successor could immediately terminate my services and replace me with someone else, whether the position was classified as a political appointment or a career service. Nevertheless, I wanted the position to be reclassified as a merit or civil service-type job and not a political position. If Interior was willing to change the classification, I would accept the offer at a pay grade of a GS-16 instead of a GS-17. At that time, a government employee could not be compensated more than a congressman, and as a result there was no difference in the pay for those at the GS-16, GS-17, or the top grade of GS-18. By making this concession to accept the job at a GS-16, I was not leaving any money on the table. Interior agreed and reclassified the position. I felt these changes better described me as a career employee instead of a political appointee, but all would prove to have been worthless later, during the Carter Administration.

There were 8,000 employees with those agencies, mainly the Bureaus of Reclamation and Land Management, who reported to my new boss, Jack Horton. Although I was deputy assistant secretary for program analysis and development, and John Whitaker, the under secretary of the Interior, had recruited me to do program analysis and development, I spent increasingly more time on daily crises and issues that needed immediate attention. Most of the employees were located in and the agency programs were conducted in the 17 most Western states. With a three-hour difference in time between Washington and the West Coast it was not unusual for me to be tied up in the office until 7 p.m. or later dealing with some issue in one of the states. With occasional 7 a.m. staff meetings in the Office of the Secretary, this work schedule meant long hours at the office like I had experienced at OMB. I had hoped that such an exhausting schedule would be history in my new job, but that was wishful thinking.

Shortly after I arrived at the Department of Interior, its secretary, Rogers Morton, left to become secretary of commerce to begin raising money for Gerald Ford's election campaign. To make matters worse, John Whitaker had a serious heart attack and eventually was forced to resign because of his health. With these developments and the long, hectic work hours, I began to wonder if by leaving OMB for Interior, I had leaped from the frying pan into the fire.

Evel Knievel

I had been at Interior for only a couple of months when I received a telephone call from what I believed would be my daily crisis from one of our offices out West, but this call was about a matter of much greater importance. It was late on a Friday afternoon after most everyone in the office had left, including my boss, who was traveling in Wyoming. Horton was contemplating running for governor and was spending a lot of time in Wyoming and less time in the office. This call was from someone who had wanted to speak with a staff member who had already left for the day and the weekend. So, I answered the call. During my chat, the caller, from the Bureau of Land Management (BLM) office in Idaho, casually mentioned that Evel Knievel, famous stunt man, was planning to jump his motorcycle across the Snake River Canyon. Immediately, red flags went up. I saw this as the making of a major fiasco. After questioning everyone later, I learned that this was either the first time anyone in my office or in the department had ever heard about the stunt or they were unwilling to admit knowing about it. I had remembered a couple of years earlier that Knievel had sought permission to jump the Grand Canyon, but Interior had rightfully nixed the idea.

I asked the caller how BLM was involved in this latest caper. The jump was to take place on the south rim of the canyon west of Shoshone Falls, Idaho. The takeoff was on non-federal property, but if he succeeded in clearing the canyon, his landing would be on BLM land. I asked if Knievel had a BLM permit, keeping my fingers crossed that someone in the field had not granted him one. I was relieved to learn that no permit had been issued, and I told the caller to make sure no federal property was to be involved in the stunt and that if Knievel wanted to kill himself, we were not going to help him do so. The caller immediately started naming all the reasons that we could not stop the stunt, giving me the impression that BLM was more involved than the caller had indicated. He explained that the jump was well publicized, that it was to be shown on pay-for-view and other media outlets, and that Interior could be sued for monetary damages if we issued a cease-and-desist order. With no one to consult or grant approval, I told the caller to have BLM inform the producers of the event that Interior was not going to issue a permit and that one would be required if Knievel landed on federal property. If they proceeded, and Knievel did land on federal property, he would be fined for trespassing. The caller asked me how much Knievel would be fined, so he could tell the promoters. I was way out of my field of knowledge and, frankly, was winging the entire thing. I told him that if the promoters asked, to say that the fine would cost them dearly, but certainly less than what they would make if he jumped.

The longest jump Knievel had ever attempted was 141 feet at Caesar's Palace, where he crashed and broke several bones and suffered a concussion. This jump across the river canyon was much longer, and he had a rocket-powered cycle, called Skycycle, specially designed and built for this stunt. The event took place on Sunday, September 8, 1974. When the Skycycle left the launching rail, the drag parachute opened prematurely, which slowed its ascent. Even with this hindrance, Knievel made it across the canyon, but the cycle drifted back because of the open parachute, and he finally landed at the bottom of the canyon. Fortunately, he did not land in the water, where he would likely have drowned because of a faulty harness that refused to release him from the cycle. He survived the jump with only a few minor injuries, and since he never landed on BLM land on the other side of the canyon, my threat of a fine of an unknown amount never came into play. Just another day at the office.

Project Independence

During the early 1970s, more than one-third of the nation's oil consumption came from mid-Eastern countries. That dependency became most evident when those Arab states cut off their supplies in retaliation to our support of Israel during the Yom Kipper War in October 1973. Egypt and Syria had attacked Israel to claim lands in the Golan Heights and Sinai, lands that Egypt and Syria had lost to Israel in a 1967 war. The United States provided aid, including military equipment to Israel, while Russia did the same for the two Arab nations. Russia's and the United States' involvement nearly led to a serious confrontation between these two nuclear-armed countries.

The oil embargo created an economic crisis that we had not experienced since the Great Depression. The Nixon Administration imposed some drastic conservation measures and implemented some major initiatives to increase domestic oil and gas production and to eliminate our dependency on foreign sources of energy. The President's energy program was called "Project Independence," and the Interior Department would play a major role in its implementation. Federal interdiction, however, did little to mitigate the oil embargo's immediate effects on the nation and its consumers, especially motorists.

To conserve fuel, the speed limit was reduced to 55 miles per hour for U.S. drivers. Gasoline was rationed and sold to motorists based on the last digit number of their automobile or truck tags. Those with an even number purchased gas on even numbers of calendar dates. Others with an odd number purchased gas on the odd-numbered dates. To make matters worse, most service stations had short supplies, and some limited sales to only five gallons per customer. The price of gas soared from 36 cents to 55 cents per gallon!

My family had taken the train to Alabama during the Christmas holidays during the embargo. I was able to take only a couple of days off at that time of the year because of work related to finalizing the President's budget. Foolishly, I decided to drive to Alabama, spend Christmas Day there, and leave the next day to drive the family back to Virginia. I knew gasoline was scarce, but I never suspected that it would be nearly impossible to buy any along a busy interstate during the holiday rush. We eventually made it back to Virginia, but it seemed as if it took nearly as long searching for a station that was open and had gas to sell as it did for the long drive. Many of the workers in the Washington area commuted by car since the metro system had not been built, and we all spent wasteful hours in block-long queues to purchase our meager five gallons of gas.

Times were even tougher in Europe, where shrinking supplies made some countries ban Sunday driving. When I was at OMB, I heard that the federal government had printed millions of gas ration tickets similar to those used during World War II, but they were never used since the embargo was lifted in March 1974 when Israel withdrew its troops from the Suez Canal, which it had captured during the 1973 war. Those five months without the flow of imported oil had a devastating impact on the nation's economy and drastically altered America's way of life for that brief period.

"Project Independence" included some bold measures to become self-sufficient for our energy needs by 1980. Those affecting the Interior Department and my office included accelerating the leasing of minerals, namely coal and crude oil, that was under federal jurisdiction. This included leasing the vast deposits of sub-bituminous coal in the so-called Powder River Basin in Wyoming, all owned by the federal government and under the jurisdiction of one of my office's agencies, the Bureau of Land Management (BLM). This is the largest coal mining region in the United States. There are 162 billion tons in seams thick enough and close enough to the surface to justify its extraction. The coal has a low sulfur content, but it burns at about two-thirds the BTU/lb. as eastern coal does. BLM was also directed to expand its leasing of oil and gas along the continental shelf, especially in the Gulf of Mexico. Except for Texas and Florida, the states that border the Gulf own rights that extend three miles offshore. Texas and west Florida own rights that extend nine miles from shore. Currently, the federal jurisdiction begins at the states' limits and extends from there for 200 miles.

In the 1950s, the federal government began leasing offshore tracts to private oil companies with most all the production rigs located in depths of less than 100 feet of water. That changed when prices of oil and gas soared because of the OPEC embargo in 1973. BLM began offering tracts in depths up to 1,000 feet. Geological and other mineral-related tests were conducted to learn more about the potential yield of offshore areas. When this information was available, and oil companies conducted similar tests, BLM advertised sales and sought bids from interested companies. The tracts designated for bidding were usually about 5,000 to 6,000 acres in size with as many as 100 or more tracts that might be offered at each sale. The oil company that submitted the highest price for a tract gained the exclusive rights to drill in that tract. On the day of the sale, the winning bidder paid the price in a lump sum of cash via certified check to the U.S. Treasury. The bids varied, depending on the potential a tract might offer for producing oil and gas. The government also received a share of the market value of the oil and gas from a producing well if the drilling was successful.

Standard procedure required someone from the Office of the Secretary of Interior to attend and preside during these sales. While this participation was mostly ceremonial, I was able to attend one of the sales. This was an active time for offshore drilling, and there was much interest in and competition for the tracts offered at the sale over which I presided. The sale generated tens of millions of dollars for the government and eventually more oil and gas needed to meet the nation's future energy needs. While there, I flew by helicopter to an offshore rig that was already in production and to another rig that was drilling for oil and gas. I wanted to learn more about these operations. It was enlightening, and I certainly gained a better appreciation of how hard these men worked, and I learned about the dangers of just being on these platforms. The workers' living quarters were impressive. They included a video or TV room with several large, comfortable chairs for relaxing, and the meals were outstanding, with snacks, desserts, and even an ice cream machine always available for that hunger moment. A heavy gas smell emanated from the production rig. It made me feel like I was sitting on a ticking time bomb. I was greatly relieved when the helicopter lifted off for our return trip to New Orleans.

Another important element of the Nixon/Ford energy initiatives was the Trans-Alaskan Pipeline. In 1968, a major oil field had been discovered on the north slope of Alaska in Prudhoe Bay. This cold, remote area presented unprecedented challenges for finding a viable means of transporting the oil to U.S. refineries. After considering several alternatives, including building a port to serve sea-going tankers on the frigid Prudhoe Bay, a consortium of private oil companies proposed to build a pipeline from the north slope oil fields, 800 miles across Alaska to an ice-free sea terminal at Valdez. The proposed pipeline drew immediate opposition from nearly all the national environmental and conservation organizations as well as some Alaska natives. The environmentalists cited a host of ecological and wildlife issues, while the natives were adamantly opposed to ceding any of their lands. Interior Department, the federal agency primarily affected by the proposal, was charged with the preparation of the Environmental Impact Statement (EIS). The department issued a draft EIS to the public for review in January 1971. The pipeline's opponents immediately attacked the draft. The 3,500-page document generated some 1,300 pages of critical comments and prompted a lawsuit alleging the Interior Department had not properly considered other alternatives to the pipeline. The Nixon Administration and pipeline supporters in congress recognized that some unusual measures must be taken if this project were ever to be built.

To solve the native lands issues, the Congress passed, and Nixon signed the Alaska Natives Claims Settlement Act in December 1971. The legislation essentially bought off the natives by getting them to renounce their claims to the land needed for the pipeline in exchange for payments of over $950 million and a transfer of ownership of nearly 150 million acres of other federal lands to the natives. The Congress addressed the environmental opposition to the pipeline by enacting its construction in the Trans-Alaska Pipeline Authorization Act, which President Nixon signed in November 1973. The law included a provision that Congress seldom incorporated in this kind of legislation by stipulating that any permits or other actions associated with building the pipeline "shall not be subject to judicial review." This provision broke the stalemate between the pipeline's opponents and its supporters by removing all legal barriers to building the project, virtually guaranteeing its completion.

The Alyeska Pipeline Service Company, composed of several oil companies, with British Petroleum, Conoco/Phillips, and Exxon/Mobil as the major partners, began construction of the pipeline in January 1974. The permafrost that existed along the pipeline's right-of-way made it impossible to bury the pipeline, which is the typical construction method. Instead, it was built above the ground with occasional passageways for migrating animals like caribou herds. Thousands of workers working around the clock completed the project in less than four years at a cost of $8 billion. In May 1977, the four-foot diameter, 800-mile-long pipe system began delivering 500,000 barrels of oil each day to American consumers.

These three initiatives and other energy projects under the responsibility of the Interior Department and my office greatly increased our workload and created seemingly endless meetings within the department and with other agencies. Environmentalists adamantly opposed all these measures, and it seemed that we were being sued by some group every week.

The Time I Met Popeye

Everyone at some time meets someone, usually by happenstance, who leaves a lasting if not unforgettable impression. I have been fortunate to meet several people who were, indeed, memorable even though our time together was brief. One was a man I met in New Orleans when I was there for a meeting with the local BLM office. I was staying at the Braniff Hotel, which offered government room rates and was located on Canal Street. I believe the Braniff, then owned by the airline of the same name, is now the Jung Hotel. A fellow coworker and I were at the hotel bar one afternoon when I struck up a conversation with a man sitting next to me. He introduced himself as Al Copeland from New Orleans, and after some small talk, he began to tell me about his business. He had started a fast-food restaurant in the city specializing in fried chicken. He intended to compete with Kentucky Fried Chicken. He said his restaurant failed because the recipe for his chicken was too bland, and it needed to be spicier. He added that he had now developed the perfect recipe and was looking for investors to reopen his restaurant and start selling franchises.

Copeland was the consummate salesman, and I became intrigued with his sales pitch. I asked him to name the amount of investment he was seeking. He said he was letting "his friends" buy in for $25,000 each, and although he and I had just met, he would consider me a friend. I told him I would think about his proposal, although I did not have that kind of venture capital. Even if I had the cash, I needed much more information about him and his new chicken restaurant before investing in such a deal. We exchanged business cards, and I mentioned we were leaving for dinner. He asked if I had ever eaten at Pascal's Manale, an Italian neighborhood restaurant that had been in the city's Garden District for generations. He volunteered to take us there since it was on his way home, but once we were outside, he discovered his car was gone from where he had parked it in front of the hotel. By then I was ready for us to go our separate ways, but he insisted that we follow him to an area underneath the interstate where the city impounds vehicles that it tows from no-parking zones. Apparently, this happened to him frequently, because he immediately stuck $50 in the attendant's hand, retrieved his keys, and we were on our way in his old Cadillac convertible.

Copeland dropped us off at the restaurant, and we said our goodbyes, and that was the last I heard from him. Several months later someone at the local BLM office told me that Copeland had reopened his new fried chicken business, and he had named it Popeye's Famous Fried Chicken. Within 10 years he had expanded to over 500 restaurants throughout the South. I could have become richer that evening after meeting Al Copeland in the Braniff Hotel bar if I had been more of a risk taker, but my regret at passing on the investment was tempered by learning that Copeland went bankrupt in 1990. A group of the restaurant chain's creditors bought his company at a fire-sale price and eventually resold it to a capital investment firm. As of 2017, there were 2,600 Popeye's Famous Fried Chicken restaurants worldwide. While I made no money as a result of my brief encounter with Copeland, the restaurant, Pascal's Manale, which he'd recommended, became one my favorites in New Orleans, and I have dined there many times since meeting "Mr. Popeye."

Wild Horses

One of the most contentious if not emotional issues while I was in Interior was managing the increasing numbers of wild horses and burros on federal lands in the West. Spaniards introduced the horses and the burros to the Southwest as early as the 1600s. In the 1800s, prospectors searching for gold and silver used burros to haul mining gear and supplies. Once the motherlode was gone, the animals were abandoned. Burros are very adaptable to the desert environment, and their numbers have greatly increased. The horses and burros are found mostly in the desert sections of Arizona, Oregon, Utah, California, Wyoming, and Nevada. Nevada has more than one-half of all the wild horses that roam in North America. In the 1930s, as many as 50,000 to 150,000 horses were roaming wild in these states, all competing for scarce grazing lands with ranchers' herds of cattle and wild animals, such as deer and mountain goats. Ranchers and poachers, with the implicit blessing of the Bureau of Land Management (BLM), began using inhumane methods to dramatically reduce the herds of mustangs, including outright slaughter like that which caused the disappearance of the buffalo herds in the 1800s. Ranchers and poachers eradicated many horses and burros by poisoning their watering holes or shooting them, and they sold the animals' carcasses to make soap. By the 1950s, the wild horse population had been decimated to only about 25,000.

The maltreatment of these magnificent animals became a national story, thanks to a crusade by Ms. Velma Johnston of Arizona, who would become known as "Wild Horse Annie." She solicited several well-known entertainers and movie stars to help her cause. Their publicizing the plight of these animals led to Congress enacting the Wild Horses and Burros Act in 1971. The law imposed a penalty of one year in jail and a fine of $2,000 for killing a wild horse or burro. The legislation also prohibited the use of airplanes or vehicles to round up and capture the animals, limiting the method of capture to the traditional way of employing a cowboy with a lasso. These restrictions on capture greatly inhibited BLM's success of corralling the horses and greatly increased the costs for each animal being corralled. Horses that were caught were offered to private owners for adoption, which was successful at first, but later the program had problems finding people willing to adopt. It was estimated that it was costing the government as much as $50,000 for each horse caught and successfully adopted. Given these staggering costs, the Congress finally relented to allow BLM to use helicopters to help catch and corral the horses. I witnessed one of these roundups in northern Nevada and one in Wyoming. The herds usually consisted of several mares, some colts, and a magnificent stallion as leader of the herd.

Today, nearly 50 years later, the management of wild horses and burros is still one of the most challenging issues BLM faces in the use of the public lands it manages. There are now about 25,000 mustangs or wild horses and about 3,000 burros roaming free on Western lands. However, this does not include some 50,000 horses that have been captured and are now living in corrals or pens at considerable expense to BLM while waiting to be sold to a private owner or adopted. The burros, like the coyotes, have now migrated to urban areas and are frequently involved in auto collisions, similar to the problems that motorists in the South face with deer. This management issue is as controversial today as it was when I was involved many years ago and will likely be the case for many years to come.

Trying Times at Work

People often ask me to describe the differences I see between the Corps of Engineers and the Bureau of Reclamation (BuRec). Both are world-class engineering and construction organizations, but there are major differences in how the two agencies respond to change and carry out directives. For example, the Corps immediately incorporates changes to comply with newly enacted laws, such as NEPA, into its programs and, like obedient soldiers, which its leaders are, it implements those reforms or new directives in an expeditious manner. BuRec, however, resists changes and will attempt to circumvent orders or directives it believes might conflict with the traditional ways the agency has conducted its programs since its founding in 1902. Both agencies are most adept at working with the stakeholders of their projects and programs and with their champions in the Congress.

BuRec's recalcitrance to comply with newly enacted laws and its not being forthright with its superiors created a major international incident for me and an embarrassment for the Department and the Ford Administration. The Missouri River is the nation's longest river and is the most extensively developed. Its six major dams create the largest system of reservoirs in the nation, storing a total of 74 million acre-feet of water for multiple uses. The river's development by both the Corps and BuRec is called the Pick-Sloan Project, named after the two agencies' leaders in the late 1940s. Lieutenant General Lewis Pick, one of the more notable commanders during the long history of the Corps, had roots in Alabama. During his early career he was a professor of military science at Auburn University. After retiring from military service, he returned to Alabama and served as one of Governor "Big Jim" Folsom's closest advisors. He is credited with being the brainchild of forming an interstate compact to help develop the Tenn-Tom. He passed away just before his concept, the Tenn-Tom Waterway Development Authority, was enacted by Congress. Although a native of Virginia, he chose to be buried at Auburn.

The Missouri River's six dams created huge lakes that flooded thousands of acres, some of which were the best croplands and grazing areas in the Dakotas and other affected states. The Garrison Diversion Irrigation Project was authorized as a component of the Pick-Sloan plan, and its purpose was to help mitigate these farmland losses in North Dakota. The project was authorized in 1955, but its construction was delayed for several decades. These setbacks were mainly because of opposition from environmentalists and eastern politicians, who objected to using heavily subsidized water from a federal project to grow crops that might be in surplus, or price-supported by the government.

I had always supported the project, even when I was a budget cutter at OMB. I felt it was the government's obligation, as promised, to replace those lands lost in North Dakota by building this conveyance system to irrigate dry land not suitable for growing crops. Some of the returned flows of water used by the irrigation district would eventually flow into the Souris and Red rivers, both of which flow north into Canada. Canada was concerned that these waters containing salt and nutrients would degrade the water quality of the two rivers, which would be in violation of a 1909 treaty between the two countries. Minnesota was also concerned about the adverse impacts on the Red River and had announced it would sue to stop any degradation of the river's water quality.

In June 1975, the State Department was meeting with the Canadian government concerning the impacts of the Garrison project. Both Canada and the State Department were relying on Interior or BuRec for data and information about these effects on the two international rivers. Unbeknownst to me, both my boss, Horton, and the commissioner of BuRec had exchanged memos agreeing to withhold the data from the negotiators because it was detrimental to the project. A whistleblower, either in BuRec or in my office (I later suspected the latter), sent copies of the memos to the U.S. House Government Operations Committee that was chaired by a Pennsylvania congressman who opposed Garrison. My first knowledge of the memos was when a *Washington Post* reporter, who had been provided copies by someone associated with the House Committee, called and asked to speak to Horton since he was the author of one of the memos. Horton was "unavailable" to the reporter. Horton came immediately to my office to explain their skullduggery. I was livid, especially when it was evident that I was the person who would have to try to come up with what to say, knowing that there was no acceptable explanation since the reporter had both the smoking guns. My lame excuse was that we had not released the data to the negotiators because of its preliminary nature, that the data was "mainly back-of-the-envelope estimates." The story and I made the front page of the *Washington Post* the next day. I asked Horton why he had not told me about his agreement with BuRec to not release the project data. He said, "I knew you would strongly object," and he was correct.

The Garrison Diversion District was originally authorized to serve 1 million acres of irrigated land. Because of its effects on the two rivers and opposition by Canada and Minnesota, the authorized acreage was reduced to less than 75,000 acres. Considerably less acreage than that is currently being irrigated. I am convinced that the chicanery of my boss and BuRec to withhold the Garrison irrigation district data and the resulting negative publicity contributed to this drastic reduction in the scope of the project, even though they believed they were acting in its best interest.

I once visited an Indian reservation while working on the Missouri River project, and it left a lasting impression on me. The Cheyenne River Sioux and the Standing Rock reservations were relocated when the Oahe Dam was built near Pierre, South Dakota. The two reservations lost 200,000 acres when the Oahe reservoir was flooded, and both were relocated to nearby lands. For the displaced Indian families, the Bureau of Indian Affairs within the Interior Department built new homes, prefabricated types like the so-called Jim Walter homes being built at that time in the South. These new dwellings were considerably better than the shanties in which the Indians once lived. When driving through the reservation, I noticed several cars and trucks apparently abandoned alongside the roads, though most all appeared to be suitable for driving. My guide told me the Indians would purchase a vehicle, put gas in it, and drive it as long as it ran. But if it became inoperable for any reason, the owner would abandon it wherever it ceased to run. Later, when they had the money, they would buy another vehicle and operate it until it quit running. Many of the houses had several derelict cars in their yards.

    The houses had either gas or electric heat, but during the first winter, the occupants had burned all the interior doors, even the toilet seats, to make fires in a large washtub in one of the rooms. They wanted to sit by a crackling fire like their forefathers had for generations. I learned that some of the younger Indians would leave the reservation to attend college or find work off the reservation. Most, though, would eventually return to the reservation. Alcoholism was rampant on the reservation, even among the younger Indians. I was so saddened to see that these once proud if not noble people were now living in such deplorable conditions. "Living" was not even the correct description. They were merely existing. For several generations, they had been completely dependent on the government to fulfill all their needs. As a result, they had lost their pride, ambition, and certainly had no self-motivation. I believe the same dependency could happen to those American families who rely solely on welfare checks, food stamps, and the government's other largesse. Some have done so for generations. I was encouraged when later I met some representatives from the Navaho reservation in New Mexico. That tribe is very industrious and has adapted very well to the modern world while still embracing its history and culture. That can also be said for the Choctaws in Mississippi, who have been successful in attracting industrial development to their reservation and have built casinos and other tourist attractions. I hope the lives of the Sioux have similarly improved.

I followed with much interest a more recent national controversy involving the Dakota Access Pipeline. The proposed route of the pipeline had it crossing the lake created by the Oahe Dam, which the Cheyenne River Sioux and the Standing Rock Indian reservations both opposed. These are the two reservations I visited in the early 1970s. Several thousand environmentalists and what I call no-growth advocates joined the Indians in opposing the pipeline. They spent weeks camping there in protest, vowing not to leave until they had defeated the pipeline crossing. The pipeline company offered substantial compensation to the tribes to obtain their approval, but they declined. Although the pipeline route did not directly affect their reservation, it would disturb their ancestral grounds now inundated by the reservoir. The company's request for a permit from the Corps of Engineers to build the pipeline underneath the reservoir was denied in 2016 by the Obama Administration. However, one of the first actions President Donald Trump took was to approve the permit. The Cheyenne River Sioux Reservation immediately filed a lawsuit complaining that the crossing violated an 1851 treaty. The construction of the pipeline in this area has now been completed, irrespective of the tribe's litigation.

Washington's Deep State Never Sleeps

Interior had been without a secretary and an undersecretary since shortly after I arrived there. President Ford in late 1974 or early 1975 nominated Stanley Hathaway, a former governor of Wyoming, to be secretary. Hathaway had lived a hard-scrabble life, grew up in a cabin, and was a self-made man. As governor, he had been instrumental in stimulating some unprecedented economic growth for his state. With my boss from Wyoming and a friend of the governor, plus all the positive things I had heard about him, I was looking forward to Hathaway's becoming the next secretary. Once his Senate confirmation hearings began, it was evident that some powerful environmental groups were determined to keep him from leading Interior. The governor was squeaky clean with regard to his personal life. The attacks mostly concerned his pro-economic development record as governor, which the environmentalists said was accomplished at the expense of the environment. A well-orchestrated attack by environmental groups and some legislative procedural maneuvers in the United States Senate, led by Senator Edmund Muskie of Maine, delayed Hathaway's confirmation vote for several months. He was finally confirmed in June 1975 with 60 senators voting for his confirmation. However, the vicious personal attacks had taken their toll on Hathaway's health, and he suffered a nervous breakdown soon after his confirmation. I don't believe he spent a single day at Interior, and he finally resigned in October 1975, three months after being confirmed. I was troubled by this destruction of such a good man, and it demonstrated to me just how mean politics was becoming. The upshot of this personal tragedy was that we in the Office of the Secretary were still without a leader one year after I joined the team. My time in the department was becoming untenable.

Horton had been pressuring me since I first arrived to get rid of a staff member in our office. The employee was career civil service, not a political appointee, and had been there for several years when one of his former bosses promoted him to a GS-16 grade. By grade he was one of the top staff members in our office. He was the consummate bureaucrat, and I agreed with Horton that his performance and contributions were far from satisfactory. So, I began taking steps to either fire him or have him transferred somewhere else in the department. I knew that it was very difficult to fire someone working for the federal government. Nevertheless, I started keeping a record of his unsatisfactory performance. When I thought I had enough justification, I started the paperwork to abolish his position and informed him of my plans.

The head of personnel in the department, whom I had known since my days in OMB, asked me to come to his office to discuss my plans to get rid of the employee. He warned me that, under government rules on abolishing a "super grade" position, since the employee had many more years of service than I did, he could potentially "bump" me for my position. He was laughing hysterically about my compiling such a meticulously strong record to justify the employee's dismissal only for me to learn that I would fire myself if we followed through with my plans. I did not think it was as funny as the personnel director did. Since my position had been changed at my request from a political appointment to a career position, with the grade lowered from a GS-17 to GS-16, the employee's career status was the same as mine, regardless of the fact I was his supervisor. I reported back to Horton and told him that, unless he wanted this employee to be his deputy, he was stuck with him as a member of our staff. This was an excellent example how any administration has its hands tied to effect change, since many government workers are unduly insulated from having to perform at a satisfactory level or obediently follow directives from a President or his administration. These bureaucrats can bide their time until the next change in administration. This kind of intransigence is part of what some refer to as the "Deep State." The employee was still there when I left Interior, still drawing top federal pay and contributing little if anything to the functions of the office.

Chapter XIII
Time Again To Move On

I was enjoying my job at Interior, and it exposed me to a lot of interesting and challenging issues. However, the working conditions were deplorable, at best. Horton and I had become friends, and it was a pleasure working for him. However, he spent increasingly more time in Wyoming exploring the prospects of running for governor. With his absence and no one in the secretary's job, I had no one above me to whom to refer matters that needed immediate attention, no one to turn to when higher authorities in the Office of the Secretary or at the White House urgently needed a decision. Waiting was sometimes not an option because some matters required immediate action, which forced me to make decisions that I knew should be made by someone at a higher level. This was especially true of issues involving politics. While I thrived on much of it, I had been working in a high-pressure environment since I first arrived in Washington nearly a decade before. In some respects, those kinds of working conditions were worse at Interior than at OMB, which I never imagined would be the case. As the adage goes, "I had enjoyed all of this about as much as I could stand."

I had not seen Glover Wilkins or talked to him since I left OMB, and I'd been too busy to even think about the Tenn-Tom. One day, though, Wilkins called me and invited me to lunch. I gladly accepted.

He picked me up in front of my building in a chauffeur-driven car. I was most impressed. Bill Timmons and Tom Korologos, both former key White House staffers who handled legislative affairs for Nixon and later for Ford, had started a new governmental relations firm called Timmons and Company. Wilkins, who knew Timmons, a Tennessean, recognized the advantages of being associated with such a long-time political operative for the waterway. The waterway authority became one of the firm's first clients and paid a very reasonable beginning retainer. One of the perks was that when Wilkins was in Washington, the firm made its car and driver available to him. The firm's influence in Washington would prove to be fruitful later during the congressional battles over the waterway's funding.

At lunch, Wilkins asked if I had ever heard of a federal program called the Intergovernmental Personnel Act (IPA) program. I was somewhat familiar with its purpose since some in OMB had been loaned to states to help improve their budgeting and programming systems. The Corps and Army had also brought in university professors or educators on a temporary or loaned arrangement, but I knew little about the details of the program. Wilkins had asked someone in Congress to research the program and found that the Tenn-Tom Authority, being a subdivision of state government, could participate in the program. He added that, while construction was progressing well, the compact was having to deal with a growing number of problems and issues, including another possible lawsuit. Further, if the details and the arrangements could be worked out to my satisfaction, he wanted me to join him on loan under the IPA program. I told him I was interested in the offer, but I needed to research the details before giving him an answer.

I learned that I could be loaned to the authority for two years at my current salary, with the authority splitting the costs. After the loan period, when I returned to Interior, I was guaranteed a job of similar pay and responsibility but not necessarily the position I had vacated. My time with the authority would count toward my federal retirement, and it provided other benefits, like paying for moving costs. I called Wilkins and told him I would accept his offer, but I feared the biggest hurdle would be getting the Interior Department to approve such an arrangement. Unlike the Corps, Interior had no program interest in the waterway to help justify loaning an employee at my level to the authority. Frankly, I had little hope of gaining Interior's approval. One afternoon after work when I likely would not be interrupted by a call or a staff member, I broached the proposal with Horton. I told him that I was not interested in participating in this loan program for career development, but that I was burned out mentally and ready to get the hell out of Washington for a while. I knew keeping my super grade position could kill the deal since those positions are authorized or allocated to the department by the Congress and that, if I retained the super grade, Interior could not fill my position at that level. I volunteered to return to a GS-15 grade while I was on loan, knowing that the top step of that grade paid the same as the salary for a GS-16. Horton did not give me an immediate answer and left town for a few days, leaving me to ponder my future. When he returned, he said that while he hated to lose me and was very complimentary of the work I had done for him and the department, he understood why I wanted to leave and would approve the loan. He said, somewhat in jest, that he wished I would find him a similar deal like that in Wyoming. My friend in the personnel office (the one who had advised me against firing the employee) took care of all the details of the loan arrangement. With no secretary or undersecretary in the front office to possibly nix the deal, the loan was approved, mainly with just Horton's blessings.

Wilkins and Horton signed the contract between the authority and Interior. I had several matters in Interior that I wanted to wrap up before leaving, and I agreed to report to the Tenn-Tom no later than October 1, 1975. While I was excited and pleased to be returning to the South, even on a loan or temporary basis, I had some troubling doubts that I was abandoning what I felt was a promising career in the federal government. Those concerns proved to be the case.

After more than 10 years in Washington, working in two very stressful and demanding positions in government, I loaded my Buick station wagon with some personal things, including a poodle and a cat, and began my 15-hour drive to Columbus, Mississippi, for my new job. The family had relocated in July, and I left at the end of September in 1975, after overseeing the packing and moving of our household goods and selling our home. I had reservations about selling our townhouse, since I expected to return after I fulfilled my two-year loan to the waterway authority, but I it was a seller's market, so I sold it. Plus, when I returned, I wanted to live closer to Washington instead of Centreville, which at that time was about a one-hour drive to D.C. on the best of days.

I had gotten to know Glover Wilkins during the many meetings we had in Washington, and I was confident that I would enjoy working for him. Still, I was anxious to meet the other six members of the team. Darlene Barels (Scoggin) was Glover's longtime administrative assistant. Pete Kelley oversaw public affairs. Assisting him was Pat Broocks (Ross) and another person whose name I cannot recall. Pete was the former editor of the *Times Daily*, a newspaper serving Northwest Alabama. Ross also had a journalism background. Other staff members were Rilla Wiley, the accountant, and Jeanne Wallace (Ferguson), the receptionist/secretary. I was succeeding Bruce Hanson, Glover's executive assistant, who had left to run a state trade association. Everyone was cordial and seemed pleased to have me on board.

Jack Horton, assistant secretary of Interior, at left, and Glover Wilkins, administrator of the Tennessee Tombigbee Waterway Development Authority watch as I sign the agreement for the Department of Interior to loan me to the authority for two years. The loan was later extended for two additional years. After that time, I resigned from the federal government and joined the authority as its deputy administrator.

Chapter XIV
A Behemoth Endeavor

When I arrived at the Tenn-Tom Authority, about 25 percent of the waterway's construction had been completed, and work was busily underway at both ends of the waterway. It was the largest and most costly and complex public works or water resources project ever undertaken, even surpassing the building of the Panama Canal. The project consisted of 10 locks and dams and the removal of some 310 million cubic yards of material, compared to about 210 million cubic yards excavated during construction of the Panama Canal. The Tenn-Tom project was so big that its design and construction were assigned to two district offices of the Army Corps of Engineers: The Mobile District (MDO), which is part of the South Atlantic Division (SAD); and the Ohio River Division's Nashville District (NDO). Apportioning the waterway's activities between two districts potentially could pose problems related to coordinating, budgeting, and program planning. Having two division commands involved could also accentuate those challenges. It was decided at the outset that MDO would have primary responsibilities for the project's program, planning, and budgeting functions and that SAD would be the lead division. Major General Carroll LeTellier, SAD commander, appointed Bob Crisp of his office to serve as the Tenn-Tom coordinator, which he did with distinction until the project was completed. Vernon Holmes, with the able assistance of Jeff Tidmore and other members of the Mobile District's budget office, had the difficult chore of preparing the annual budget requests for the project. After receiving input of the Nashville District's funding needs from its budget chief, Bill Eastland, and his assistants, Jim Goad and Tom Cayce, and after close coordination with both districts and the divisions, Holmes and his team prepared a joint budget that prioritized the allocations of those funds to the various features of the project. During the latter years of construction, the annual funding exceeded over $100 million and reached as high as nearly $250 million in FY 1980, a record amount of Congressional appropriations to fund a project by the Corps of Engineers in a single fiscal year. The working relationships and cooperation among the Corps employees from the two districts involved in building the waterway during its 12 years of construction could not have been better.

The 234-mile waterway has three distinct elements: the so-called River Section; the Chain of Lakes or Canal Section; and the Divide Section.

River Section

The southern section of the waterway begins at its junction with the Warrior-Tombigbee Waterway just north of Demopolis, Alabama. It generally follows the natural course of the Tombigbee River for 149 miles through west Alabama and Northeast Mississippi. Four locks and dams were needed to circumnavigate a total drop in elevation or a slope of the river of 117 feet. These structures are now called Howell Heflin Lock and Dam (L/D), Tom Bevill Lock and Dam, John C. Stennis Lock and Dam, and Aberdeen Lock and Dam.

Heflin L/D in Sumter County, Alabama, was well under construction when I arrived in late 1975. Heflin is located near Gainesville, and the lock has a lift of 36 feet. Environmental groups filed a lawsuit that delayed the start of construction for nearly 18 months. After the federal judge lifted the court injunction and dismissed the suit, construction of the lock finally began on December 12, 1972, signifying the start of construction of Tenn-Tom.

Contracts had also been awarded to start construction of Bevill L/D and Stennis L/D, but little work had been accomplished when I arrived. Aberdeen L/D as well as most of all the rest of the waterway was still in the design stages. Bevill L/D is located in Pickens County at Pickensville, Alabama, and its lock has a lift of 27 feet. All of the lock chambers on the waterway are 110 feet wide and 600 feet long, which can accommodate eight standard-sized barges and a tow boat in a single lockage. Stennis L/D is the first waterway structure in Mississippi and is located in Lowndes County near Columbus. Like Bevill, it also has a lift of 27 feet. The last structure on the River Section is the Aberdeen L/D located in Monroe County, and it, too, has a 27-foot lift.

While the waterway's navigation generally followed the natural course of the river, some cutoffs of the river were made to better accommodate the typical barge tows plying the waterway. The 35 cutoffs and straightening of some bends shortened the channel by as much as 40 miles. Nearly 85 million cubic yards of material were dredged from the River Section to provide a 300-foot-wide navigation channel at a depth sufficient to float a barge loaded to 9 feet. Prior to Tenn-Tom, materials dredged or excavated during the building or maintaining an inland waterway were deposited along the riverbanks. This method of disposal was not only unsightly, but some of the material would wash back into the channel and have to be removed again. The Mobile District chose another method of disposal; it placed all the dredged material in so-called upland disposal areas. These areas were enclosed with dikes and designed to allow the liquid part of the pipeline deposit to return to the waterway after the solid materials had filtered out. The disposal areas were located out of eyesight of the waterway and left with native plants and trees to attract wildlife. They were located along the waterway where they were needed for construction and would be accessible for future maintenance dredging. In the River Section alone, over 9,000 acres were acquired just for dredged disposal areas. This method for dredged disposal became standard practice for the Corps.

Some 85 million cubic yards of material were removed to provide the navigation channel along the so-called 149-mile River Section or the southern reach of the waterway. This massive excavation work was accomplished using pipeline dredges, and for the first time, all the material was pumped into diked upland spoil areas instead being dumped along the riverbanks. The channel improvements also included 35 cutoffs for better alignment of the meandering river which shortened the navigation channel by 40 miles.

Mobile's design and constructions teams also implemented another procedure that became a standard for building locks and dams. One of the challenges of building these kinds of structures is controlling the presence of water at the construction site. In layman's terms, cofferdams are installed to lessen seepage from groundwater or from water bearing soils for excavation needed to build the structure's foundation and other associated work. A cofferdam is built by driving interlocking sheet piling below grade. It is an expensive process, and it is difficult to prevent all leakage into the work site. After construction is complete, the sheet pilings need to be removed. MDO decided to use a new method of controlling seepage called a slurry trench. As an alternative to a cofferdam, a slurry trench, first developed in Italy, proved to be easier to install than a cofferdam and much less costly. The process involved digging a trench with a clamshell or similar machine and backfilling the trench with a mixture of the excavated material, bentonite, and water, creating a water barrier that had a low permeability. These new, innovative techniques helped to reduce construction costs and, in some cases, helped lessen its adverse impacts on the environment.

Chain of Lakes Section

The original design concept for this reach of the waterway was called a perched canal. The upper reaches of the Tombigbee River are nothing more than a small, circuitous stream, and to continue following the river itself would have destroyed its semblance and natural amenities. The perched canal was just what the term implies, a canal with high levees on each side for a distance of 46 miles. It presented a host of problems such as incoming drainage or streams that would be traversed or affected by a diked canal, requiring a system to convey any affected water flows underneath the canal itself. It also had serious environmental consequences, including destroying the headwaters of the Tombigbee and its ecological values. As an alternative, the Mobile District engineers, led by Bud Cronenberg, developed an alternative plan they called a "Chain of Lakes." The plan called for construction of five locks with relatively small impoundments formed by dams and a series of levees on the western side to help provide adequate channel depths in the small lakes and avoid adversely affecting the nearby headwaters of the Tombigbee River. The eastern side of the lakes would be allowed to seek its natural elevations, depending on the lifts of the locks. Five locks would be built to overcome a difference in elevation of 140 feet along this reach of the waterway. This plan was approved because it was much more cost effective and preserved the upper reaches of the Tombigbee and its natural and ecological features.

The five locks were originally designated by the alphabet, A, B, C, D, and E, but Congress later named them after some of the waterway's champions. Thad Cochran Lock (A) is the southernmost structure in this section and is located in Amory, Mississippi. Glover Wilkins Lock (B) is near Smithville, followed by Fulton Lock (C). The Tenn-Tom Waterway Development Authority, by resolution, has requested Congress to name the lock at Fulton in honor of Senator Roger Wicker, a longtime and influential supporter of the waterway, upon his retirement from the U.S. Senate. The final two in this section of the waterway are John Rankin (D) and Sonny Montgomery (E) locks. Rankin is located in Itawamba County, and Montgomery is in the northern part of that county near the boundary with Prentiss County. The locks at Cochran, Rankin, and Montgomery have lifts of 30 feet, and those at Wilkins and Fulton are 25 feet.

A controversy developed in the late 1970s concerning these locks when the Corps recommended that Rankin not be built, and Montgomery be relocated farther south of its current location. This could be accomplished by raising the elevations or lifts of the remaining locks. The Rankin site was a swampy, low-lying area, and soil conditions there were not conducive to supporting a massive structure like a lock chamber. The authority favored this modification because it would reduce lockage times to transit the waterway, and this would be beneficial to commercial navigation. What's more, the larger lakes formed by the remaining locks would generate more recreational benefits. Eliminating a lock would also reduce the cost of the project and would lower operation and maintenance (O&M) costs during the life of the waterway. Some were concerned that the proposed changes could have serious implications on the lawsuit that was in the federal courts. One of the plaintiffs' main charges in that case was that the Corps had overstepped its legal authorities by making previous changes to the project. Local citizens and their leaders were also strongly opposed to eliminating the lock, contending the Corps was reneging on prior promises if not commitments it had made to them about the development of the waterway. The authority was not able to persuade those in opposition to acknowledge the significant benefits of the proposed change, and they were able to convince Congressman Jamie Whitten to kill the proposal. This was most unfortunate for all concerns, including the local beneficiaries. The poor soil conditions at Rankin were overcome by radically changing the lock's design from a gravity type to a floating or bathtub type of structure. All the other locks in the Chain of Lakes and River Sections are a gravity type where the immense weight of the lock secures its stability and permanence. Rankin was changed to a bathtub type where the structure floats because of the poor load-bearing soil conditions. Whitten Lock is of similar design.

Divide Cut Section

The northern portion of the waterway, where there was no stream to follow and which traverses the highest elevations of terrain in Mississippi, was arguably the most challenging to design and build. The Nashville District was given the responsibility of building Whitten Lock and Dam, which created the 6,700-acre Bay Springs Lake, and constructing a 29-mile canal to connect that reservoir with the commercial navigation channel at Pickwick Lake on the Tennessee River. It took eight years to complete this monumental project.

Construction of Whitten Lock and Dam includes a massive 100-foot-high, rock-filled earthen dam one-half mile long. At 84 feet, it is the fourth-highest single lift lock in the nation. The dam is unique in that it does not include a spillway. The only water released from its reservoir into the waterway downstream is spillage from lockage. There is also an O-ring valve used to release a small amount of water downstream for water quality purposes. Connected by the Divide Cut canal, Bay Springs Lake has the same fluctuations as that of Pickwick Lake on the Tennessee River, with drawdowns during the winter months for flood control storage and higher elevations during the summer months for recreational purposes. As an extension of the much larger 43,000-acre Pickwick Lake, a break or rupture of the dam at Whitten could release millions of gallons and cause catastrophic devastation downstream. It was identified as a potentially high-risk target after the terrorist attacks on 9/11.

Building the 29-mile canal to connect Bay Springs Lake with the Tennessee River was arguably the most challenging feat in building the waterway. It would involve the largest earth-moving project ever undertaken. The canal would have to traverse some of the highest elevations in Mississippi. The average depth of excavation would be 50 feet, with the deepest cut as much as 175 feet. At that depth, the width of the excavation work spanned some 1,400 feet from one ridge line to the other and sloped down to the canal, which was 280 feet wide and 12 feet deep. It was truly Mississippi's Grand Canyon.

The Nashville District consolidated about 11 miles of the canal into one contract. The successful bidder was a consortium of three of the largest construction contractors in the nation: Morrison-Knudson Corporation of Boise, Idaho; Brown and Root, Inc. of Houston, Texas; and Martin K. Eby Construction Company of Wichita, Kansas. The group called themselves the Tenn-Tom Constructors. The consortium's low bid of $271 million was the largest contract the Corps had ever awarded for a civil works project. Fearing that the federal judge could enjoin the award of any new contracts until the ongoing lawsuit could be fully adjudicated, there was enormous pressure to get as many contracts underway as possible, including this mega contract. It was rumored that Colonel Bob Tenor, commander of the Nashville District, locked his contract evaluation staff in a room and told them they could not come out until they finished their review of the bid proposal. The contract was awarded in March 1979, in record time.

Whitten Lock and Dam shown here under construction is the largest of the 10 such structures on the Tenn-Tom. Also shown here is the newly constructed Natchez Trace Parkway bridge, one of 13 highways and six railroads that had to be relocated to accommodate the 234-mile waterway.

Whitten Lock and Dam is shown here after its completion at a cost of nearly $75 million, a pittance compared to today's costs for similar projects. Its 6,600-acre lake offers some of the most scenic vistas along the entire waterway. Standing at 84 feet, the lock is the fourth-highest single lift in the nation.

There has never been as much uncertainty about the supply of oil and its price as there was when this contract was awarded. The oil embargo in 1973 and later the oil crises in Iran in 1979 that threatened production there made future prices and supplies of fuel highly speculative, at best. Although fuel costs were a major component of the costs for excavation work of this kind, surprisingly, the contract did not include a fuel cost-escalation clause, which was a huge risk for the contractors. By all accounts the assumptions they made on projected fuel consumption and costs proved to be on target.

Another major component of the expense to accomplish this enormous work was the costs for heavy construction equipment. It was rumored that the consortium bought $40 million of new equipment and expected to fully depreciate it by the end of the contract. The companies that enjoyed these sales had representatives and service teams on site to address any issues that might affect the performance of the equipment. Soil samples indicated that the material to be excavated was alluvial-type soils, fine silt, clays, and other similar types that were conducive to excavation by typical machines. There was no rock or other hard material requiring blasting. The only rock encountered throughout the 234 miles of the waterway was located at the northernmost end of the waterway, where it connected to the Tennessee River. After blasting, the rock and other material were removed by floating plant and used as fill for developing industrial sites associated with Yellow Creek Port.

Tenn-Tom Constructors developed an ingenious way to remove the softer materials by using New Holland scrapers (a company more noted for its agricultural equipment). Two bulldozers pushed and pulled the scrapers, and as the material was scraped, it was deposited on a system of conveyors and side cast into large dump trucks. It was a continual operation with a flag man riding on the scraper. The flag man would wave off the dump trunk once it was loaded and direct the next one that was in line to be loaded. Fifty-ton dump trucks were loaded in about one minute, then they carried the materials to nearby designated spoil areas. The Nashville District designated deposit areas along the canal route such as in valleys between hills, without significantly altering the landscape. Once filled, the areas were seeded with native grasses, and some had small ponds for waterfowl and other wildlife. The other, coarser materials were excavated using large two-engine scrapers typically used in highway construction.

A series of pumps were installed along the canal to lower the water table and stabilize both the canal bottom and the slopes leading to the canal. The system was so effective that homeowners several miles away complained that the dewatering had dried up their wells, the primary source of water in the rural areas of Tishomingo County at that time. Nashville District investigated nearly 200 complaints, and when the canal's dewatering system was determined to be at fault, the government reimbursed homeowners for the expense of boring deeper wells. Also, scores of structures had to be built to convey water from interrupted streams and drainage areas into or from the canal. Other challenges included the relocation of a railroad, including a new bridge, while not interrupting service; the relocation of three highways; and the removal of a hamlet called Holcut. Although a total of about 110,000 acres of private property were acquired for the waterway, Holcut, in Tishomingo County, was the only settlement affected by its construction. The small rural community sat in the path of the canal, and Nashville District purchased all the property and demolished it. A memorial was erected near the village site to commemorate what its citizens lost for the benefit of progress.

Arguably the most daunting task for the Corps of Engineers in building Tenn-Tom was the so-called Divide Cut. The 27-mile-long canal through Mississippi's highest elevations connects Tenn-Tom with the Tennessee River. Some 150 million cubic yards of material were dug, more than that needed to build the Suez Canal. Six highway and railroad bridges had to be relocated before the project was completed at a total cost of nearly $490 million.

The Nashville District awarded a $271-million contract to a consortium of three of the nation's largest contractors to build the canal's largest section of the Divide Cut with its deepest excavation of 175 feet. It was the largest contract ever awarded by the Corps at that time. All the excavation for the 12x280-foot canal was accomplished one year ahead of schedule. Shown here celebrating that herculean accomplishment are Jerry Ranier, Nashville District's project manager, on the left, and Glover Wilkins of the waterway authority.

One of the greatest challenges in building the canal was the disposal of 150 million cubic yards of excavated material in a cost-effective and environmentally compatible manner. Most all the material was deposited in the undulating valleys alongside the canal. As shown here, it is difficult to discern where these spoil areas are compared to the natural conditions of the countryside. Landscaping, planting native grasses, and building small ponds for waterfowl helped mitigate any unsightly or environmentally harmful effects.

CHAPTER XV
Construction's Local Benefits

The Tennessee-Tombigbee Waterway wound its way through four counties in west Alabama and six in Northeast Mississippi, mostly all rural and sparsely populated areas. Some of these counties were the most economically depressed in the nation with the lowest per capita income and chronic unemployment rates as high as 40 percent. The Corps would employ 125 prime contractors to build the waterway, most of them headquartered outside the two states. They would in turn utilize some 1,200 subcontractors, many of whom did not live in the 10 waterway counties. All this work would create thousands of new jobs during the 12 years the project was under construction. Building such a large public works project in such a rural, economically depressed setting could create boom and bust conditions, which would be very harmful to the impacted area unless the authority took steps to mitigate the potential harm.

Most of the waterway corridor did not have the infrastructure to accommodate a large influx of workers and their families. The workers' short-term stays made it impractical to address the increased needs for housing, schools, and other requirements to support these new, albeit temporary residents. The Corps, working with the waterway authority, undertook measures to lessen the negative effects of these major construction activities on the waterway corridor, while creating new employment and business opportunities for its citizens. For example, a local hiring preference clause was included in all the awarded contracts that stipulated the contractor must try to hire at least 80 percent of its workforce from the local area. The provision was a goal and not a legally binding obligation, but the contractor had to show evidence of its attempts to comply and to keep records of its progress or success in meeting the hiring goal.

The local hiring preference clause was a laudable objective, but there was a dearth of workers in the local labor pools who were qualified and possessed the trade skills the heavy construction industry needed. This shortcoming was especially prevalent within the minority population. Living in abject poverty with little hope of getting a meaningful job, many did not have reliable means of transportation to travel to work, and some didn't even have an alarm clock to get them up early. It was most evident that an aggressive and comprehensive training program and some cultural changes had to be implemented rapidly if those disadvantaged citizens living in the waterway corridor were to be gainfully employed. The civil rights laws enacted during the 1960s were followed by implementation of several affirmative action plans and programs, including the so-called Philadelphia Plan. This plan, adopted by both the Johnson and Nixon administrations, required contractors of federally funded construction projects in the city of Philadelphia to meet certain goals by specific dates for hiring minorities. The building trades unions in the city had a history of not allowing minorities to join the membership. Similar plans were adopted for other cities and for the Tennessee-Tombigbee project. The Tenn-Tom plan was the most aggressive of all the affirmative action programs adopted for federally funded construction projects. Instead of setting an overall goal for employing minorities for the project, it established goals for each of the involved trades, which increased annually during the construction period. In other words, a contractor could not hire most all its minority workers as laborers, masons, or lower-paying trades to help it meet its goal, while falling short of hiring electricians, iron workers, and the other more skilled and higher-paying trades.

The Minority Peoples Council (MPC) pressed for more minority participation in the waterway's construction. The local organization claimed to have more than 4,000 members from a dozen or more chapters and was led by Wendel Paris, John Zippert, and other leaders in west Alabama. MPC's advocacy for more jobs and business opportunities for minorities led Congress to enact section 185 of the Water Resources Development Act of 1977. That legislation established a goal of 30 percent of minority hires for each craft being utilized and authorized worker trainee programs to place more minorities at the entry level for these crafts. It also required that prime contracts include provisions requiring set-a-sides for subcontracting to minority businesses and that a Tennessee-Tombigbee Affirmative Action Committee (TTAAC) be established. TTAAC, composed of the relevant federal agencies and non-federal interests, including the waterway authority, and chaired by the Corps' division engineer, met regularly and was responsible for establishing the policies and programs to meet the goals set forth by Congress.

Trained workers were most urgently needed. The unions were very cooperative in that regard. Some, like the operating engineers, the plumbers, the ironworkers, and the laborers conducted training courses that were supplemented by local vo-tech schools like the LA Dow Technical School at Carrollton, Alabama, and the Golden Triangle School at Columbus, Mississippi. While these programs produced more minority workers, the most effective program involved an agreement among the Corps, the contractors, and the trade unions that allowed contractors to hire trainees who would spend time on the job learning a specific trade. The Corps offered reimbursement for part of the workers' time spent training. It was a very successful endeavor.

Similar efforts were undertaken to increase the involvement of minority-owned businesses. Such efforts established goals for subcontracting or set-aside work, depending on the type of work to be accomplished and the capabilities of known minority businesses in the area. An office was established in Columbus to help minorities prepare government bids, related documents, and employ better business practices. Tutorials by Sam Pilkington, Tom Epps, and Esther Harrison, as well as others there, not only helped these fledgling businesses to secure waterway-related business, but also led many to continue growing as profitable enterprises. Some of these companies, as well as many of the minority workers who had become journeymen of their trades while building the Tenn-Tom, took their business acumen and skills to help build the Red River Waterway and other federally funded projects.

All of these social engineering efforts helped accomplish a more equitable increase in the local economic benefits derived from the waterway's construction. Those contractors employed by both the Mobile and Nashville Districts not only met the 80 percent local hiring goal but also exceeded it, which was commendable. The goal of hiring 30 percent minority workers in the different building trades was not achieved, but its failure was not because of a lack of effort. The primary impediment was the low populations of Blacks living in the northern part of the waterway where so much of the work occurred. For example, the 2020 census, 40 years since the waterway was under construction and despite growth in the overall population, showed that only 7 percent and a mere 2.7 percent of those living in Itawamba County and Tishomingo County, respectively, were Black. Nevertheless, employment of minorities, who enjoyed higher paying jobs working on the waterway, still ranged from the low to mid-20 percentile during construction, certainly another commendable achievement. The utilization of minority businesses was also a success. I once heard Esther Harrison, who would later become the first Black woman elected to represent the Columbus area in the Mississippi State Legislature, say at one of the early TTAAC meetings that a goal of $50 million of contract set-asides would likely exceed the capabilities of all the minority business within the waterway area. More than that amount of business was later realized by minority-owned enterprises.

The two Corps Districts, their employees, and the contractors whose workers built the waterway can all take personal pleasure and much pride in accomplishing one of the engineering wonders of the world. They built 10 locks and dams, 234 miles of navigable channels, and numerous recreational and environmental facilities within just 12 years. In doing so, they excavated as much material as what was dug for the Panama and Suez canals combined, poured some 2.2 million cubic yards of concrete, and used some 33,000 tons of steel. The waterway was completed in December 1984. Amazingly, all that was accomplished faster and at less cost than would be needed to build one lock and dam today.

More details about the waterway and its components are included in Appendix A. Appendix D includes a list of Corps of Engineers employees at the Mobile District who made important contributions to the waterway. The list includes those who helped plan, design, construct, operate the project and provided other services required to complete it. Appendix E includes similar recognition of those employees with the Nashville District, who also made valuable contributions and provided services to the waterway. Recognition of these individuals was compiled from memory, and therefore, some deserved ones have likely been inadvertently omitted. If so, I apologize for the oversight.

CHAPTER XVI
Bridges Too Far?

Federally authorized inland waterways are planned, designed, constructed, operated, and maintained by the federal government. The only exception was that the affected states were responsible for the relocation of highway bridges across a waterway. Any railroads affected were a federal responsibility. In 1946, when Congress authorized the Tenn-Tom, Alabama and Mississippi agreed to assume responsibility for any highway relocations, and the costs of doing so were well within the financial capabilities of the two states. At that time, fewer highways were affected, and no highways were four lanes. Thirty years later, the non-federal costs associated with the waterway had soared because of building and upgrading more crossings and increased costs caused by new federal environmental and safety laws and regulations.

As soon as construction of the waterway began, the Corps started pressing the authority to provide more formal assurances that the highway bridges would be relocated in accord with the construction schedule of the waterway. The compact states had not given the authority the responsibility to carry out the bridge relocations. The Corps assumed that Alabama and Mississippi would be responsible for their bridge relocations. In the 1960s, the Alabama State Legislature passed a $10 million bond issue to finance the state's financial obligations associated with the waterway. With prices rising because of inflation and more burdensome federal environmental and safety regulations, an additional $25 million was needed to relocate Alabama's three highway crossings. The earlier bond issue was intended to fund a new bridge at Gainesville for State Highway 39 at the site of the lock and dam construction. The additional $25 million was needed to relocate U.S. Highway 17 in Pickens County and U.S. Highway 11 in Greene County. Legislation authorizing the additional bond issue was approved in 1976, pending approval by the state voters in the general election that fall.

Voters tend to vote against money measures they perceive to offer no direct benefit to them or to their part of the state. The authority knew it faced a formidable challenge to ensure that a majority of the voters would approve the Tenn-Tom bond issue. Immediately after the governor's approval of including the bond issue in the fall election, Pete Kelley and other authority staff began sending press releases to every daily and weekly newspaper in the state touting the local, regional, and national benefits of the waterway, especially those impacts for the state. Since little was known about the Tenn-Tom outside its corridor, especially in the northern and eastern counties, Pete Kelley, a former newspaper editor, met with daily newspapers throughout the state to request op-ed space for waterway-related articles. He also met with radio stations to schedule recorded radio spots about the waterway. The authority developed a 20-minute program with slides to use at civic clubs, and requests were sent to many local organizations to speak at these meetings. The entire staff was marshaled to accommodate the response. Most clubs are always looking for a program or speaker, and we spoke to both large and small groups throughout the state.

I kept reminding everyone that the Trinity River project that would have provided barge transportation from the Texas coast to Dallas also required a similar statewide referendum to finance highway relocations. The project's supporters were confident that with such strong local support and with President Lyndon Johnson's support only smooth sailings were in store for their waterway. That proved to be wrong when the state voters decisively voted down the bond measure, effectively killing the project. It was never built, and the same could have easily happened to the Tenn-Tom. Therefore, we were anxiously watching the election returns the evening of the vote and learned that all our hard work of spreading the word about the Tenn-Tom had paid off. More than 80 percent of the voters approved the bond measure.

Mississippi would be a much harder nut to crack, and the Corps' patience was wearing thin. Attempts to pass a $10 million bond issue in 1972 failed, and the State Legislature rejected another attempt the following year to pass a $15 million measure. With the costs to relocate 10 bridges along the Mississippi portion of the waterway approaching $150 million, there was growing concern that the nation's poorest state could not meet such a financial requirement. The prospects of Mississippi not being able to comply were not lost, even by its opponents, who were whispering to the congressional committees about this potential roadblock for the waterway. The Corps of Engineers was also growing impatient and wanted more assurances that the two states' financial obligations were forthcoming. Major General Carroll LeTellier, the South Atlantic Division commander, was receiving a lot of pressure from headquarters to either secure the agreements from the two states or delay the award of any new contracts. At the risk of hurting his Army career, the general gave the authority until March 1976 to resolve the problem.

All the legislators along the waterway in Northeast Mississippi were strong supporters of fulfilling the state's obligations, and State Representative Jerry Wilburn from Itawamba County and others were able to garner Speaker Buddy Newman's agreement to help. However, the earlier bond legislation had failed because of the lukewarm support of those legislators from the western and southern sections of the state. It was apparent that getting approval of the funding would be very difficult, at best. The seriousness of the state's inability to fulfill its funding obligations was brought to the attention of the Mississippi congressional delegation. Waterway opponents, mostly national environmental organizations, were whispering to people on Capitol

Hill about the failure of the state to meet its financial commitments. The authority and others were seeking advice if not solutions from the waterway's congressional supporters.

During the 1970s, the state enjoyed some of the most powerful members of any state serving in Congress. There are some who advocate for term limits for those serving in Congress. If implemented, it would mean that the most important positions like chairing the key congressional committees would not be based on seniority of service but by elections among the membership. That would be a huge advantage for the larger, more populous states. States like New York and California would have many more members to vote for leadership positions in the House than smaller states like Mississippi and Alabama. As a result, the larger delegations could virtually name the chairmanships of the most important committees like appropriations, rules, and armed services. Seniority or years of service helps ensure that representatives of less populated states like Mississippi can serve in leadership positions. A colleague from Ohio once asked me how Alabama and Mississippi always seemed to have so many congressional supporters for their water resources projects, with representatives serving on the right committees to advance those projects. My response was that the voters have an uncanny ability to initially elect someone who is young, intelligent, an effective campaigner, and who can relate to constituents. In most all cases, the voters keep re-electing them, and over time they gain enough seniority to have a lot of influence in Washington. That description of the ideal congressional candidate certainly fit those representing the waterway compact states, including Mississippi, during the years the waterway was under construction.

Jamie Whitten, the dean of the state's congressional delegation, was "Mr. Agriculture" and served on the appropriations committee, which he would chair beginning in 1979. By the time he retired in 1992, Whitten had served for 50 years in the U.S. House of Representatives, the second longest tenure in history at the time. Trent Lott and Thad Cochran were both elected in 1972 as Republicans, a rarity for the state in those days. Both soon became leaders in the

House, with Lott serving on the Judiciary Committee and as the minority whip for the Republican leadership. Cochran gained a seat on the Public Works and Transportation Committee, a position of great importance to the state's water resources development, including the Tenn-Tom. He resigned after serving three terms and was elected to the U.S. Senate in 1978. Lott followed Cochran 10 years later, and both had impressive careers in the upper body. Lott became majority leader, and Cochran chaired Appropriations. David Bowen and Sonny Montgomery also made lasting contributions to government during their time in the House. Montgomery was champion of American veterans. He served as the chairman of Veterans Affairs and wrote the GI Bill of Rights. Bowen was a key member of the Merchant Marine and Fisheries Committee. In 1978, he helped pass some important reforms to the Endangered Species Act that were of much importance to economic development projects, including the Tenn-Tom.

Mississippi's two senators wielded even greater influence on Capitol Hill. Senator James Eastland chaired the powerful Judiciary Committee for 23 years of the 35 years he served in the U.S. Senate. Until he retired in 1978, he was also president pro tempore, a position that honors the senator with the most seniority. John C. Stennis served even longer, for 42 years, before retiring in 1989. During that time, he chaired the Armed Services Committee from 1969 until 1981 during the Cold War and Vietnam War buildup of the nation's military power. He also served on the Appropriations Committee, including as a member of the Water Resources and Energy Subcommittee that funded the Corps of Engineers. He chaired the full committee for the last two years of his tenure. He was so well-respected by his colleagues that they called him "Mr. Integrity." He was the first chairman of that body's Ethics Committee. During the Watergate scandal, President Nixon felt Stennis would be impartial to listen to the infamous White House tapes and objectively report his findings back to Congress, void of any political embellishments. This so-called Senate Compromise, as an alternative to releasing the tapes to the public, was never accepted, and eventually the release of the tapes and their contents led to Nixon's resignation.

After close consultation with Congressmen Whitten and Bob Jones of North Alabama, who chaired the House Public Works and Transportation Committee, Congressman Cochran sought to add a provision to a pending federal highway bill. His proposed legislation would have transferred the funding for the waterway-impacted highway relocations to the U.S Department of Transportation. Although the proposed language was general in nature and did not name either a state or a specific project, it was no secret it pertained to the Tenn-Tom. Waterway opponents learned of Cochran's proposal and were able to kill the measure in committee.

Not to be deterred, Whitten was able to include similar language in the Federal Aid (no pun intended) Highway Act of 1976. As a senior member of the Appropriations Committee, he was able to deflect any efforts by other members to strike the provision from the bill, even though the waterway opponents were urging some to do so. They knew the Tenn-Tom was "Whitten's project" and were reluctant to cross swords with the soon-to-become all-powerful chairman of Appropriations. The waterway opponents, though, were persistent. After the enactment of the Federal Aid Highway Act, opponents were able to get the Ford Administration to request a rescission of that specific provision in the enacted law. In the end, Congress rejected the President's request.

This authorization not only relieved the two states of their obligations for those crossings, but it also enabled other crossings that had been assumed to be abandoned. There were numerous private ferry crossings along the Tombigbee River, including one at Pickensville, Alabama, and the Nashville, Waverly, and Barton ferry crossings in Mississippi. Under the new federal authority, a bridge would be constructed at State Highway 50 between Columbus and West Point to replace the Waverly and Barton Ferries. The persistent efforts of Pickens County Probate Judge Robert Hugh Kirksey led to a new bridge crossing at Pickensville, which replaced the ferry there. The new bridge was accessible to users of the nearby Nashville Ferry, which was also abandoned. The Pickensville bridge appropriately bears the judge's name.

This masterful legislative work by Congressmen Cochran, Whitten, and Jones resolved the issue of financing the bridge crossings, the costs of which had soared beyond the financial capabilities of the state of Mississippi. By doing so, it eliminated the threat that the Corps would halt construction of the waterway until the state met its obligations. There was fear that, if that happened, work might never be resumed. However, we soon learned that we had little time to celebrate this victory because another threat, potentially even more serious than the funding for bridges, was about to arise.

Chapter XVII
Carter's Hit List

The presidential election of 1976 was one of the more interesting races of that era. President Richard Nixon appointed Gerald Ford in December 1973 as his vice president after Spiro Agnew resigned because of criminal charges that stemmed from his time as governor of Maryland. Ford was the first vice president who was approved under the provisions of the 25th amendment that says the President nominates his candidate who must then be approved be a majority of the members of the U.S. House of Representatives and members of the U.S. Senate. Ford was overwhelmingly approved, but after he became President when Nixon was forced to resign, he fell out of favor with many when he pardoned Nixon for unspecified crimes he might have committed. Ford said he did so for the good of the nation, but the controversial pardon likely caused his defeat in 1976, when he ran for another term. He became the Republican nominee after beating back a challenge by former California Governor Ronald Reagan and by replacing his first choice as his vice president, Nelson Rockefeller, with U.S. Senator Bob Dole. That move was made to appease the more conservative members of the party.

The race for the Democrat presidential candidate was even more of a crap shoot. Seventeen candidates qualified for the primary, which most likely was a record. Included in the field of candidates were several of the most powerful members of Congress, such as senators Henry "Scoop" Jackson of Washington, Walter Mondale of Minnesota, Frank Church of Idaho, Lloyd Bentsen of Texas, and U.S. Representative Morris "Mo" Udall of Arizona. Governors vying for the nomination were Jerry Brown of California; George Wallace of Alabama, the "law-and-order" candidate now confined to a wheelchair because of an assignation attempt in 1972; and a little-known governor from Georgia, Jimmy Carter.

Carter campaigned as a Washington outsider and ran a grassroots campaign using volunteers organized as Carter's Peanut Brigade, who went nationwide knocking on voters' doors. It worked. He did well in all except two Sunbelt states, while the other candidates fought each other for the other states. Brown, of course, carried California. There was not a clear-cut winner when the national convention began, but after many negotiations and some old-fashioned horse trading, Carter emerged as the party's nominee. He chose Walter Mondale as his running mate. The general election was hotly contested, but Carter was victorious over Ford by a slim margin, winning 50.1 percent of the popular vote and 55 percent of the electoral votes.

I found both candidates appealing but voted for Ford since I had worked as a member of his administration. I expected to join him again at the end of my two-year loan to the authority, assuming he was reelected. The position I vacated at Interior was a Schedule C or a political appointment and not a civil service one. I had acquired the job not through party politics, but through my association with John Whitaker, a top White House aide. Nixon had appointed him as deputy secretary of Interior, and he asked me to join him there. I realized that the new Carter team at Interior would treat me as a pariah and not allow me to return to a position comparable to my previous responsibility and pay when I left the agency in 1975. The loan program, the Intergovernmental Personnel Act, did not guarantee the returning government employee his or her old job, but the agency was required to offer one at a similar level within the department. I knew the new administration would assume I was a Ford holdover. No doubt they were already scheming about how to get rid of me.

Within a few months of completing my two-year loan, I learned that my prediction was true. Some friends still at Interior were telling me that at staff meetings, even at the secretary level, the question was routinely asked: "What are we going to do with Waldon when he returns?" I was convinced I likely had no future in Washington as long as the Carter crowd was in charge.

The Corps of Engineers had proposed building three dams on the Flint River south of Atlanta, mainly for meeting the growing water supply needs of that expanding metropolitan area. The feasibility study of one of the dams, called Sprewell Bluff, was the first one completed and was available for review and comments beginning in 1972 during the first years of Jimmy Carter's term as governor. Years earlier, before becoming governor, Carter had voiced support for the plan to develop the Flint River. The Corps' plans for Sprewell Bluff were widely circulated for review and were generally accepted and supported by the public and elected officials, except for a small, loosely organized group of environmentalists and now Governor Carter. One of the governor's main concerns was that the Corps had underestimated the project's estimated cost of $133 million. The costs of the project that are allocated to water supply, a primary purpose of the project, are totally reimbursed by those entities, including possibly the state, that contract to purchase the municipal and industrial water supplies provided by the dam. Thus, the reason Carter was so concerned about the costs of the federal project. Much to the delight of the environmental opponents and to the disgust of the project's supporters, Carter vetoed the building of the dam. The Corps never recommends construction of a water resources project unless it is supported by the governor of the affected state. As a result, Carter's disapproval effectively killed the development of the Flint River. The three dams, including Sprewell Bluff, were never built. The elimination of these projects to help meet Greater Atlanta's water supply helped precipitate the "water wars" litigation involving the states of Alabama, Florida, and Georgia concerning each state's rights to water available from the Chattahoochee and Coosa River basins. The Flint River proposal left Carter with a suspicion of, if not a dislike of, the

Corps, and he brought that with him to the presidency.

Shortly after coming to Washington, Carter met with Lieutenant General Jack Morris at the general's request. At the time, Morris was the commander of the Corps. The general knew that Carter had campaigned to put the Corps out of the dam business, and he wanted an opportunity to try to mend fences between the agency and the President. I am sure the general also took the opportunity to inform the President of the Corps' international reputation for its premier engineering and construction capabilities, both for civil works and for the military. The meeting lasted for two hours, much to everyone's astonishment.

While the long meeting with Morris might have lessened the President's dislike for the Corps as an agency, it did little to temper his disdain for water projects. As part of his first budget to Congress, Carter sent a separate message on February 21, 1977, calling for major reforms to better measure the worth of these projects. As an example, he included a list of projects that his budget recommended to be terminated. It included eleven Corps projects and eight of the Bureau of Reclamation. He further announced that he had instructed both the Corps and Reclamation, working with the Office of Management and Budget and the Council of Environmental Quality, to review all 500 or more projects in their budgets with the purpose of terminating those found to be uneconomic or those that would cause significant harm to the environment. He gave them only two months to complete that herculean exercise. The review resulted in the President adding an additional 30 projects to his hit list, including the Tenn-Tom and the Red River Waterway.

Carter no doubt underestimated how strongly powerful members of Congress supported the projects he targeted. Many members of Congress who didn't even have a project on the President's chopping block were incensed that he had the gall to institute his own set of criteria for evaluating water projects, rather than follow the Corps' criteria, which was used by Congress and previous administrations. Some of Carter's closest advisors warned him that the money saved and the reduced adverse impacts on the environment if these projects were terminated would not come close to being worth all the political backlash and acrimony his administration would receive from Congress.

Public hearings were held for each project as part of the review process, and all had to be conducted within a very tight timeframe. The Corps alerted the authority that the Tenn-Tom hearing would be held in Columbus, Mississippi, on March 29, 1977, a week or so before it was officially announced. We used that time to begin preparing for what had to be a huge demonstration of local support for the projects. Elected officials in the waterway region, including governors, congressmen, and senators, as well as members of the state legislatures, were notified and urged to attend and to testify in favor of the waterway. Similar requests for statements of support were sent to all the chambers of commerce and economic development organizations. Contractors working nearby on the waterway were encouraged to let workers have time off to attend the hearing and to bring their hard hats.

These were extraordinarily busy times. In addition to addressing the ominous threat of Carter not supporting the waterway, a lawsuit filed against the Corps and the waterway by L&N (CSX) Railroad and the other environmental plaintiffs earlier in November was now gearing up to full steam. With the help of the national media, the waterway's opponents were doing a masterful job of nurturing more opposition from the public and within Congress. All these threats to the waterway were placing heavy demands on the waterway authority's resources, especially on its small staff and limited funding.

When the day arrived with much of the national media on hand, we were ready to show the Carter administration as well as the world how much public and political support the Tenn-Tom enjoyed. Much to our delight, some 5,000 supporters had traveled from near and far to show their support. For example, Decatur and Mobile had chartered buses to enable its citizens to attend, and others traveled from as far away as Tennessee and Kentucky to be there. Governors, congressmen, state legislators, and other state and local officials were there to voice their support. Mississippi's governor, Cliff Finch, led a hard hat parade of construction workers through the streets of Columbus by driving a large front-end loader machine with a couple of attractive female construction workers riding in the bucket.

Arguably the largest attended public hearing ever held by the Corps of Engineers occurred on March 29, 1977, in Columbus, Mississippi, when an estimated 5,000 Tenn-Tom supporters came to voice their opposition to President Carter's proposed termination of the waterway. After several hours of testimony, the hearing was mercifully cut short by a bomb threat, but the evidence of such overwhelming support for Tenn-Tom was a factor in Carter's approving the waterway for funding.

The authority has had some outstanding governors as members of the waterway compact during the 65 years or so. Those who served during the 1970s and 1980s spent inordinate amounts of time helping lead the project through difficult times, while at the same time serving the needs of their respective states. None were more engaged than Cliff Finch of Mississippi. He was elected governor in 1975 by running a unique grassroots campaign as the working man's candidate. To attract blue collar workers' support, he carried a metal lunch box to all his campaign stops, and one day each week he performed various jobs, such as working at a construction site, pumping gas, or even bagging groceries. The gimmicks worked, and he beat some better-known Democrats to win the primary and later the general election.

Finch never missed an authority meeting, including those in Washington. He also made available for the authority's use the Huey helicopters of the Air National Guard stationed at Tupelo and, when needed, provided the Guard's larger transport airplanes. The availability of the state's aircraft was a godsend, with activities taking place along the entire 250 miles of the waterway. We learned that he had worked in heavy construction and had operated heavy equipment while working his way through college. When we approached him about leading the hard hat parade, he was exuberant about the opportunity. He insisted that he drive a bulldozer, but the city of Columbus vetoed the idea out of fear it would tear up the streets. Finch was, nevertheless, very excited to drive the front-end loader and to be the first speaker at the hearing, as governor of the host state.

One of the more memorable experiences I had with Governor Finch occurred several weeks after the public hearing. With no advanced notice to the authority the governor had scheduled an emergency meeting with the governors from the waterway states to discuss important matters related to the project. On the afternoon before the meeting, his office called to invite the authority to attend and also to prepare an agenda for the meeting. I drew the short straw, went home to pack for an overnight stay, and immediately left for Jackson. My mind was completely occupied with developing an agenda worthy of an emergency-called meeting involving governors. That task became even more challenging when I learned that Finch had invited Edwin Edwards, the governor of Louisiana. Edwards was not a member of the waterway compact but likely considered it to be in competition with his state. After driving for several minutes, I realized that I had left a bag at my house and had to return home. This, along with stewing about the next day's meeting, upset me so much that I decided to take my anger out on an empty five-gallon bucket lying in the middle of the highway. The bucket became wedged underneath my car. After several attempts to dislodge it, I finally gave up and drove about 100 miles listening to an awful noise that sounded like everything underneath the car was being destroyed. Miles down the road, the bucket finally disintegrated. At that point, I couldn't have cared less about the car, as long as it got me to the governor's mansion.

Mississippi Governor Cliff Finch, a former heavy construction worker, led a "hard hat" parade through the streets of Columbus prior to the Carter hearings. Some of the waterway contractors gave their workers time off to attend the hearing. Their attendance was both noticeable and very effective for the waterway.

The next morning, I worked frantically with the governor's staff to develop an agenda for the luncheon meeting. We added some energy-related issues to justify inviting Governor Edwards to attend. Much to my surprise and certainly much relief, the luncheon went well, as did a later press conference that covered both the Tenn-Tom and energy issues facing the states. Governor Finch was very pleased with the day's events, except when Governor Ray Blanton of Tennessee ordered a cocktail at lunch while others had iced tea. Finch's staff took forever to find Blanton some bourbon. That day had all the prospects of being an embarrassment if not a colossal public relations disaster for Governor Finch, but it turned out to be a classic example of the old adage of putting lipstick on a pig.

Authority staff had written statements for each member who planned to attend the Carter hearing and had them prepped to make an oral presentation if needed. I went by the hotel to check on one of our Mississippi members, Rhett Eaton, and asked him if he had read or had any questions about the statement we had prepared for him. He said he had never spoken before to a group at a public meeting, and that he was so nervous he had been standing in front of a mirror practicing for hours. I assured him that he would do just fine. Much to his relief there were many more registered to speak than time would allow, and we did not have to call on him.

The Corps was responsible for conducting the hearing and recording its proceedings. Colonel Charlie Blalock, commander of the Mobile District, and Colonel Hank Hatch of Nashville were in charge of conducting the hearing and maintaining order. There were concerns that some of the waterway opponents might try to disrupt the proceedings, but that did not happen. Blalock retired that year from the military and became head of Mississippi's Department of Natural Resources. Hatch would advance quickly through the ranks of the Army and become commander of the Corps as a lieutenant general. The Carter administration had an observer there who seemed bored with the long, drawn-out proceedings. I surmised that he likely had formed a negative opinion about the waterway before he arrived at the hearing.

The venue for the hearing was the Whitfield Auditorium on the campus of the Mississippi State College for Women (now Mississippi University of Women or MUW). Its seating capacity of about 1,200, by far the largest in Columbus, was woefully too small to accommodate the estimated 5,000 who came to show their support for the waterway. A section of the auditorium was reserved for all the dignitaries, and we had also reserved a section for construction workers wearing their hard hats and holding handmade placards. This staged visual had a very positive effect on the media covering the hearing and on everyone in the audience.

The first couple of hours were devoted to statements made by the governors, members of Congress, and other dignitaries, all of whom spoke in favor of the waterway. State Senator Bill Burgin of Columbus and the principal partner of the law firm that represented the authority, accomplished during his remarks another important visual that benefited the waterway. Burgin was a large man with a booming voice, and at that time he was arguably the most powerful member serving in the State Legislature. Although all the speakers had been warned not to conduct any antics that might detract from the decorum of the hearing, Burgin asked all those in the audience to stand up if they supported the Tenn-Tom. Practically everyone in the auditorium stood with resounding hooting and hollering. He then asked those who opposed the waterway to stand. After a long pause when you could have heard a pin drop, about a dozen or so sitting together reluctantly stood up at the jeers of everyone else. Burgin's stunt made it clear who was there supporting the waterway and who was not, much to the chagrin of the few opponents in attendance.

In addition to pulling out all the stops to demonstrate the strong political and public support of Tenn-Tom, we also addressed allegations about its economics and its compliance with the various environmental laws and policies. For example, Dr. Joseph Hartley, an economics professor at Indiana State University, was employed to conduct an independent analysis of the project's benefits-to-costs ratio and present his findings. Dr. Hartley had conducted similar studies for the St. Lawrence Seaway and commercial navigation activities on the Ohio River. Sverdrup and Parcel, one of the nation's most prominent engineering firms, was employed to critique the project's Environmental Impact Statement, including the deficiencies alleged by its opponents. One of the firm's young engineers, Ron Coles, presented the findings at the hearings. Ron, who later left the firm to start his own business, went on to play a key role in the development of the waterway and in its leadership, including serving as a member of the authority and chairman of its sister organization, the Tenn-Tom Waterway Council.

After many witnesses spoke during the course of the day, someone called in a bomb threat, which mercifully, led to the hearing's adjournment. Although it ended in such a manner, with many disappointed they were unable to voice their support for the waterway, Tenn-Tom supporters were very pleased with the hearing. The event had achieved its objective of providing a very positive record of the waterway's public and political support for consideration by the Carter administration. The Corps reported that it was the largest-attended public hearing it had ever conducted. Carter continued to receive backlash from members of Congress, including Tenn-Tom supporters, about his negative actions against water resources development. The growing criticism from members of both parties led some of his aides to question the political cost of taking on such a relatively unimportant endeavor. However, Glover Wilkins, the waterway authority's administrator, did not want to leave one stone unturned and did not want to claim premature victory. He launched an aggressive lobbying effort to firmly secure the President's blessing. We had learned by happenstance that one of the authority members, Ed Browder of Harriman, Tennessee, could hold a key to that end. Browder was a very successful businessman and a self-made multi-millionaire, primarily from oil and gas distributorships, banking, and car dealerships. One of his ventures in banking was with Jake Butcher, a relative, who was chairman of the United American Bank, headquartered in Knoxville, Tennessee, and one of the largest banks in the state. Browder was much involved behind the scenes in the Democrat Party at both the state and national levels. He knew that I often traveled to

Washington, and he would send me tickets to some of the biggest, most elaborate receptions, mainly fundraisers for key politicians. I went to them, waved the Tenn-Tom flag, and no one ever knew I was there thanks to our benefactor, Mr. Ed.

President Carter had appointed Bert Lance, a banker from Georgia, as his director of the Office of Management and Budget. We just so happened to learn through Browder that Lance and Butcher were close friends. Glover immediately saw this friendship as a possible way of getting an audience with the person responsible for the President's budgets. At the request of Browder, Butcher was most willing to call Lance and tell him how important Tenn-Tom was to the future economy of the South and that the President's stance against water projects was hurting him politically and damaging any prospects of getting congressional approval of his other program initiatives. Last, Butcher asked Lance to meet with a group to discuss in more detail the merits of the waterway. The director agreed to meet with the Tenn-Tom delegation.

With little notice and a short time to schedule and attend such an important meeting, four of the five compact governors rearranged their busy schedules and flew to Washington to meet with Lance. Those attending this important meeting were governors Ray Blanton of Tennessee, Julian Carroll of Kentucky, Cliff Finch of Mississippi, and George Wallace of Alabama. The governors reiterated the importance of the waterway to their respective states and reminded Lance that the voters in their states had strongly backed the President. Further, they wanted to report back to their constituents that the President would endorse and fund the waterway. After that quid pro quo, Lance excused himself and went into an adjoining office to make a telephone call. After a few minutes, he returned to report that the President would approve the waterway once the ongoing review process was completed. We never knew whether Lance called the President or someone of high authority in the White House. Regardless, he returned to the meeting with a presidential commitment in hand. Later, Lance, one of Carter's closest friends, was forced to resign after being charged for some banking irregularities for which he was later acquitted. Butcher was not so fortunate. He later served time for bank fraud.

As an affirmation of the adage that "all politics is local," a Tenn-Tom authority member from Tennessee had a connection with Bert Lance, President Carter's budget director, that led to a crucial meeting with the former Georgia banker. The overwhelming turnout of waterway supporters at the earlier public hearing and because four governors attended the Lance meeting on short notice convinced the budget director and later the president to support continued funding for the waterway. The governors shown here meeting with Lance are, from left: Julian Carroll (Kentucky); sitting, George Wallace (Alabama); Bert Lance; Cliff Finch (Mississippi); and Ray Blanton (Tennessee). That meeting and its outcome were some of the most important turning points or milestones for the waterway.

Word soon reached the environmental groups that the President was backing away from his opposition to the waterway. They aggressively lobbied key players in the White House, and their efforts began to have some staff members contemplate asking the President to reverse his decision. Any possible reconsiderations were finally nipped in the bud, though, when it was decided that any negative action against the waterway by the administration would be inappropriate at that time since that could affect the outcome of the ongoing lawsuit in federal court. Waterway proponents would later use the same reasoning when lobbying Congress for appropriations, but to no avail.

On April 18, 1977, when the President announced his much-awaited decision to support the Tennessee-Tombigbee Waterway, I was less than six months from ending my time on loan to the authority from the Department of Interior. Carter had picked Cecil Andrus, former governor of Idaho, as the secretary of Interior, and most all the appointees at the departmental level were environmentalists or conservationists, including the person occupying my former position. They were aware that I had been very involved in getting the President to change his position on the waterway and that I was heavily involved in preparing for the defense of the ongoing lawsuit. They also continued to believe I was a Nixon/Ford Republican, all of which made it unlikely for me to return and work at the departmental level.

After reviewing the rules and regulations of the law that established the loan program, I learned that a government employee could be on loan for a total of four years, but no longer. As expected, when I contacted the department and requested it to extend my time on loan for another two years, I got an immediate no and was told to report to the Interior Department on a certain day. I reminded them this was not the Army, and I was not going anywhere until I was told what position I would fill. I knew then that the only way the new team at Interior would ever approve continuing the loan would be through political pressure. The master chef of concocting such a brew, Glover Wilkins, went to work. He asked most all the Democrat members of Congress from Alabama and Mississippi, as well as some from Tennessee and Kentucky, to write the President or call the White House to extend the loan for another two years. Governor Julian Carroll of Kentucky and the other compact governors who knew Andrus from prior associations as fellow governors, contacted the secretary on my behalf. Jokingly, I told Glover had I garnered that kind of political support earlier I could have been head of Interior instead of trying to get some lower-level position. The effort worked, and it was not long before I got a call telling me that the department had changed its position and would support extending the loan for another two years. The caller later asked that I "call off the dogs."

I innocently asked, "Do what?"

He said, "Call those who are contacting the White House about your loan and tell them to quit." Concerned that they might later renege on the two-year extension, I suggested that the secretary or someone at the White House call those who had made the requests on my behalf. I knew then that the White House had reversed those at Interior, which pleased me, but I also realized that I had burned my last bridge to ever work at Interior while Carter was in office. I resigned from the federal government at the end of the loan in 1979 and joined the Tennessee-Tombigbee Waterway Development Authority as its deputy administrator.

After all of Carter's early negative statements and actions, including putting the waterway on his "hit list," his administration later included the waterway as a national demonstration project as part of his rural development initiative. Tenn-Tom was selected as an example of how a large public works project could be built in a sparsely populated rural setting and create much-needed high-paying jobs and with careful planning preclude boom-or-bust conditions that normally occur in the project area. We worked closely with Jack Watson, one of Carter's aides in charge of this initiative, and were able to get some much-needed positive publicity for the waterway. Toward the end of Carter's administration, a meeting was held in Columbus to report on the progress of the demonstration project. The First Lady, Rosalynn, along with Jack Watson, attended, and both spoke to the group. It was evident that the First Lady was suffering from too many campaign stops that week and appeared tired and befuddled. However, she was most gracious and allowed me to take some photographs of her with some authority members. Ironically, all of them were staunch Republicans. Mrs. Carter's tiring campaign work was for naught since, later in November, Ronald Reagan decisively defeated her husband's reelection bid. All the Tenn-Tom states were included in the 44 states that voted for Reagan.

CHAPTER XVIII
Back In The Courts

While the victory of the first court battle was sweet, the case's national publicity became the clarion that began to rally opposition to the Tenn-Tom by well-financed national environmental organizations. It also emboldened opposition to the waterway by the rail industry, especially from the L&N (now CSX) Railroad and its national trade association, the Association of American Railroads (AAR). A CSX official had worked behind the scenes with CLEAN during its litigation, offering advice. Rumors swirled, saying that CSX helped fund CLEAN's operations. With Tenn-Tom now under construction, AAR started openly opposing the waterway by testifying before Congress against its appropriations.

Almost before the ink had dried on the final proceedings of the first lawsuit, L&N and EDF simultaneously filed separate lawsuits in the U.S. District Court of D.C. The EDF suit also included CLEAN and three individuals as plaintiffs,: G. Randall Grace, Glenn Clemmer, and F. Glenn Liming, all of whom were members of both CLEAN and EDF. Later during the trial, the National Audubon Society, the Birmingham Audubon Society, and the Alabama Conservancy joined as plaintiff-intervenors. The case was assigned to Judge Joseph Waddy, who immediately ordered that the two complaints be consolidated into one lawsuit. As Yogi Berra would say, "It was deja vu all over again." It seemed like a reoccurring bad dream. The authority immediately joined the Corps as a defendant-intervenor, as did TRVWMD. Hunter Gholson and John Gullet were retained to represent the authority, and Ralph Pogue of Aberdeen would be legal counsel for TRVWMD. All agreed that the first order of business was to have the case transferred to a district court in the waterway region, preferably assigned to Judge Keady. The defendants had learned much from the previous lawsuit, as had EDF. The environmental group believed that the change in venue contributed greatly to its losing the earlier case. Therefore, we knew the plaintiffs would strongly resist any efforts to move the case.

Dr. Frank Davis from Corinth, Mississippi, and a long-time member of the authority, was a close friend of Senator Jim Eastland. He had traveled with the chairman to Europe on one of the early flights of the Concorde, the supersonic jet passenger service. Glover asked Dr. Davis to contact the senator and request a meeting to discuss the lawsuit. Glover, Hunter Gholson, Dr. Davis, and I met with the chairman early one evening in his office. It was a memorable meeting that showed me firsthand how Washington politics work. Most everyone in the senator's office had gone home for the day, and the chairman offered us a cocktail while he was briefed on the new lawsuit. President Jimmy Carter had just been inaugurated, and his attorney general, Griffin Bell of Georgia, had recently been confirmed by Senator Eastland's committee. The senator and Bell had become close acquaintances during the confirmation process. We asked the chairman for his help to impress upon the attorney general the importance of making the waterway's trial a high priority within DOJ and of appointing one of his senior attorneys to represent the defense. The attorneys who had worked on the earlier lawsuit had left DOJ and returned to private practice. We also stressed the importance of moving the case from the D.C. district court, recognizing the presiding judge had sole discretion about whether to retain jurisdiction of the case or not. Neither Chairman Eastland nor the attorney general could order a change of venue.

After he had heard enough, he buzzed his secretary and told her to "get the attorney general on the phone; I need to speak to him as soon as I can." My immediate thought was that since it was long after normal working hours, there was little likelihood that Bell was still in the office. I supposed he would call back the next day. This, obviously, was before cell phones. Much to my surprise, the secretary buzzed back and said that Mr. Bell was on the phone. After dispensing with some pleasantries, the chairman told him about the lawsuit and stressed how important the Tenn-Tom was to his state and to him personally. He conveyed our two requests, though we heard only the chairman's side of the conversation. I realized later that he had purposely not put the call on his speaker phone. Bell pleaded that he had no jurisdiction over the district judge and that he was very reluctant to talk to him about our request. The senator was unrelenting and asked him again if he would talk to Judge Waddy and explain to him the similarities of the two cases and impress upon him that it would be reasonable to transfer this latest case to Judge Keady, who had adjudicated the earlier case. Chairman Eastland also asked Bell to consider this case a top priority within his department and assign to it some of its best, most seasoned, and qualified attorneys. We left feeling somewhat encouraged, but frankly, I had little hope about a change of venue. Hunter followed up with a meeting the next day with one of DOJ's senior officials and briefed him about the current case as well as the court's prior rulings.

None of us ever knew whether the attorney general ever talked to Judge Waddy or whether the chairman did so. However, the district judge held a hearing in March to weigh the arguments for or against a change of venue and announced he was relinquishing jurisdiction of the lawsuit and transferring the case to Keady. The Justice Department also complied with Chairman Eastland's request about the importance of the litigation and assigned the case to Edward Christenbury, one of DOJ's senior trial attorneys. This case was much more involved and sophisticated than the previous case, since it not only threatened the waterway, but it also attacked the Corps' policies and procedures. Also, L&N Railroad, now a plaintiff, had deep pockets with the ability to finance a long and protracted trial. Nevertheless, we were now in a much better position to possibly win the case, thanks to Senator Jim Eastland and his influence.

The consolidated lawsuit contained 15 complaints against the Corps or the waterway. Judge Keady's dismissal with prejudice of those charges contained in his earlier ruling meant that they could not be revisited, including the one pertaining to the waterway's environmental impact statement. By far, the most novel charge and the most troubling one was that the Corps had overstepped its discretionary authority by making substantive changes and additions to the waterway without seeking specific congressional approval. In an earlier trial involving Lock and Dam 26 on the upper Mississippi River Waterway, Joseph Karaganis, the lead attorney for the plaintiffs, had successfully challenged the Corps' practice of making "post authorization" changes. A coalition of railroads and national environmental organizations had successfully won a court-imposed injunction against construction of that project by challenging its economics, its environmental impacts and the Corps' authority. That court victory encouraged the plaintiffs to raise similar charges against the Tenn-Tom.

It was evident this litigation would tax the authority's capabilities, both its funding and its small staff. Hunter Gholson was the only member of the defendant's legal team who had been involved in the earlier lawsuit and would become a more active and critically effective litigant for the defense. While certainly justified, legal expenses and expenses related to expert witnesses would be substantial for a trial that was expected to last for several years.

Karaganis and his legal team spent days if not weeks during the discovery process of the litigation that Keady had approved. It allowed them to search the Corps' files, including those at its headquarters, and conduct interrogatories and depositions. The authority was also subjected to discovery, and one of its attorneys spent a couple of days going through our files in Columbus. As I recall, Glover had to answer an interrogatory, and he was deposed. I had acquired the habit of maintaining my own personal files on what I considered to be the most important current issues. I wanted to have immediate access to the information and frankly. I never trusted the filing systems of office secretaries. During discovery, all official files must be made available to the plaintiffs and copies made of any documents that might be requested. I had taken my files home since they were "not official" and encouraged Glover and others to do the same. A careless filing of a document came close to disrupting our case during the trial.

Glover had a meeting scheduled with the Corps commander of the South Atlantic Division, and he asked me to prepare a short briefing paper for him that outlined what we believed to be some of the most critical issues in the lawsuit. I gave the paper to him and stressed the importance of keeping it very confidential, no copies, etc. He agreed, but later during the actual hearing of the trial before Judge Keady, the plaintiffs offered my memo to Glover as an exhibit as evidence for their case. I was sitting in the courtroom watching the proceedings and saw Hunter's concern about the document; he questioned its authenticity. While these discussions were taking place between Hunter and Karaganis, Keady called for a timely recess. Hunter immediately came to me, and I could tell he was very agitated. He showed me a copy of the paper. He asked, "What is this?" It took me a minute to answer his question since I had written so much about the case. I finally realized that it was the briefing I had prepared for Glover's meeting with the general.

Hunter instructed me to leave the courtroom, since Karaganis and team members knew me and could call on me to testify about the authenticity of the document, since I was its author. I spent the rest of the day sitting in a stew in the courthouse snack bar, worrying that the judge's clerk or someone else would come and drag me before the judge to verify the document. After recess, Hunter decided not to object to having the paper added as an exhibit, and possibly because of Hunter's feigned disinterest in challenging the document, the plaintiffs strangely decided not to use the paper's potentially damaging contents as part of its case. I was upset with Glover, and when I returned to the office, I told him what had happened. I asked him why he made a copy of the briefing paper and why he filed it when I had warned him against doing so. He thought for a while, then said

JOURNEY TO THE RIVER

that after his meeting, the general asked for a copy of the briefing paper. Glover, not wanting to make copies of the paper, had given the general the original copy on the condition that it was solely for his personal use and was not to be included in the Corps' official files. Apparently, during discovery, a plaintiff lawyer discovered the paper in the general's personal files.

One of the more serious of the plaintiffs' charges concerned the extent of the Corps' legal authority to make changes in a congressionally authorized project without seeking approval by Congress. What better way to gain a sense of the Congress about the extent of the Corps' discretionary authority than to ask the longtime chairman of the House Public Works Committee? Robert "Bob" Jones had served 30 years representing North Alabama before retiring in 1977. During that time, he had served on the Corps' authorization committee and had been instrumental in the passages of all the Corps' authorities during those three decades in the House. Wilkins, Gholson, and I traveled to Scottsboro, Alabama, where Congressman Jones was living to get his views on this charge now before the courts. He greeted us warmly, and it was evident that he was pleased to have visitors break the monotony of retirement. He had a small cottage in his back yard that he had furnished with his desk from when he served in the House and decorated with all the memorabilia he had accumulated during his years of service. It certainly gave the impression of meeting with him in his office on Capitol Hill. It was clear that he spent most of his days there.

Gholson briefed the former chairman on the plaintiffs' allegation and asked if his committee ever questioned the Corps' discretionary authority to modify previously authorized projects or whether that had ever been an issue. The chairman turned to me (I assumed he picked me since I was the junior member of the group) and ordered me to get Les Edelman on the phone. I knew Edelman since he had been the staff director of Jones' committee and was now head of the Corps' Office of Legal Counsel. I responded that I did not have Edelman's number. Obviously, used to barking out orders, he told me to get the number from his wife, which I did. Much to my surprise,

Edelman, in just a few minutes, was speaking to his old boss. By hearing only one side of that phone conversation, we learned that the committee had never formally complained to the Corps or considered any legislation about it overstepping its limits of authorities in this regard. I always wondered why Gholson or the DOJ attorneys never deposed Congressman Jones or included him as a witness, but they were reluctant to do so, since Edelman, who was now the top lawyer for the Corps, the defendant in the lawsuit, had been the chief staff member of Jones' committee. The three-hour drive to Scottsboro and the opportunity to discuss this legal question concerning the Corps' discretionary authority to make substantive changes to federally authorized projects, like Tenn-Tom, with two foremost authorities on the issue were most enlightening. I concluded after the meeting that, if the House authorization committee never questioned the Corps' discretionary authorities, why should a federal judge do so? It would not be long until I learned that answer.

One of the other charges the plaintiffs made was that the waterway was not an economically feasible investment for the federal government. Unlike individual projects or activities of other federal programs, water resource projects must demonstrate their benefits and show that increases in national income will equal or exceed its costs. Regional economic development benefits are not included in the equation since those benefits induced by the federal investment come at the expense of other regions and do not add to a net increase in national income. The project's worth is measured in terms of a benefit-to-cost ratio (BCR), which is calculated by discounting its construction costs and its anticipated operations and maintenance costs over the economic life of the project. Although navigation projects have been known to be operational and generate benefits for longer than 100 years, a conservative economic life of 50 years is used to determine its BCR. A similar process is used to determine the project's average annual benefits, mainly measured in savings in transportation of identified shipments of commerce compared to that of an alternative mode of transport, generally rail.

I spent eight years analyzing water projects and preparing the

President's annual budgets for the Corps and other programs during the Johnson and Nixon administrations. I, therefore, was very sensitive about the BCR for the Tenn-Tom and concerned about whether it would continue to demonstrate that it was a worthwhile investment. Its estimated cost, when it was initially approved for construction, was nearly $359 million, but its cost had increased over four-fold — to nearly $1.5 billion — at the time of the lawsuit. The cost escalated because of increased price levels for heavy construction, due in part to the recent oil embargo, but most of the increase was attributed to more detailed design and greater knowledge about what building such a large and complex project would entail. Tenn-Tom's BCR had always hovered around unity (one dollar of cost for each dollar of economic benefit), and it became a concern whether economic restudies could find enough benefits to maintain such a marginal justification.

My concern about the waterway's economic justification was not so much how Judge Keady might rule on this technical issue. If proven that the Corps had followed the principles and standards prescribed by the Congress in measuring the worth of the project, he, being a conservative judge, would defer that issue to Congress. Both the House and Senate appropriations committees held hearings each year on the Corps' budget, including the level of funding for scores of individual projects like Tenn-Tom. The hearings include testimony by Corps officials as well as project stakeholders, like the Tenn-Tom Authority. Therefore, the members of Congress were kept abreast of the status of projects and were fully informed about any issue affecting a project. My prognosis was correct, and the judge tossed that ball to the Congress, where it would become the most serious threat the waterway ever faced.

Judge Keady divided the 15 charges into different groups for separate hearings, e.g., the Corps' authorization charges and those related to the economics of the project and another concerning its effects on the environment. Through the discovery process, the plaintiffs microfilmed literally thousands of pages of Corps documents at all levels of the agency and learned intricate details about its planning and decision-making processes. For example, they learned that the Corps had assumed that significant improvements to the Black Warrior-Tombigbee Waterway (BWT) below Demopolis, Alabama, would be required to support the increased barge traffic needed to maintain a favorable BCR for the Tenn-Tom. We were not aware that the Corps planners had made such an inappropriate assumption in its economic restudies. If so, we would have strongly objected, since the BWT is a separately authorized project, and any such improvements for that project had never been studied, much less authorized, by Congress. Nevertheless, the plaintiffs alleged that these added improvements on the BWT, including duplicate locks at Demopolis and Coffeeville, were needed to make the Tenn-Tom a viable waterway. The plaintiffs argued that adding these needed improvements to the BWT increased the total cost of the Tenn-Tom by an additional $1 billion, nearly doubling the project's cost. The plaintiffs began an effective campaign by spoon-feeding the national media about this "discovery" and other information they had learned that could be interpreted as detrimental to the waterway. For example, the National Campaign to Stop the Tenn-Tom printed hundreds of handbills resembling greenbacks that depicted the Tenn-Tom as a $3 billion ditch, calling it the nation's biggest pork barrel project. Although the plaintiffs had won other lawsuits against other Corps projects, they began the groundwork to take their fight to the Congress in case Judge Keady ruled against them. While the court might delay construction of the waterway or hinder its progress, the Congress is the only entity that can kill a federally authorized project. The opponents, with the negative stories and bad publicity they were promulgating, could possibly persuade Congress to do just that. They fed to the media and environmental groups everything they found during discovery, the interrogatories, and depositions that they felt were derogatory. Their campaign was very successful. It seemed like every week there were more negative stories appearing in the major newspapers throughout the nation. More environmental groups, including some in the waterway region, were joining the ranks of others opposing the waterway. The Birmingham Audubon Society and the Alabama Conservancy had never publicly opposed Tenn-Tom but changed their positions and joined the lawsuit as late plaintiff intervenors. The negative public relations campaign also generated more opposition within the halls of Congress, which portended more troubles.

Judge Keady held his hearings at the federal courthouse in Greenville instead of Aberdeen, the venue for the first trial. While Greenville was not as convenient as Aberdeen for some of us, it has one of the best steakhouses, if not the best, in the state. Doe's Eat Place has been owned and operated by the same family since 1941. The restaurant is in the family's original dwelling in a downscale neighborhood. Its building and location's unattractiveness make first-timers question whether to dine there. But once inside, a diner will experience the food and service comparable to that of a five-star restaurant. Most of us associated with the trial ate dinner there almost every evening. Doe's was as famous for its hot tamales as for its steaks. About one dozen of the delicious treats were packed in large tin cans, each tamale wrapped in a corn husk. I would always have requests from the office to bring several cans back to Columbus. With my trunk loaded with tamales, the aroma permeated the car, making it nearly impossible to keep from stopping and sampling a couple.

One evening, members of the defense team and the plaintiff group were waiting at Doe's for table space, and I happened to strike up a conversation with a man and his party who were also waiting to be seated. He turned out to be one of those individuals of unforgettable character whom you meet by happenstance but never forget. He was curious what our business was, and I told him we were in federal court, and about half of the group was trying to save a multibillion-dollar project while the other group was trying to kill it. Doe's served only beer, and he had come prepared with a large bottle of Crown Royal whiskey in its purple velvet bag tied by its drawstrings to his belt. He gleefully shared some with all of us. I learned he was in the construction business in Louisiana, and he and his group were in the area on a hunting trip. Our table was finally ready, and I bid him farewell. After our meal, I asked the waiter to bring me our tab. Occasionally, our attorney or I would pay for our group's meal, which we had planned to do that evening. The waiter told me that the bill had already been paid. After Hunter told me that he had not paid for the meals, I questioned the waiter again, and he pointed to my new friend from Louisiana, saying he had paid for the entire group, including the plaintiffs. Fearing that he might be inebriated and not using good judgement, I insisted that I pay for our meals. He said he wanted to treat us, hoping that his "small gesture" would some way help the two parties resolve their differences. I told him that it would not likely happen, but we all appreciated his generosity. When we left the restaurant, he waved back at us as he drove off in a late-model Cadillac convertible. Judging from the car's muddy and dented appearance, he obviously had been hauling his dogs and fellow hunters to and from the duck blinds. I failed to get his full name and contact information, and throughout the years I have thought about him and hope he is still fun-loving and gregarious.

Most everyone involved in the trial stayed at the same hotel, the Ramada Inn in Greenville. It had a bar/lounge where we would occasionally gather for a nightcap before retiring for the evening. After a full day of hearings before Judge Keady, the trial was the last subject anyone wanted to discuss over a drink. One evening was an exception when one of the plaintiffs got into a heated discussion about the trial with a representative of TRVWMD (his name will remain anonymous). Their argument escalated until both were on the floor trading punches. We were finally able to separate them and saw that the plaintiff had gotten the best of his sparring partner. We took our colleague to the emergency room for treatment of his cuts and bruises. The next morning, I called the man's wife and suggested that she bring someone to help her get him home. That evening ended any future social interaction between the two parties.

The first hearing was on the charges related to the Corps' authorities, especially the agency's discretion to make post-authorization changes to a project without seeking congressional approval. The lawsuit threatened Tenn-Tom's future and could have great repercussions about how the Corps administered its civil works program. Given the seriousness of those charges, the Corps' headquarters, especially its general counsel's office, was fully engaged in the trial proceedings. One of the key witnesses for the defense was Lieutenant General Jack Morris, commander, or the chief of engineers, for the Corps from 1976 until 1980. He had a long and distinguished career in the Army. He was a graduate of West Point and served as combat engineer in the Pacific during the Second World War and later in Vietnam. Later he was district engineer of the Tulsa District and in the 1960s was heavily involved in building the Arkansas River Navigation Project. The waterway is now called the McClellan-Kerr Waterway, named after two of its champions. U.S. Senator Robert S. Kerr of Oklahoma and U.S. Senator John L. McClellan of Arkansas. While serving at headquarters, General Morris led the Corps to quickly adapt its programs to those changes dictated by NEPA and other environmental laws and policies, without the agency losing its basic focus on developing the nation's water resources. The Sierra Club and others awarded him for his leadership in reforming the Corps. As mentioned earlier, he is also credited with softening President Carter's long-held dislike for the Corps and its programs. The general was an outstanding witness for the defendants, and I believe his testimony had a compelling effect on the judge.

The nation was most fortunate to have had three of the most qualified and able Corps commanders to ever wear the "green suit" during the 1970s and 1980s, a time when the waterway faced some of its biggest challenges. Lieutenant General Joe Bratton followed Morris as chief of engineers from 1980 until 1984. General Bratton was commander of the South Atlantic Division before being promoted to chief of engineers and was very familiar with Tenn-Tom and its issues and with the role of the authority. He had a master's degree in nuclear engineering from MIT and held top-level positions at Army headquarters in the Pentagon and at the Department of Energy. Lieutenant General Elvin "Vald" Heiberg succeeded Bratton and served as Corps commander until 1988. Heiberg was once the district engineer in New Orleans and in 1975 and 1976 was commander of the Ohio River Division. The Nashville District and its Tenn-Tom activities, including the challenging Divide Section, were part of his command.

I enjoyed a close working relationship with these three outstanding military leaders and was honored that they continued to be friends after they retired. Sadly, all three passed away several years ago, Bratton in 2007, and both Morris and Heiberg in 2013. Bratton and Heiberg are buried at Arlington Cemetery, while Morris chose West Point for his final resting place. God rest their souls.

The trial of complaints related to Corps authority ended when the judge rendered his decision in March 1979. He deferred from addressing the merits of the plaintiffs' claims by dismissing all of them, citing the equitable doctrine of laches. Keady admonished the plaintiffs for bringing up these charges at that time when most had been known as early as nine years before. He called it "inexcusable." He also said the defendants would suffer undue harm if their belated claims were now approved since the waterway was well under construction. While the judge's decision was great news for the defendants, it was far from being a decisive victory. The overriding question about the Corps' discretionary authority to make significant post-authorization changes in its projects, including the Tenn-Tom, remained unanswered. As expected, the plaintiffs immediately appealed to the Fifth Circuit Court of Appeals and included a motion for an injunction, pending appeal, which they expected would take several months. The appeals court denied the motion for a temporary injunction, but it scheduled expedited oral arguments on its appeal of Keady's ruling. In March 1980, one year after the lower court findings, the Fifth Circuit Court of Appeals denied the plaintiffs' appeal by affirming that Keady's use of the laches doctrine to dismiss their charges was appropriate. As a last resort, EDF appealed its case to the U.S. Supreme Court, which denied it in October of that year. CSX Railroad chose not to join EDF to seek a writ of certiorari. In the meantime, waterway construction continued, unabated by litigation.

Judge Keady had waited until the appeals process of his Corps authority ruling was over before he scheduled hearings on the other charges. These dealt with the plaintiffs' economic and environmental allegations. They charged that the Corps had not complied with long-established laws, polices, and regulations in determining the waterway's economic justification. They alleged the project's benefits were overstated, and its costs were underestimated. It attacked the use of a 3.25 percent discount rate used for computing the project's benefits-to-costs ratio. At that time, banks were charging as much as 20 percent for a 30-year home mortgage loan. However, the defendants testified that while the discount rate appeared to be unreasonably low compared to the average cost of borrowing at that time, the Congress had approved it for the Corps and other agencies to use for all water resource projects, including the Tenn-Tom.

The plaintiffs' charges concerning environmental issues were based on an erroneous assumption that the Corps was actually building two projects: the Tenn-Tom project from Demopolis to the Tennessee River and another one concerning improvement to that part of the Black Warrior-Tombigbee Waterway below Demopolis to Mobile. The Corps had speculated that improvements below Demopolis, including channel widening and duplicate locks at Demopolis and at Coffeeville, might be needed to support the increased commerce identified in its latest economic study for the Tenn-Tom. The opponents alleged that this was an additional project whose costs could equal those of Tenn-Tom and that it required its own environmental impact study. The Corps contended that those navigational improvements had not been studied, much less authorized, and that an EIS to determine its potential environmental impacts would not be required until then.

In October 1980, the judge essentially dismissed all the complaints associated with the economic and environmental charges. The plaintiffs immediately appealed to the Fifth Circuit Court of Appeals. They also filed a motion for an injunction to stop construction, pending a ruling by that court. The appeals court immediately denied the injunctive relief for the plaintiffs, but did schedule oral arguments in April 1981, six months after Judge Keady's ruling.

That hearing led to significant reversals of Keady's earlier decisions. It ruled that the Corps' use of the 3.25 percent discount rate be discontinued, although its use had been approved by Congress. It also directed the Corps to prepare a supplemental EIS for any waterway changes, such as those in the Chain of Lakes section, that had been made since the original EIS was prepared. The judge's order went further by barring construction of any of those changes until the Corps had prepared the supplemental EIS and the court had approved it. This injunction especially affected any further work for the five locks in the Chain of Lakes section and in any cutoffs of river bends in the lower River Section needed to improve commercial navigation but not identified in the original EIS.

Recognizing that the appeals court ruling would delay the completion of the waterway and add to its final cost, the authority sought approval for a rehearing. The DOJ attorneys opposed such a request, and Gholson, alone, on behalf of the defendant-intervenors requested the rehearing. The request was denied, but the appeals court significantly modified its earlier injunctive directive by giving Judge Keady discretion and latitude to delay construction of only those elements that would not cause "irreparable harm" to the government or to the project. Finally, Judge Keady ordered both parties to work together to determine elements that could be delayed without seriously disrupting the orderly progress of construction. Surprisingly, those negotiations bore fruit, likely because the plaintiffs finally recognized their chances to stop the waterway by litigation were not in the cards. Their best chance to kill the waterway was taking the fight to Congress, where they had already been working diligently for several years to nurture more opposition.

In the meantime, the Corps worked night and day to prepare the court-ordered supplemental EIS. This herculean effort was accomplished in less than one year, thanks to N.D. "Skeeter" McClure and others in the planning division of the Mobile District. The opponents raised a litany of specific accusations concerning the adequacy or thoroughness of the supplemental EIS draft. Nevertheless, it was approved in June 1982 by Major General Vald Heiberg, then director of Civil Works, the decision maker at Corps headquarters for such documents. It was then sent to Judge Keady, who accepted it as fulfillment of the 1981 appeals court directive.

After all the defendants' appeals had been exhausted, Judge Keady made his final ruling in favor of the defendants on May 9, 1983, finally ending the nearly decade-long litigation against the waterway. As a non-legal close observer of the trial and its proceedings, I believed the judge to have been both fair and impartial in his rulings. He did not permit personal or political biases to creep into his rulings, and as result, his rulings were not vulnerable to appeals. He deserves the thanks and appreciation from those who will benefit from the waterway.

Chapter XIX
The Last Battle

The 1970s were tumultuous and challenging years for Tenn-Tom and its supporters. The decade had been a hotly contested race that seemed to have no finish line. It began with President Nixon endorsing the project and its funding. Following that, an environmental lawsuit delayed the start of construction by about 18 months before it was finally adjudicated in the federal courts. With construction then underway, the states of Alabama and Mississippi faced the dilemma of building the highway bridges across the waterway, and costs far exceeded their capability to finance, especially in the case of Mississippi. That issue, which threatened to stop construction of the waterway, was resolved when Mississippi Congressman Jamie Whitten deftly formulated a legislative remedy by transferring those responsibilities to the U.S. Department of Transportation. The rationale for the abdication was that a large part of the bridges' costs were brought on by federal environmental and safety regulations imposed on the states. The bridge-funding issue had hardly been resolved when President Jimmy Carter arrived in Washington and decided to reform water resources development, including terminating some 30 projects, including the Tennessee-Tombigbee Waterway. The Tenn-Tom Waterway Authority, led by its administrator, Glover Wilkins, marshaled a legion of public and political support never witnessed before at such a level for a public works project, which helped convince the President to eventually support the waterway. Two months before Carter's inauguration, L&N (now CSX) Railroad and several environmental organizations and individuals filed another lawsuit to stop the waterway. Although court proceedings were still underway by the end of that decade, it was evident to the plaintiffs that their chances of killing the waterway in the courts were futile. With these setbacks, the waterway's ever-persistent opponents viewed the United States Congress as their last hope to terminate the Tenn-Tom.

Some national environmental organizations had been trying to cultivate anti-waterway allies within Congress ever since Nixon first approved the project for construction. The Environmental Defense Fund (EDF), a national organization headquartered in New York City, was the principal litigator for environmental causes at that time. EDF was a plaintiff in both Tenn-Tom lawsuits and in other cases involving Corps projects. Its counterpart group to build public and political support for environmental causes was the Environmental Policy Center (EPC). EPC, under the direction of Brent Blackwelder, led and coordinated an effective national campaign designed to generate enough congressional support to stop construction of the Tenn-Tom by eliminating its federal funding. To that end, it organized a coalition made up of national environmental organizations, such as the Sierra Club, National Wildlife Federation, National Audubon Society, Friends of the Earth, and the Natural Resources Defense Council. Joining them was a formidable group primarily concerned with government spending, including the National Taxpayers Union, Common Cause, and the League of Women Voters.

The Association of American Railroads (AAR) also joined the cause. AAR opposed all funding for waterway projects, contending that commercial water transportation was an unfair competitive mode for rail since it was so heavily subsidized by the federal government. Until 1978, waterways were built, operated, and maintained solely with federal funds, and commercial users paid no fees or taxes to use them. That changed when Congress passed The Revenue Act of 1978, which imposed a special fuel tax on commercial carriers using the 12,000 miles of the nation's inland waterway system, including the Tenn-Tom. The U.S. Treasury collects that money and deposits it into a trust fund to use to improve waterways. The initial tax was 4 cents per gallon, and it stands at 29 cents per gallon today. Ned Breathitt, a former governor of Kentucky and later vice president for public affairs for Norfolk Southern Railroad (NSR), once told me that NSR had been strongly urged to join L&N in its legal fight to kill the waterway, but it had made a corporate decision not to do so. However, it and the other Class I railroads likely supported their national trade association's effort to do their bidding by opposing projects like the Tenn-Tom.

The authority began assembling some allies of its own to help backstop the waterway's congressional supporters. The authority was a member of most all the major national water resources trade associations, such as the National Waterways Conference and the Water Resources Congress. That active involvement helped develop relationships with many of their members, who were politically involved, especially with members of Congress outside the Tenn-Tom region. Two other important members of the Waterway's A-team were the AFL-CIO and the Association of General Contractors (AGC). The prime contractors building the waterway were large national or international companies, and they were unionized. Although Alabama and Mississippi are right-to-work states, the majority of the 4,000 to 5,000 workers building the waterway carried union cards. The threat of these workers losing their jobs if the project were terminated was the motivation for AFL-CIO's interest. Also, if the opponents were successful in stopping the largest water project, they would be encouraged to challenge other projects, thus threatening more union jobs. One of the more active members of AGC's governing body at that time was Kirk Fordice, a heavy construction contractor from Vicksburg, Mississippi, and a supporter of the waterway. He made sure that his association was totally engaged with all its resources and influence in the battle for congressional votes. Fordice would later be elected president of AGC. He also served as Mississippi's 61st governor. While governor, he was a strong supporter of the waterway and served as the authority's chairman in 1994 and again in 1998.

The Tenn-Tom war in Congress began when Senator Gaylord Nelson of Wisconsin proposed legislation to strip the funds President Nixon had included in his 1972 budget to start construction of the waterway. Strangely, however, EDF and the other plaintiffs in the first lawsuit asked that Nelson withdraw his bill and allow the federal court to kill the waterway. He complied. Presumably, they were so confident of the success of their litigation, they wanted to get all the credit for terminating the waterway and not share with the senator any glory for the kill. Nelson was the Senate's "conservationist" and had founded Earth Day. He was also instrumental in the enactment of landmark environmental laws during the 1970s, such as the Clean Water Act, the National Wild and Scenic Rivers Act, Clean Air, and a host of others. He firmly believed that economic development should not take precedence over protecting the environment, and he advocated for controlling the world's population for the environment's sake. He would continue to be one of Tenn-Tom's most formidable opponents until he retired in 1981.

Nelson's fellow senator from Wisconsin, William Proxmire, made his reputation as the Senate's crusader against what he perceived as wasteful government spending. Every month during his many years of service, he identified either a public official or federal agency to receive his Golden Fleece Award for what he claimed to be squandering public funds. The Corps of Engineers twice received this dubious award. The Corps received the award in 1976 for what the senator believed was the worst agency of all for cost overruns. Several projects then under construction were cited for large cost increases, including a reported escalation of over 300 percent in estimated costs for the Tenn-Tom.

Annual appropriations for the Tennessee-Tombigbee Waterway and other Corps water resources projects, along with several other agencies, are included in an omnibus piece of legislation called the Energy and Water Development Appropriations Bill. The specific amount of funding for each Corps project is not noted in the bill itself, but all the projects are lumped into a total amount in the construction, general account. The amount that the Appropriations Committee approves for each project is included in the Conference Committee Report that accompanies the legislation. The appropriations bill as well as the conference committee report may also include specific directives or comments to the Corps concerning specific projects or programs.

Once the Energy and Water Development Appropriations Subcommittee approves the bill and its contents, the bill is forwarded to the Appropriations Committee, made up of members from all thirteen subcommittees. There, the bill is "marked up" and subject to amendments and changes before it is approved to be offered for a vote by all members. Before it is presented for a vote, the Rules Committees decide which amendments may be offered by individual members on the floor during the bill's debate. The House and Senate have the same committee structure, but the senators are not as constrained to propose amendments as the House members are by its Rules Committee. Ideally, both the House and Senate pass bills, and the differences in the two bills are settled by a conference committee composed of selected members from both the House and Senate subcommittees. This legislative process, particularly in the House, somewhat limits debate and amendments concerning an individual project like the Tenn-Tom, but that was about to change.

Senator Gaylord Nelson, as he had told the plaintiffs he would do, did not take any action against the Tennessee-Tombigbee until the first lawsuit was finally adjudicated. Disappointed that the courts ruled in favor of the Corps and the waterway, he prepared legislation to have the project deauthorized. One of the principal complaints of EDF's and L&N Railroads's second lawsuit alleged the Corps did not have authority to implement major alterations to the project without specific congressional approval. Nelson's legislation not only addressed that issue but also went much further by deauthorizing the entire project. He was able to get Senators Howard Metzenbaum of Ohio, Donald Riegle of Michigan, and William Proxmire of Wisconsin to sign on as co-sponsors of the proposal.

Nelson chaired the Senate Committee on Small Business, but

his legislation to kill the waterway came under the jurisdiction of the Environment and Public Works Committee, chaired by Jennings Randolph of West Virginia, a close friend of Senator Stennis. Its subcommittee had scheduled a week of hearings with a previously set agenda regarding the Corps' water resources program as part of what is now referred to as the WRDA Bill. The subcommittee chairman, Mike Gravel of Alaska, with the backing of the committee chairman, Randolph, refused to alter its agenda to include Nelson's amendment. One of the stated reasons for denying the request was not to address the issue of the waterway's authority while that matter was being adjudicated in court. Disappointed with Gravel's decision, Nelson threatened to conduct his own hearings before his Small Business Committee, but he backed off since he would have violated one of the Senate's longstanding rules on committee jurisdiction. He finally abandoned his attempts to deauthorize the waterway, but he and his allies vowed to continue their fight to eliminate its funding.

Recognizing the threats of the ongoing litigation and the growing opposition to the waterway in Congress, the Mobile and Nashville Districts were building the project at their full capabilities. Congress had appropriated $165 million in fiscal year 1980 to support such an aggressive schedule. Tom Bevil, chairman of the Energy and Water Development Appropriations subcommittee, and Jamie Whitten, chairman of the full Appropriations Committee, could claim credit for the record amount of funding in the House-passed bill. Their "mark" was supported by Stennis and other key backers in the Senate. As the Corps' largest project under construction, the Tenn-Tom was receiving by far the largest annual appropriation ever for a water project. To meet the Corps' accelerated construction schedule, it had reprogrammed an additional $23 million to Tenn-Tom from surplus funds available from other projects. The total availability of nearly $190 million was still woefully short of what was needed to meet contractor earnings for that fiscal year. The Corps, for the first time ever for the waterway, asked Congress for an additional $58 million in supplemental appropriations. Supplemental appropriation bills are generally approved to fund unforeseen emergencies, such as natural disasters, but can also include other needs, like the funding shortfall for the Tenn-Tom. Unlike the 12 appropriations bills for which the Rules Committee tightly controls amendments, House members have more latitude to amend supplemental bills. In hindsight, it was a grave mistake for the Corps to request additional funding, which opened the door for the waterway opponents to attack its funding for the first time. Slowing construction to decrease contractor earnings would have been a much more plausible option.

U.S. Representative Joel Pritchard, a Republican from the state of Washington, and a Pennsylvania Democrat, Representative Robert Edgar, introduced an amendment to strike the $58 million for the waterway (the only amount on the table, since their amendment pertained to only the supplemental bill). The National Taxpayers Union, which endorsed the amendment, aggressively lobbied other House members to support it on the pretense of reducing federal spending, making the argument that the $189 million already available for such a controversial project was more than enough. The amendment caught everyone by surprise, but the House supporters, led by Tom Bevill and Jamie Whitten, were able to marshal enough members to defeat the amendment by a vote of 230 to 185. While the vote was not that close, it showed that opposition to the waterway was growing, as clouds on the horizon grew even darker.

By the time the supplemental bill reached the Senate, it had grown to include a total of nearly $17 billion, including emergency spending associated with the disaster caused by the Mount St. Helens volcanic eruption. Nevertheless, the relatively paltry amount of $58 million quickly drew the attention of Senators John Chafee, a Republican from Rhode Island, and Daniel Moynihan, a New York Democrat. Moynihan had just become chairman of the Water Resources Subcommittee of the Committee on Environment and Public Works. His subcommittee had responsibility for the Corps' authorization legislation. He would later use that position to create a lot of grief for the waterway. Chafee offered his amendment to delete the $58 million that precipitated a floor debate. Senator Stennis led the opposition to the measure with help of other senators from the waterway region, including Senator Howell Heflin, a Democrat from Alabama, and Republican Howard Baker from Tennessee. Some felt that this challenge was just the beginning of future debates about federal funding and programs that would pit those representing the Sunbelt states against those from the northern so-called Rust Belt. Senator Chafee's amendment was defeated 47 to 36. It also did not go unnoticed that 17 senators did not vote, with most choosing to take a walk rather than vote against the waterway and offend its supporters. Everyone, including the Corps, vowed to never seek additional funding through a supplemental appropriations bill, regardless of need. It had opened Pandora's box and had shown that the waterway was losing congressional support, mainly because of its detractors' effective media and lobbying campaign. The waterway's future funding was in peril.

The next challenge would be passage of the 1981 appropriations bill. The fight over appropriations would require me to, over two years' time, spend many days in Washington working with our congressional supporters and the waterway's coalition. Everyone, including those who had worked so diligently for more than a decade to stop the Tenn-Tom, realized the fight over the waterway's funding in the next two appropriation bills would likely determine the fate of the project. After then, it would cost more (contractor claims, mothballing costs, etc.) to stop it than to complete it.

EDF and L&N Railroad were spoon-feeding the national media as well as those Tenn-Tom detractors in Congress with any aspects of the ongoing federal lawsuit that could be promulgated as negative publicity for the waterway. Brent Blackwelder of EPC and his coalition of national environmental groups were working overtime to do the same. It seemed like every week a national publication or newspaper published an article or editorial attacking the waterway. With everything going on in the world, why were *Readers Digest*, the *Wall Street Journal*, the *Los Angeles Times*, *New York Times*, other major newspapers throughout the nation, including those in Miami, St. Petersburg, and Atlanta, devoting so much print space to attacking a project located far from their circulation? No one ever questioned whether L&N Railroad was spending vast amounts in legal fees to kill the waterway on account of the fact that the waterway would be a competitive transportation mode for coal shipments from Appalachia and Illinois. If it was such a "boondoggle" project, why was there so much effort to stop its construction? I finally concluded that the national environmental groups had zeroed in on the Tenn-Tom because it was the largest project ever undertaken in the United States. It became the poster child for all the no-growth advocates because, if they could terminate its construction with all its strong local and political supporters, other projects would be fair game and could also be terminated. By stopping the Tenn-Tom with the influence it enjoyed in the Congress, other economic development projects would be easy pickings. The opponents were flush in funding, well-connected, and certainly capable of accomplishing their goal. We supporters had our work cut out for us if we were to save the waterway.

The 1980 elections brought about a sea of change in Washington politics. Ronald Reagan handily beat Carter to win the presidency. In doing so, 34 new House members and 12 new senators rode into the Congress on Reagan's coattails, dramatically changing the party makeup of both the House and Senate. With Reagan being a staunch conservative and having campaigned for less government and reduced federal spending, opponents of the Tenn-Tom felt they now had an ally in the White House who would not support the waterway. They were mistaken. Thanks to the influence of the waterway's Republican congressional members, such as Senators Howard Baker of Tennessee and Thad Cochran of Mississippi and Representatives Trent Lott of Mississippi and Jack Edwards of Alabama, the President and his administration not only approved the waterway but also included $200 million for the project in his first budget, FY1981. Throughout the coming years and until the project was finally completed, President Reagan's support never wavered.

There was little time between the deliberations on the supplemental bill and the beginning of the FY1981 appropriations process. As expected, Pritchard and Edgar offered an amendment to cut the waterway's funding from what the House Appropriations Committee had approved, but with a different twist from before. This time, they wanted to reduce the Appropriations Committee's mark of $225 million ($25 million more than Reagan's request of $200 million) by $200 million, with the remaining $25 million to finish ongoing work between Demopolis, Alabama, and Columbus, Mississippi. The rest of the project between Columbus and Pickwick Lake would be mothballed, pending the Congress' reevaluation of completing the project. As chairman of Appropriations, Congressman Whitten had the discretion to set the time for a vote on the bill that contained the Tenn-Tom funds. At the last minute, he announced the bill would be debated on the House floor on a Tuesday instead of Thursday, the typical day such votes are scheduled. That wily legislative maneuver likely caught the opponents off guard. The amendment was defeated by a vote of 216 against and 196 for passage. The amendment's defeat was certainly a victory for the Tenn-Tom, but it was evident the waterway was losing supporters on each succeeding vote.

As promised, Senator Moynihan used his position as the new chairman of the Water Resources Subcommittee to delve into the economic worth of the waterway. He scheduled three days of hearings in July. While it was obvious his intent was to besmirch the waterway, the hearings were coined in a broader context of investigating the transportation needs of coal. Moynihan, a former professor at Harvard, was considered an intellectual and an expert in urban affairs and welfare, although some of his "thinking" was considered racist by progressives. He had held cabinet-level positions in both the Kennedy and the Nixon/Ford administrations and was a formidable adversary for the Tenn-Tom.

The authority was invited to testify, and Glover chose Hunter to be Tenn-Tom's witness and asked that I prepare the statement. In addition to including some positive points about the waterway, I took the opportunity to tell the chairman, who had a limited knowledge of the federal water resources program, there were several projects in his state that were justified using the same evaluation criteria for which the Tenn-Tom was being attacked. In other words, if he and other members of Congress did not agree with how water projects were justified, then they should change the standards, such as the much-criticized low discount rate. I apparently touched a nerve, and Moynihan exploded into a rant, saying that the hearing concerned the Tennessee-Tombigbee Waterway and not projects in New York. Hunter was very upset with my putting him in such an embarrassing situation. He later calmed down when Glover explained to him that we had scored some points by describing for the record that all projects are evaluated using the same principles and standards. Forty years later, the Corps, with the blessing of Congress, continues to use basically the same criteria for determining a project's economic justification. Much to the disappointment of the waterway opponents, the hearing proceedings played a limited part in the Senate's funding deliberations. However, the Tenn-Tom's detractors ridiculed the waterway by using Moynihan's moniker: the Tenn-Tom was just "an attempt to clone the Mississippi River."

As was the case in the House, each vote pending in the Senate brought out the opposition. Senator Chafee initially introduced again his amendment to delete the waterway's funding but revised it to more conform with the House amendment that had just been defeated. His revised amendment called for deleting $200 million of the $208 million that the Senate Appropriations Committee had just approved for the waterway, leaving the remaining $8 million to help complete work underway south of Columbus. Senator Alan Simpson, a conservative Republican from Wyoming, and Senator Moynihan spoke in favor of the amendment. After a much-spirited debate on both sides, Chafee's efforts were defeated by a roll call vote of 52 to 37.

Even before the ink was dry on President Reagan's signature enacting the 1981 Energy and Water Development Appropriations Act that included $212 million for Tenn-Tom, plans were underway to address another expected battle in the House. Congressman Bevill was much aware that "his project" was in jeopardy. The waterway was losing the support of Bevill's colleagues, mainly because of the environmental groups' and the railroad trade association's effective nationwide campaign, supported by the media, to discredit it. Bevill began reaching out to his fellow waterway supporters for help. He asked Trent Lott, a Republican from South Mississippi, to solicit support from the 34 freshmen Republicans. Many of the new members were conservative and had campaigned to cut federal spending. Bevill knew this would be a difficult chore to convince them to support such a large amount of funding for a project that would likely not directly benefit their constituents. Lott was a rising star in Congress and a leader in the House as its Republican Whip and a member of its powerful Rules Committee. He would later move on to the U.S. Senate, where he would be elected Majority Leader, arguably the nation's third most powerful position in government. Lott accepted the challenge and assigned the task to Roger Wicker, one of his young staff members, to begin working with the staff members of the newly elected representatives to convince them to support the waterway. Wicker would later be elected to Congress to represent North Mississippi, including all the counties along the waterway. In 2007, when Lott retired, Wicker would succeed Trent Lott as one of Mississippi's senators. Wicker continues to serve as an influential senior member of that body.

Congressman Bevill had acquired the respect if not friendship of many of his colleagues because of his willingness to use his influence to fund members' water and energy projects of importance to their districts, regardless of their political affiliation. He was the epitome of a Southern gentleman and was one of the House's most respected and well-liked members. In past years, he had befriended Ohio Congressman Louis Stokes of Cleveland. At the time, he headed the House Black Caucus and was the first African American to serve on the House Appropriations Committee. At Stokes' request, Bevill helped secure some much-needed funds to improve Cleveland's port. Bevill explained that the waterway had one of the most aggressive affirmative-action programs, and many minority workers and minority-owned businesses would suffer if the waterway were terminated. Since his wife was a native of Noxubee County, Mississippi, one of the waterway counties, Stokes was familiar with the demographics of the waterway area. Stokes assured Bevill he would vote for the waterway and would work hard to convince other members of the Black

Caucus to do the same. Bennie Turner, a member of the Tenn-Tom Authority and a Mississippi state senator, was also very effective in working with members.

Bevill began organizing trips to the Tenn-Tom region for his fellow members to tour the waterway and see firsthand its advanced stage of construction and the care taken to minimize its impact on the environment. He first invited those members he felt were wavering in their support. Later, he extended the invitation to any member who expressed an interest in going. Typically, the trip began on a military aircraft that left Washington and flew to the Columbus Air Force Base, where they were met by the Corps, given a briefing, and then taken on an inspection of work underway at the locks and dams. A high-ranking officer from the Corps' headquarters accompanied each group. Before the group returned to Washington, the authority would host a delicious Southern-cooked meal at Gates Lodge near Aliceville Lock and Dam, which was later named in honor of Bevill.

Representative Robert Edgar of Pennsylvania, one of the waterway's most vociferous opponents, was part of one of the delegations. He saw that the project was more than half completed and that stopping it at Columbus made no economic sense. He seemed genuinely impressed with what he had seen. He also fell in love with the homemade banana pudding with home-made custard filling that was served at lunch. He asked for a second helping. I thought the tour would convince him that it was not practical to stop the waterway with so much of it already completed or under contract and, if not, surely his newly found love for banana pudding would convert him. Regrettably, I was wrong on both counts. While the trips were an imposition on some, especially Bevill, I believe they were worthwhile and likely convinced some undecided members to support the waterway.

Congressman Tom Bevill hosted "fly-ins" on military aircraft to enable fellow members of the U.S. House of Representatives to personally tour the waterway. These one-day trips helped convince some members that construction was too far advanced to terminate the project. Senators Howell Heflin and Jeremiah Denton of Alabama conducted similar tours for their colleagues in the U.S. Senate. These fact-finding trips proved to be critical when later the Congress narrowly approved the waterway's continued funding. Shown here, from left, are Bevill briefing four of his House colleagues, including Congressmen Vic Fazio (California) (second from the right); and Louis Stokes (Ohio), on the right; both of whom later voted for the waterway.

Bevill invited those who could not take an inspection trip to a luncheon meeting that he hosted in his committee room in the House Rayburn Office Building. There, one of the Corps' general officers would conduct a briefing about the Tenn-Tom. Afterwards, the authority would treat attendees to a steak lunch. I attended all these luncheons but kept a low profile. I learned a lot about the concerns and issues some of the members expressed, most all related to opponents' allegations. One common misconception was that it would require an additional $1 billion of improvements to the Lower Tombigbee River below Demopolis before navigation could effectively function on the Tenn-Tom. That allegation would also be one of the most consistent attacks in the Senate, where some were calling it the "$3 billion ditch!"

The luncheons were served on a long conference table with about a dozen members usually attending. Chairman Bevill was successful in getting Tip O'Neill, the Speaker of the House, to attend one of the luncheons, which was a coup. It just so happened the Speaker was seated across from me at lunch. I usually did not eat until after the luncheon had ended so I could concentrate more on the chitchat and try to learn more about any concerns or issues they had. The Speaker noticed I hadn't eaten my slice of cherry pie. I caught him eyeing it, so I asked him if he would like to have it. He had the physique of a pie lover. He thanked me as he reached for it. After lunch, he called Bevill to the side and said the waterway and its opposition had taken up too much of the House's attention and that it was finally time to put the matter to rest. To me, that meant he was ready to take whatever steps necessary to finally end the debate. As Speaker of the House, he controlled when bills were scheduled for a vote and could influence the Rules Committee's decisions that could limit a bill's debate. It was encouraging that he seemed to be on our side. I enjoyed telling in jest the chairman and others that it was my slice of pie, not the Corps briefing, that had swayed the Speaker to our side.

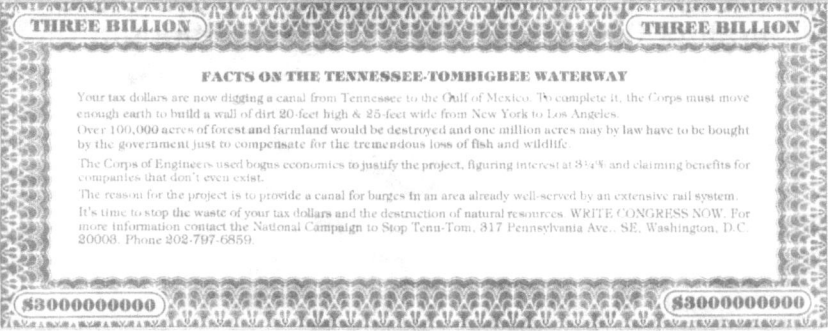

One of the waterway opponents' effective ploys was distributing this handbill alleging that it would take an additional $1 billion of improvements to the connecting Black Warrior Tombigbee (BWT) project to make the $2-billion Tenn-Tom operable. Over four decades later, since that claim was made, not one dollar has been spent to improve that section of BWT to benefit Tenn-Tom's operations.

Both the House and Senate Energy and Water Appropriations Subcommittees held public hearings each year for non-federal interests to testify about project funding. The Tenn-Tom hearing was always scheduled on a Monday with the House hearing chaired by Congressman Bevill during the morning, followed in the afternoon with the Senate hearing, usually chaired by Senator Stennis. A group of congressmen and senators from the waterway area would always attend to hear the testimony. Indiana Congressman John Myers, the ranking member of the House Subcommittee, also attended these hearings. Although of different political stripes, he and Bevill were not only colleagues but also personal friends. Water resources development has never been in more supportive hands than during those years when those two led that committee.

Given the hearing's importance, all authority members, including the governors, were encouraged to travel to Washington and attend. The authority would conduct a business meeting while there, which obviated the need for one of its quarterly meetings. Most all the governors would adjust their busy schedules to attend the hearings. I was intrigued by the number of security and staff members who usually accompanied some of the governors. The number ranged from one or two to as many as six or more. The exception was Governor Lamar Alexander of Tennessee, who later served as a U.S. Senator. Alexander always traveled alone, with no security nor an aide. I was most impressed that he had not succumbed to all the trappings of his office, and I admired his obvious independence and self-confidence.

Each year, the authority would invite organizations or groups from the waterway area to testify at these hearings. They were encouraged to offer testimony to help demonstrate grassroots support for the waterway. I was responsible for coordinating their testimony and "baby sitting" them while in Washington. For some, it was their first trip there. Two of those delegations immediately come to mind. One of those groups was from Northwest Alabama and included a probate judge, a state legislator, and state senator from Lamar County, and a mayor from adjoining Marion County. Both of the counties were in Bevill's congressional district, and he knew the delegates on a first-name basis. In addition to testifying in support of the Tenn-Tom, they were there to promote a local project, including building a reservoir, to help control flooding of Buttahatchee River. They arrived on different flights. I met them in Atlanta before our flight to Washington and immediately recognized them before I reached the departure gate. The state senator who owned a clothing store had brought houndstooth hats for everyone, similar to the one Alabama football coach Paul "Bear" Bryant wore. They stuck out in the crowd like a sore thumb. When we arrived in Washington, they were insistent that we all ride in one taxi to the hotel. Although the state legislator was a very big man, we nevertheless packed ourselves into one cab with the big guy in the front seat and four of us stacked in the back. I noticed that the cab driver kept looking intently at us. He finally asked,

The waterway compact governors always took time from their busy schedules to testify before the Congress in support of the waterway's funding. Representing the waterway authority at this U.S.House appropriations hearing were, from left: Glover Wilkins, authority administrator; Gov. Fob James (Alabama); Gov. William Winter (Mississippi); and Gov. Lamar Alexander (Tennessee). Similar hearings were held in the U.S. Senate. Authority staff members were responsible for preparing the witnesses' testimonies.

"What's with the hats?" His substantial front-seat mate responded, "We are the University of Alabama's track team, and I'm the high jumper!" That retort ended any further conversation with the driver. After everyone had checked into their hotel rooms, and I was looking forward to a couple of hours to relax before dinner, I got a call from the probate judge, who was in a panic. He had left his small carry-on bag containing his heart medicine in the cab. I had not made note the taxicab company but hoped the hotel doorman might remember. While I was talking to the doorman, the cab arrived, and the driver got out with the judge's bag. Although he had completed a couple of fares before discovering the bag, he knew it belonged to "those guys with the crazy hats," which saved the day for the judge and his medicine. We convened in the hotel lobby for dinner, and everyone was present except the mayor. Someone said he was likely working on his testimony since the group had elected him to speak on their behalf. After we waited for some time for him to show, someone went to his room but could not get an answer. Fearing the worst, I had a bellman unlock his door. He was passed out on the bed. I learned later that he was an alcoholic but had been on the wagon until he discovered the mini bar in his room with all its miniature bottles of liquor, many of which he had consumed. We left him as he lay, and we went to dinner, where I told the others they needed to select someone else to testify. Much to everyone's surprise if not shock, the mayor arrived for breakfast the next morning and was insistent that he deliver their statement. It was obvious that he was suffering from a terrible hangover, and he was drawing off his most inner strength just to function. However, he did a very credible job delivering the statement, much to everyone's relief. I was most relieved to see them depart for their homes that afternoon. A couple of weeks later, I received a package from the state senator. He sent a note thanking me "taking care of them," and he gave me a leisure suit, which stylish at the time, that fit me perfectly. The man was certainly a haberdasher first and a state senator second.

Another group I remember fondly was from Northeast Mississippi. On the pretense of cheaper air fares, they had arrived in Washington on a Saturday before the hearing on Monday. We were staying at different hotels, but I joined them for dinner that evening. When I arrived at their hotel, it was most evident that some had already had a few libations. After a very long dinner, including too many cocktails, someone mentioned that he had never been to New York City and that the rail service (Amtrak) between D.C. and New York was both cheap and frequent, with a train leaving Union Station that evening at about midnight. They all liked the idea of seeing the sights of New York, and despite my pleas to not go, it was off to the Big Apple! Either while touring the Empire State Building or at the Windows of the World restaurant on top of the World Trade Center, we discovered one member of the group had disappeared. No one seemed overly concerned until on the return trip to Washington when everyone became distraught about the whereabouts of the lost companion. The train ride to and from New York was an experience by itself. All the worry and concerns about their colleague ended when they entered the suite at the hotel to find their missing member sleeping on the couch. Everyone, of course, was relieved to see him safely back at the hotel but also irate about his causing so much worry and anxiety. He explained that he told the cab driver at the Trade Center to take him to his hotel. The driver concluded that he thought he was in Washington and not New York and took him back to the train station where, somehow, he managed to book a seat on an earlier train back to Washington. I was especially glad to see him since he was also a member of the Waterway Authority and one of my bosses. I told the authority later that they were was not paying me nearly enough to "host" these groups.

As the appropriations vote approached in the House, I was spending more time on Capitol Hill. Some weeks I would spend the weekend in Washington. I had a desk in Bevill's office where I could work and make or receive phone calls. I had similar arrangements in the Senate where I used one of Senator Stennis' hideaway offices. With no cell phones then, these accommodations were a godsend. In today's political climate, congressional rules would strictly prohibit such privileges. In those days, someone familiar with Capitol Hill could travel from each House office building to the Capitol by underground tram, walk through the Capitol from the House side of the building to the Senate side, and from there take a tram to the three Senate buildings. This convenience greatly facilitated conducting business at the Capitol without one's ever having to venture outside the complex. That's not possible now because of security restrictions, unless one is escorted by a member of Congress or a staff member.

We established a team made up of House staff members and others, who would meet frequently to discuss issues and start counting votes. The House team members included Ed Nolan of Bevill's office; Nancy Tippen, representing Jack Edwards of Alabama; Hal Decell from Whitten's office; Bill Rascoe and Pete Kelley, representing Flippo of Alabama; Roger Wicker from Lott's office; and Guy Land, representing Bowen of Mississippi. Everyone concluded the pending vote on appropriations would be close, at best. Our concerns about the waterway were well-founded.

On July 23, 1981, the Energy and Water Development appropriations bill for fiscal year 1982 came to the House floor for debate and passage. The Edgar amendment was hotly debated but failed by a very slim margin of 208 to 198, with one voting present and 28 members not voting. They likely chose not to vote for the waterway but were reluctant to go on record for casting a vote against Bevill's and Whitten's favorite project. That evening, the team of staffers and others who had contributed so much to the outcome of the vote gathered at a popular watering hole on Capitol Hill to celebrate the victory. After a couple of libations, Roger Wicker and I joked that we, rather than Bevill, Whitten, or Lott could claim credit for the victory. While nothing could have been further from the truth, he and I still reminisce over 40 years later about that evening and our joke. Seriously, Wicker can very well claim much credit for what he and his boss, Representative Trent Lott, did to convince many of the first-term members to either vote against the Edgar amendment or take a walk, which was as good as an anti-amendment vote. All kidding aside, I know that I personally was not directly responsible for a single vote (except possibly by my offering my slice of pie to the Speaker).

I do, however, believe the authority's involvement and its aggressive campaign to marshal and coordinate a team of waterway supporters helped convince 208 members to vote to defeat the amendment and save the waterway. The authority and other waterway supporters working in harmony made the difference between victory and defeat. The approaching funding battle in the Senate proved to be even more challenging, even though there were 100 members there to convince to support Tenn-Tom, compared to 435 in the House.

The 1980 election not only resulted in a Republican President, but the voters also dramatically changed the makeup of the U.S. Senate. That year, there were 34 seats up for election, of which 22 were won by the Republicans, including 12 elected for the first time. Those victories gave the Grand Ole Party a total of 53 seats and majority rule, with Howard Baker of Tennessee becoming Senate Majority Leader. Senator Baker had always been a proponent of the Tenn-Tom and was a close friend of John Waters, a member of the authority representing Tennessee. That close relationship would prove to be of great benefit to the waterway. Chairmanship of the committees also changed. Senator Mark Hatfield of Oregon became chairman of the Energy and Water Development Appropriations Subcommittee, and J. Bennett Johnston from Louisiana was the ranking member for the Democrats. Senator Hatfield had voted for the waterway during the two previous debates, as had Johnston. Senator Stennis would later ask Johnston to lead the debate to defeat any proposals affecting the waterway's funding. Senator James Abdnor of South Dakota, although newly elected, would chair the authorization subcommittee for water resources. My colleagues from the Dakotas, who were fellow members of the Water Resources Congress, had assured me he was a Tenn-Tom supporter.

Senator Stennis would follow the same strategy that was successful in the House. He asked newly elected Senator Jeremiah Denton of Alabama to work with the other 11 newly elected Republicans to persuade them to support the waterway. Denton was a war hero who had spent eight torturous years in North Vietnamese prisons, including the infamous Hanoi Hilton, after he was shot down during a bombing mission. As one of the top officers who was captured, he was subjected to constant torture and horrible living conditions, but they never broke his will. He said his strong religious beliefs helped him survive his ordeal. He retired from the Navy as a rear admiral. He and I became friends, and I would meet with him after normal working hours to get feedback on his efforts with the freshmen senators. He once told me that while he was a POW, he promised himself that, if he survived, he was going to do two things: go fishing more often and have a cocktail in the evenings after a hard day of work. He lived in Mobile, my hometown, and he and I swapped stories about fishing there. He always invited me to join him for a cocktail after work. He had installed an old-fashioned popcorn machine in his reception room, and the aroma of freshly popped corn permeated the entire floor of the office building. Being a lover of popcorn, I did not need any other excuse to visit his office. I admired him so much and considered it one of my greatest honors to have known him.

Howell Heflin, Alabama's senior serving senator by only a couple of years, had supported passage of a $1.5 billion loan in 1979 for the Chrysler Corporation. Knowing of his conservative nature, the senators from Michigan and the upper Midwest were especially appreciative of his vote for the bailout. Stennis asked Senator Heflin to persuade those senators from the upper Midwestern states to return the favor by supporting the Tenn-Tom. Such reciprocity helped save the waterway. Both Senators Denton and Heflin sponsored inspection trips to the waterway, patterned somewhat after Bevill's tours. Moynihan, one of the Tenn-Tom's nemeses in the Senate, accompanied Heflin on one of the waterway trips.

The Environmental Policy Center (EPC) and its collaborators, including the Sierra Club, the National Taxpayers' Union, the League of Women Voters, and a smorgasbord of other groups were working overtime to finally stop the waterway's funding. All were very effective adversaries. They had recruited new torch bearers to sell their cause in the Senate. Senator Charles Percy of Illinois and seven other senators circulated a "Dear Colleague" letter to all the senators announcing they would be offering an amendment to strike the Tenn-Tom funding. Earlier in March 1981, Senator Pete Domenici, a Republican from New Mexico, and Senator Alan Simpson of Wyoming had been successful getting a majority of the members of the Authorization Committee (not appropriations) to adopt a position to complete the waterway only to south of Columbus and abandoned the northern portion. This vote was very disconcerting since it was a complete reversal of the past supportive stances the waterway had enjoyed. Fortunately, its recommendations got no traction within the Senate, but Simpson and Domenici vowed to continue the fight when the appropriations bill came up for a vote.

Like in the House, a team of staff members were assembled to solicit votes and begin the tenuous process of counting votes by working with their counterparts in the other Senate offices. James Jordan, legislative director for Stennis, would lead the group. Jordan, a Carolinian and a former Navy captain, was one of the most intelligent and capable people I ever had the pleasure to know. With all the advanced technologies in weaponry being procured by the military, Stennis asked the Pentagon to recommend someone who could assist him in discharging his responsibilities as chairman of armed services, including staying abreast of all the new and innovative advancements. The Pentagon sent him Jordan. The regular members of the Senate staff team besides Jordan were Jim Lofton, representing Cochran of Mississippi; Charlie Mitchell, representing Heflin of Alabama; Teresa Miller, representing Denton of Alabama; Ed Graves, representing Huddleston of Kentucky; Mike Walker, representing Sasser of Tennessee; and occasionally others. The team would be invaluable when time came to start counting votes.

I had become consumed with the tasks of preparing for the impending vote and the consequences of its outcome. Being so closely involved, I soon learned to tell who was earnestly lobbying on behalf of the waterway and who was just pretending to do so. The National Waterways Conference Inc. (NWC), a member of our team, is a national trade association for the barge industry. Its president was Harry Cook, a native of Mississippi and a former employee of the Waterway Authority. Glover Wilkins was responsible for his becoming the founding president of the trade group. I was concerned about the apparent lack of support coming from the group and met with Cook in his Washington office. He began giving me suggestions about what we should be doing to generate more votes. It had been a long day, and I exploded, telling him, "I don't need any advice. I'm already getting enough of that. What I need is more votes!" He told me NWC was not in the business of lobbying but mainly dealt with federal policies pertaining to commercial navigation. I knew that some of the larger barge companies that primarily operated on the Ohio and Mississippi rivers were concerned that the Tenn-Tom was diverting funds from the needs of those waterways and that it was also generating a lot of negative publicity for the industry. Some were privately opposed to the waterway. I reported to Senator Stennis about my meeting with Cook. The senator and Cook were from the same county in Mississippi but were not personal acquaintances. He invited Cook to meet with him, and the senator, in his typically gentlemanly manner, explained how important the Tenn-Tom was to "their" state and that its opponents were working hard to kill it. He ended the very brief meeting by telling Cook that he needed NWC's help. With my presence at the meeting, it was evident to Cook that I was responsible for his subtle dress down by the senator. He complained to others later, saying I had set him up. However, the meeting resulted in NWC and its members becoming much more active and helpful.

Wilkins knew that Barrett Shelton, an authority member from Decatur, Alabama, had been one of a few very influential Democrats in Alabama who had supported John F. Kennedy's presidential election. Shelton was publisher of the *Decatur Daily*, a Roosevelt Democrat, and an advocate of the Tennessee Valley Authority and its programs. He was largely responsible for the impressive number of heavy industries that had located in that part of North Alabama. Kennedy had rewarded Shelton's loyalty and support by appointing his very capable assistant, Maynard Layman, to some important positions in his administration. With nothing to lose, Wilkins asked Shelton to call the President's younger brother, Senator Ted Kennedy, and ask for his support. Shelton reported that he had talked to Kennedy and that he promised to vote for the waterway if his vote "was needed." That was great news, since everyone on our team had assumed he was a "no" vote for the waterway.

One afternoon, a couple of days before the vote was scheduled, I met Bartley O'Hara and another lobbyist for AFL-CIO in a corridor of a Senate office building. O'Hara represented the Teamsters Union and was one of the more active lobbyists working for Tenn-Tom. He asked how the vote counting was shaping up, and I told him that we needed more supporters. I mentioned several senators who had been aggressively pursued but still appeared to be solid "no" votes, including Democrat Senator Chris Dodd of Connecticut. Dodd was newly elected with the strong backing of AFL-CIO and was the son of Thomas Dodd, who had previously served two terms in the Senate. By coincidence, O'Hara said they were on their way to meet with Dodd and would urge him to support the waterway and its several thousand unionized construction workers. I thanked them and wished them luck.

Jim Jordan and the Senate staff team met more frequently with the time approaching for deliberations of the Energy and Water Development Appropriations Bill. Each meeting concluded that the waterway was short of votes. The senators were told they needed to work harder for more votes, and Stennis and Majority Leader Baker used their clout to postpone the bill for a vote. The bill was deferred several times until it was finally decided by the Senate leadership, win or lose for the Tenn-Tom, to bring the bill up for debate and a vote on November 4, 1981.

Not being a staff member, I was not allowed on the Senate floor but found a seat in the gallery, where I could witness the proceedings and the fruits of our labors, and hopefully not its shortcomings. Senators Simpson and Domenici made impassioned pleas to strike the $189 million in the bill for the Tenn-Tom. Senator Johnston, with the able assistance of Proctor Jones, the subcommittee chief staff member, led the defense of the funding. I learned later that Jones and Simpson got into a heated argument when Jones confronted Simpson's legislative assistant for providing the senator with false information about the Tenn-Tom. Simpson demanded that Jones be removed from the Senate floor, but with Johnston's backing and support, he refused to leave. After the vote, Simpson apologized for the episode and, using an old Wyoming adage, commended Jones for "sticking to his guns."

During the debate, I noticed that Heflin was huddled in deep conversation with Senator Carl Levin of Michigan. Charlie Mitchell, Heflin's legislative director, was listening to the senators' conversation. Mitchell knew I was in the gallery and came to report that Levin wanted to vote against the amendment but had been persuaded against doing so by the opponents' allegation that $1 billion more would be needed to make the waterway functional. The environmentalists had launched a very effective nationwide campaign portraying the Tenn-Tom as a "$3-billion ditch," and Levin had drunk the Kool-Aid. I explained that the allegations were ludicrous and that improvements were not needed on another waterway to make the Tenn-Tom navigable. Mitchell, through Heflin, told Levin that the $3 billion charge had no merit. Not wanting to take Heflin's staffer's word, he wanted to include an amendment in the bill stipulating that funds were not being sought for any improvements of the Black Warrior-Tombigbee Waterway (BWT) to aid navigation on the Tenn-Tom. Mitchell and I hurriedly drafted language for the senator's amendment without any time to consult with anyone, including the Corps. After we prepared a couple of drafts, the senator finally accepted the language and offered his amendment for a vote. It passed with no debate and since then is referred to as the "Levin Amendment." He later returned the favor to Heflin for supporting the Chrysler bailout by voting against striking the waterway's funds. When the Corps learned of the Levin Amendment, some in the Mobile District were upset that I had sold out any future improvements to the BWT. I reminded them that such language in an annual appropriations bill is in effect for only that fiscal year. Since there were no funds in the bill for any BWT improvements, the amendment was meaningless, but it gave the Michigan senator an out to support the Tenn-Tom.

After the debate, a roll-call vote was taken. In the Senate, most members cast their votes in what is referred to as "in the well" by standing within sight of the clerk recording the vote and giving a hand signal of a thumbs up or down. After the vote, the presiding president of the Senate (generally a senator from the majority party) announces the results of the vote on the public address system. From my perch above the Senate floor, I watched with keen interest as each senator came to the well to announce his or her vote. I was ecstatic to learn that O'Hara and his fellow lobbyists for AFL-CIO had been successful in getting Senator Dodd to vote against the amendment. I watched with much interest as Senator Kennedy, standing near the well, carefully watched the voting and, at the last minute, voted in favor of the amendment once it was certain that it would be defeated, albeit by a razor's edge. The final tally showed 48 senators voted to defeat the amendment while 46 voted for it, with five choosing not to vote, most of those likely in deference to Stennis, like Senator Barry Goldwater (R-Arizona) and Senator Ted Stevens (D-Alaska). The unexpected votes by Dodd and Levin, with Kennedy's vote in reserve, proved to be the difference in the waterway's victory. I was very disappointed that both senators from Florida, a waterway compact state, chose not to support the Tenn-Tom. Senator Lawton Chiles voted for the amendment, and newly elected Senator Paula Hawkins, who had earlier indicated her support to Senator Denton, voted "present."

There was no victory party like we'd had after the House vote. Everyone was too exhausted to celebrate. Although nearly $400 million of additional funding would be needed to complete the project, no one knew at the time that the Senate vote we just witnessed would be the last up-or-down vote for the Tenn-Tom. The waterway's opponents smelled blood with the very narrow votes in both the House and Senate and began preparing to finish off the Tenn-Tom in the next fiscal year. They were determined to eventually prevail in their decade-long battle to kill the waterway, just as they had done to the Cross Florida Barge Canal.

Reagan and the Corps requested $189 million for the Tenn-Tom in the FY1983 budget. The Appropriations Committee failed to schedule and pass the Energy and Water Development bill before the end of the fiscal year or by September 30. Failing to do so required the passage of a Continuing Resolution (CR) and the Corps' funding, including the $189 million for the Tenn-Tom, was incorporated into that bill. Failure to pass appropriations on time is now common, but it was unprecedented in the 1980s. Whether the delay was unintentional or purposeful is conjecture. I believe the latter, since Appropriations Chairman Jamie Whitten knew that the Rules Committee limited the number of amendments that could be offered for a CR. Congressman Edgar again proposed his amendment to cut the project's funds, but the Rules Committee denied his request, although it approved similar amendments for three other water and energy projects that led to their loss of funding. I have always suspected that the Rules Committee's decision to deny Edgar's request was influenced by Speaker O'Neill's commitment to Congressman Bevill to support the waterway's funding. I facetiously attributed that to the slice of cherry pie I gave the Speaker during the luncheon, and the briefing that helped seal the deal. Congressman Trent Lott was a member of the Rules Committee, and I am confident he helped influence the committee's decision to deny Edgar's amendment. In any event, $189 million of funding for the waterway made its way through both the House and Senate without a challenge.

There remained an additional $200 million in the next three years needed to complete the waterway. Chairman Bevill concocted a unique, if not unprecedented, legislative ploy to provide those funds without the fear of any opposing amendments. Instead of identifying a specific amount of funds in the Energy and Water Development bill for FY1984, language was included directing the Corps to complete the waterway with funds already available to the agency. The Corps' annual construction program totaled nearly $1 billion and involved scores of projects. Some of these projects incurred savings in contract costs or slippage in construction schedules. Any such unspent funds were to be reprogrammed to the Tenn-Tom and used to meet its needs in subsequent years until it was completed. Understandably, the opponents were outraged and cried foul, some contending it was unconstitutional to commit such funding for future years. Nevertheless, both the House and Senate both adopted and enacted the provision. I believe that, by then, most members of Congress, like Speaker O'Neill, were ready to rid Congress of all the controversies surrounding the Tenn-Tom. Senator Stennis congratulated Bevill on his solution to finally end the waterway's funding challenges and commended him for what the senator said was "the best legislative job I have seen done here." That statement was most telling of what had just been accomplished: the end of the Tenn-Tom's funding war, assuring the project's completion and the fulfillment of the dreams of many generations.

CHAPTER XX
Changing of the Guard

With victories to celebrate in Congress and in the federal courts, it was time to begin planning for the waterway's completion and its development. With all the needed funds now available, the Mobile and Nashville Districts, under the command of Colonels Bob Ryan and Pat Kelly and Colonels Bob Tener and Lee Tucker, respectively, accelerated construction of the remaining features of the waterway. Its supporters, including the authority, exhaled sighs of relief with the major challenges to the waterway now in their rearview mirror. We started looking forward to its completion less than two years away.

Glover Wilkins, the authority's long-time administrator, had been instrumental in keeping the waterway from running off the rails and staying on track, despite his experiencing some health problems. While his illness limited his travel to Washington, he continued to work from the Columbus office, making contacts in Congress and with others that only he could make. I marveled at his ability to nurture true and lasting relationships, if not friendships, with those from all walks of life. For example, he became close friends with Congressman John Rhodes of Arizona, who was the House Republican leader. Although his constituents would not benefit from the Tenn-Tom, he not only supported the Tenn-Tom, but traveled to Columbus to attend an authority meeting and spend the weekend with his friend, Glover. Glover had an admirable ability to attend a reception or a large gathering of people and to later remember the attendees' names and affiliations. He said that most people don't concentrate on the introduction and are looking at the tie or dress they are wearing or succumb to some other distraction. Instead, Glover orally or mentally repeated the person's name or thought of some association that would help him remember the person's name. Whatever his technique, he was the best I have ever known to have had such a gift.

Although he had dedicated most of his adult life to promoting the waterway and was universally known as Mr. Tenn-Tom, Glover had two or three members of authority who never wasted an opportunity to give him grief. He was devastated to learn that most of his difficulties with the three members (as much as I want to divulge their identity, I will not name them, all of whom now deceased) stemmed from a member of the authority staff spreading malicious gossip about him. Once he and I attended a meeting and were away from the office for two days. While we were gone, the three, all from out of town, met in the office with the authority's outside accountant and rummaged through all the financial files. As expected, they found no irregularities, but the quickly called meeting was evidence that someone on the staff had let them know that we were out of the office. I also started receiving some negative connotations from the three. I confronted one of them about why they seemed to be searching for reasons to criticize me, mostly with petty complaints. His response was that they had some resentment toward me because I was Glover's "fair-haired boy." I told him that I considered that a compliment. Because of my genuine affection for Glover and the disdain I had for those who were making life so miserable for him, that was the darkest, most troubling time during my 30 years with authority.

The authority held a quarterly meeting in Mobile in January 1984 at a time when there was much to celebrate about all the positive things that had transpired since the last meeting in the fall. Instead, Glover made a bombshell announcement that he was retiring the following June. Glover might have shared his plans with some of his closest friends, but it was a complete surprise to everyone, including me. One of the three dissidents immediately proposed that a committee be formed to start a search for his replacement. Jack Paxton, a member from Kentucky, who had learned about the men's backstabbing of Glover, forcefully countered with a motion that the members vote right then instead of keeping everything in a state of flux for three months or longer until the next meeting. We held a secret ballot, and I was elected to succeed Glover effective on July 1, 1984. I would hold the position for the next 21 years. I asked the member who counted the votes to confidentially tell me how many votes I had received. I wanted to know if most, if not all, of the members had supported me. If not, I was hesitant to accept the position. She said that of the 24 members voting, I had received all the votes except three, undoubtedly the three members who had been giving Glover so much grief. I decided I could overcome any opposition from them with the other members in my court, until their governors replaced them. Two of them resigned later that year, and eventually the other one did, too.

One of the main topics of the January meeting was to discuss the future role, if any, for the authority since its primary mission of getting the waterway built had now been fulfilled. Such discussions had been going on since 1981 but had been sidetracked with the funding battles in Congress and the litigation. Some of the members felt that the compact had fulfilled its intent and that consideration should be given to phasing the authority out of business. The most vocal ones of that view were the same three members who had maligned Glover. Most of the members, however, felt there might be an important role for the authority to help promote and market the development of the waterway and its economic potential. Corps officials had voiced their support to continue the compact to help ensure that federal appropriations were sufficient to properly operate and maintain the waterway. The Corps of Engineers, as a federal agency, cannot openly lobby Congress for funding. Fulfilling the waterway's funding needs would be dependent upon its stakeholders, represented by a regional body like the authority. The states of Arkansas and Oklahoma had a similar organization that worked in a cooperative way to improve the Arkansas River for commercial navigation from its mouth with the Mississippi River to Tulsa, Oklahoma. They disbanded once the project was completed but later recognized that a two-state coalition was just as important during the operation and development stages of the waterway as it had been during its construction. Changes in the political climate had prevented them from reestablishing such an organization.

The authority members had established a Planning and Development Committee to help identify which activities, if any, would be relevant and would be supported by the compact states by continuing their funding to the compact. The committee was composed of one member from each of the five states. Fred Bush, a well-known attorney from Tupelo, Mississippi, and a member of the defendants' legal team for the recent litigation, chaired the committee. The group held quarterly meetings along with some ad hoc meetings and concluded there was an important role for the authority as long as its activities did not conflict with those of the member states. As Bush stated to the members at the January meeting, "We are now in the development stage of the waterway . . . Investment decisions involving new plant locations and expansions as well as decisions by commercial interest to ship on the waterway will be based on detailed, factual information concerning the waterway . . . The Authority is the most logical source for developing and disseminating this valuable information to the member states, their political subdivisions, and regional development agencies for use in industrial promotion, as well as for increasing shipments on the waterway.

"I believe the authority should be concerned with the total development of the waterway to the extent it can provide needed services to the states, local communities, potential shippers, and other interests."

Except for a couple of naysayers, the members appreciated Bush's eloquent courtroom delivery of his vision for the authority's future. The members instructed the staff to begin formulating a work program commiserate with Bush's committee's recommendations. Further, it was time for the authority to devote most of its energies and resources toward ensuring the realization of the waterway's potential benefits to the member states and to the nation. This most meaningful work by the Planning and Development Committee in charting the future of the compact can be attributed to the vision of Bush and his fellow committee member, Alex Chamberlain of Kentucky, who was connected with the Blazer family, who founded Ashland Oil. His long-time experience with the barge industry was invaluable to the compact as it implemented its new role.

Development Opportunities Conference

With the construction of the Tenn-Tom about a year away from completion, the authority held a conference in Mobile in November 1983 to begin focusing attention on capturing the waterway's economic development potential for its region. The meeting was a huge success, with more than 800 attendees from throughout the waterway region, including governors and members of Congress. It was one of the largest attended meetings of waterway stakeholders ever held, and its two-day program focused mainly on some of the economic development opportunities of the Tenn-Tom, including recreation and tourism. Initially, the plan was to hold the meeting each year in various locations within the waterway region. Two of the earlier meetings were held in Knoxville, Tennessee, and two took place in Paducah, Kentucky. A couple of those meetings helped set a high standard for future annual conferences. At one of the conferences in Knoxville, a reception and dinner was held at a replica of an old Appalachian village near the city. When we arrived, I happened to notice Alex Haley was also entering the village. Haley's very successful novel, *Roots*, had just been produced into a very popular TV series. Haley had a vacation cabin nearby and was there to visit his friend, the proprietor of the village. I introduced myself, and during our conversation, I invited him to join us for dinner. Much to my delight, he accepted. At that time, Haley was in much demand as a speaker and was earning a hefty fee describing his lineage. After dinner I asked him to make some remarks, and we were all spellbound as he described his ancestors who came from Africa and later were slaves. It was a memorable evening with the famous author.

About that time, I had the pleasure of meeting another renowned author when the agent for James A. Michener called in late 1985 to request an interview. Michener was a prolific writer who wrote over two dozen novels, including *Tales of the South Pacific*, for which he won a Pulitzer Prize for fiction. He was one of the most popular writers of his era, with many bestsellers, including *Alaska*, *Texas*, *Hawaii*, and the critically acclaimed *Centennial*. He arrived casually dressed in a pair of khaki trousers and a flannel shirt and said he was interested in writing about transportation. I was struck that he took notes with only nub of a pencil and wrote in a small notebook that fit into his shirt pocket. He did not have a tape recorder or other means to retrieve information from the interview other than his apparent remarkable memory. I answered his questions about the Tenn-Tom, but he seemed more interested in the people along the waterway and their customs and culture. He was very pleasant and agreed to autograph my copy of *Centennial* to my son. It was one of my son's favorite novels. Michener's visit lasted most of the morning, and he left with an arm full of brochures and other information about the waterway, including its history and demographics about the region, which were compiled during the Tenn-Tom Corridor Study. I surmised after our meeting that he was contemplating a novel about the Deep South and its culture, since that was about the only part of the United States he had not already written about. Most all his other novels were more about the people than the setting, and I speculated the Tenn-Tom could possibly be the setting for his writing about the Deep South and its people. I was very disappointed that he never published such a novel. I learned later that he was suffering from kidney disease and after several years of dialysis treatments died at the age of 90 in 1997. I never knew whether his health issues precluded his writing a novel centered on the Tenn-Tom and its region, or whether he just lost interest.

The two meetings in Paducah were held at the sprawling Executive Inn located on the bank of the Tennessee River at its confluence with the Ohio River. The hotel, which has since been demolished, had a Las Vegas-style showroom that could accommodate several hundred people. It routinely booked notable musicians such as the Temptations and other popular groups from that era. The hotel management allowed conference attendees to enjoy the entertainment if we booked one of our dinners at the showroom. One of the backup musicians was Jason D. Williams, a rockabilly pianist, who was rumored to be the illegitimate son of Jerry Lee Lewis. He was a bonified copy of the Killer on the keyboards. I tried every year to book him for one of the conferences but was never able to do so until about 2000, when we were meeting at the Grand Hotel in Point Clear, Alabama. Since he and his band would be traveling through South Alabama from Texas to a gig in Florida, I was able to book him and his group for a nominal fee, plus overnight accommodation for the group at the hotel. Knowing the reputation of the group, I did not allow any food or drinks to be charged to their rooms. Knowing Jason's style of playing, the hotel also required that I pay for a tune up of the hotel piano. Jason gave such an unforgettable performance that night we who were there still talk about that evening nearly three decades later.

During those early years of meeting at the Grand Hotel, the authority rented one of the hotel's small cottages as a hospitality suite and kept it supplied with plenty of food and drinks during the evenings. Joining us with a similar watering hole was the city of Aliceville, The hospitality was solely financed every year by its mayor, Roth Hook, who epitomized Boss Hogg on the popular TV series, *Dukes of Hazzard*. Its hosts were Alan Harper, a banker and later a state representative, and Mike Oakley, the city chamber director who later became mayor of Centerville, Alabama. Oakley was an accomplished guitar player, and most evenings evolved into sing-a-longs, with everyone having a good time and perhaps a hangover the next morning.

One of our most memorable speakers during those early years was Jim Rogers, who with George Soros established the highly successful Quantum Fund, making both very rich. Rogers was fond of saying that he, growing up in Demopolis, Alabama, had always heard about the Tenn-Tom and that he now saw it as an important economic tool for the region. He had written a pair of bestsellers about his two trips around the world, once on a motorcycle with this girlfriend and later in a specially designed vehicle, custom built for him by Mercedes Benz. His two presentations about the countries he visited and his assessment of investment opportunities there were most interesting. Once you meet Rogers, you can see why he has been so successful in the financial world, and no one enjoyed the hospitality suites more than he did. During one of his generous moods, he joined the Tenn-Tom Council as a member and offered as a door prize a weekend for four at his Brownstone mansion in Manhattan. The lucky winner of the drawing and his three companions spent a weekend there, with Rogers gladly serving as their host. He later married and moved to China, because he foresaw its becoming a financial powerhouse with unlimited opportunities for making money. The legendary investor now lives in Singapore with his family, and for several years while living abroad, he would call the Tenn-Tom office just to say hello and get a report about the waterway and its activities.

The so-called Development Opportunities Conference has been held every year since 1983 and remains a popular annual event. The 41st conference was held in August 2023 at the Grand Hotel in Point Clear, Alabama, with Mitch Mays, the authority's administrator, presiding. George Crawford of Starkville, Mississippi, was recognized as the only person who has attended every conference since that first one some 41 years ago. The overwhelming success of those early annual conferences helped affirm the importance of the authority's role in promoting the development of the waterway and its economic potential by enabling its beneficiaries to reap the rewards.

Tenn-Tom Council

For some time, I had been pressing the authority members to establish an advisory group or an organization to represent companies and individuals interested in the waterway. By law, the makeup of the authority was limited to the five governors and their five appointees from each of their states, thus necessitating the need for a separately chartered sister organization. I had little success, not so much because of opposition but because of a lack of appreciation by the members, who didn't recognize the importance of creating such a group and who thought doing so could be postponed. That attitude changed at my first meeting as administrator, held in Paducah in conjunction with the second annual Development Opportunities Conference. I reported that the Tennessee River Valley Association was incorporating the Tenn-Tom and its following into its organization. It was looking for opportunities to attract more members to help alleviate its deteriorating financial situation. Now was the time for the authority members to decide to establish a waterway users' group, or someone else would do so. The threat worked, and I was given permission to charter such a group and develop its by-laws.

I named the new organization the Tennessee-Tombigbee Waterway Development Council and chartered it in Mississippi as a 501(c) organization. To avoid any possible conflicts between the two organizations, I named the authority's administrator as the president or CEO of the new council and domiciled it at the authority's headquarters. Officers and the board of directors are elected by the membership, and its membership fee structure was purposely set at a low level to attract more members. The initial announcement about the council's establishment and a solicitation for membership immediately attracted over 300 people from a dozen or more states. Its first organizational meeting was held in Columbus, Mississippi, in January 1985. The attendees elected the following officers: T.L. "Bud" Phillips of Columbus, chairman; Tim Parker of Tuscaloosa, vice chairman; Bobby Harper of Columbus, treasurer; and Ron Boutwell of Aberdeen, Mississippi, secretary. As the authority's administrator and according to the new organization's by-laws, I became the council's first president. The group also elected its founding board of directors. The council has remained an effective and viable organization and has played a vital role in the waterway's development, especially regarding commercial navigation.

The Corps completed construction of the waterway in December 1984, below estimated costs and several months ahead of schedule. The last segment of the channel was removed to complete the waterway on December 12, 1984, exactly 12 years to the day after construction began. The removal of the "plug" of earth from the navigation channel occurred near the State Highway 6 bridge crossing at Amory, Mississippi, symbolically signifying the long-awaited "mixing of the waters" of the two rivers, the Tombigbee and Tennessee. The total costs for building ten locks and dams, 234 miles of navigation channel improvement, recreational facilities, and environmental and visitor centers were slightly less than $2 billion, a bargain compared to today's costs for waterway projects.

There was so much interest from the barge companies to have the distinction of being the first to transit the entire length of the waterway that the Corps decided to hold a lottery. Waxler Towing, Inc. of Memphis was the lucky winner. The towboat, Eddie Waxler, pushing two tank barges loaded with about 2.7 million gallons of petroleum products, left Mobile on its way to Decatur via the Black Warrior-Tombigbee Waterway, connected with the Tennessee-Tombigbee Waterway at Demopolis, and eventually entered the Tennessee River. The route of this inaugural barge tow, involving three different waterways, symbolized Tenn-Tom's emerging brand as a new connecting link for the nation's inland waterway system. By coincidence, the barge tow arrived at Columbus during the waterway council's organizational meeting. The meeting was adjourned early so everyone could rush out to the lock and dam and greet the voyage. Throngs of well-wishers gathered at each lock along the waterway, despite bitter cold weather, to witness this historical event.

After 12 years of construction and at a cost of nearly $2 billion, the waterway was finally completed on December 12,1984, by removing the final plug of earth from the navigation channel at Amory, Mississippi. Symbolically, this permitted "the mixing of the waters" of the Tennessee and Tombigbee rivers and was the realization of the dreams of many generations.

Chapter XXI
Mother of All Celebrations

After decades of disappointments and setbacks for the Tenn-Tom, the waterway authority and other project supporters yearned for an opportunity to celebrate as the project neared completion. It was the fulfillment of their dreams. The Nashville District completed construction of the Divide Section in early 1984, nearly one year before the construction of the entire waterway was accomplished. What better way to start celebrating the waterway's culmination than by having a ceremony to dedicate arguably the most difficult section of the waterway to design and build? The authority in partnership with the Nashville District scheduled such an event on May 6, 1984 at the Bay Springs Lock and Dam, now named after Jamie Whitten. Several thousand came, mostly North Mississippians, both to celebrate the work accomplished for the waterway and to show their appreciation to Congressman Jamie Whitten for his 50 years of congressional service.

The congressman and some of the other dignitaries arrived at the ceremony aboard the motor vessel M/V *Mississippi*, the Corps' flagship and the largest towboat on the inland waterway system. Never missing an opportunity to ridicule the waterway and its supporters, the national media chastised the congressman as the King of Pork sailing down the Tenn-Tom, comparing him to Cleopatra floating down the Nile. My response to these bitter opponents who spent untold time and expense trying and failing to kill the waterway: "Eat your heart out and watch us as we laugh our way to the bank."

Congressman Whitten and Glover Wilkins moderated the ceremony's program, which mainly consisted of remarks by some of the waterway's greatest champions. It would be Glover's last official act since he was retiring as the authority's administrator the following month. In addition to Whitten, other notable dignitaries who attended and spoke included Mississippi senators John Stennis and Thad Cochran; Governor George Wallace of Alabama; former Mississippi governors William Winter and J.P. Coleman; currently serving congressmen Jack Edwards (Alabama); John Myers (Indiana); and Don Sundquist (Tennessee); and former congressman Tom Abernathy (Mississippi). All of the speakers followed the "five minutes" rule, and the program was both brief, considering the number of speakers, and very informative. I was especially pleased to hear the remarks by governors Wallace and Winter, who served as members of the authority during the time the compact's future was being questioned with the waterway nearing completion. Both supported the authority's new role in promoting the development of the waterway. Both said during their brief remarks that "we must now maximize the benefits offered by the waterway." The event attracted two of the waterway's early champions. J.P. Coleman, who served as governor of Mississippi when the waterway compact was founded in 1958, and former congressman Tom Abernathy, who kept the proposed project alive in the Congress during the 1960s. I was surprised by Governor Wallace's presence at the ceremony, considering how hard it was for him, wheelchair-bound, to travel. In the 1980s he was still a national celebrity and political icon, and by the crowd's reactions, he was as popular as Whitten was at his own event.

With the Tenn-Tom at last completed in December 1984 and open to navigation the following month, it was now time to begin planning for the waterway's dedication or its grand opening. There was a consensus that the event should be held later in the spring or early summer to hopefully have weather suitable for an outdoor event, and that much time was needed to plan what some were calling the "Mother of all Dedications." Everyone, including the authority's chairman (and my boss) George Wallace, seemed to have different opinions about where the event should take place, its time frame and its theme or context. I made a special trip to Montgomery to get his input, only to find I had a serious problem complying with his wishes. He told me that if he and Alabama had anything to do with the celebration, it would be held in Mobile, where in 1971 President Nixon had announced his decision to initiate funding for construction of the waterway. That event had been held on the docks of the Port of Mobile with thousands of supporters attending and the governor presiding. While the Mobile event was certainly one of the milestones for the waterway, I tried desperately to convince the governor to agree that the grand opening should be held somewhere on the waterway. The logical location was Columbus, Mississippi. I tried to explain to him that the waterway had been so maligned by its detractors, who contended that it was a boondoggle and a scourge on the environment. Holding the dedication somewhere other than on the waterway would confirm that we were hesitant for the public to see for it themselves. The meeting ended with him still adamant that the event would be in Mobile if he had anything to do with it. At that time, I had been administrator for a little over six months, and it appeared that I was about to be fired over a disagreement of an event's venue. The authority administrator serves at the pleasure of the members and can be immediately discharged with or without cause.

The Corps has had lots of experience in planning and conducting dedication ceremonies. The Corps can pay for the official ceremony, but the authority and the waterway's congressional supporters wanted the Tenn-Tom celebration to be much more than just a ribbon-cutting event. The costs for all the other related activities would be the responsibility of the waterway supporters. Because the Mobile District was under his command, Brigadier General Forrest "Ted" Gay, commander of the South Atlantic Division, would be in charge of the Corps' activities. I would be in nearly daily contact with him or his deputy, Colonel Jonathan Nottingham, for nearly four months.

Everyone agreed the event would be held on June 1, 1985. To placate Governor George Wallace and possibly preclude my dismissal, I offered a compromise concerning the location of the event. The dedication ceremony would be held that Saturday morning in Columbus at the Columbus Lock and Dam (now named after Stennis), with some ceremonies held the previous afternoon and evening. After the adjournment of the ceremony at Columbus, the dignitaries would fly to Mobile for ceremonies there, including a Mardi Gras-style parade and a dinner that evening. Two ceremonies over 200 miles apart would create logistical challenges, and each would undoubtedly detract from the other, especially regarding attendance. However, it was a workable proposal, and the plans pleased Governor Wallace. Ceremonies in two locations or cities to commemorate the completion of the largest water resources project ever built were certainly appropriate.

I never knew what the Corps spent on its part in the event, but a goal of $500,000 was set to finance the non-federal activities. Tommy Lott of Columbus, the principal partner of the authority's accounting firm, agreed to serve as chairman of the finance committee. The primary sources of funding came from donations, including those from the compact states, and some from fundraising activities. For example, we sold placards to those who wanted to honor someone who had worked to build the waterway or who had some other interest in or association with the waterway. We placed on a wall at the ceremony the placards bearing the honorees' names. So-called flotilla flags bearing the newly copyrighted logo for the waterway were sold to recreational boating interests. These and other fundraising efforts generated several thousands of dollars. There were doubts, including those of our Corps partners, that we would be capable of raising such an ambitious amount of funds in such a short period of time, but Lott and his committee proved the doubters wrong.

The plans called for the main ceremony to be on the western side of the waterway near the lock, with attendees sitting or standing on the slope of the dam and the dignitaries sitting on deck barges anchored in the waterway. A festival of communities would take place on the eastern side of the waterway. To resolve the problem of attendees getting from one side of the waterway to the other, an Army National Guard from Alabama built a portable bridge, called a Bailey Bridge, across the waterway for pedestrians. Sadly, one of the guardsmen, PFC Lloyd Dewayne Hayes of the 145th Engineering Battalion, was killed while transporting the bridge components from an upstream area. That site is now a permanent and popular recreational area and in the guardsman's memory, is called Dewayne Hayes. Workers also assembled deck barges on the eastern side for festivities planned there for the afternoon before the main ceremony.

The much-anticipated dedication of the waterway's completion was held on the morning of June 1, 1985, in Columbus, Mississippi, with another equally impressive ceremony held later that day in Mobile, Alabama. Celebrations throughout the waterway region, some as far away as Paducah, Kentucky, preceded that historical day. Some newspapers described these events as the most celebrations to occur in the waterway region since the ending of World War II.

The Alabama National Guard built a Bailey's steel bridge across Columbus Lake next to the lock and dam for pedestrian access to and from the east bank, where a festival occurred to the west side of the lake where the grand opening ceremony was held. Tragically, one of the guardsmen, DeWayne Hayes, was killed installing the bridge. To honor his memory and recognize him, the Corps of Engineers named one of the waterway's recreation areas after him.

I learned quickly there were too many aspects of this event for me to cope with. I delegated the responsibilities for planning and organizing all the festival activities on the eastern side of the lock to Pat Ross of the authority staff and her legion of local volunteers. I also asked Darlene Scoggins, another member of the staff, to prepare invitations for all the distinguished guests. She was also responsible for coordinating their travel plans and other needs. They both did a superb job, but the event's success can be attributed to the many volunteers who worked selflessly during the weeks leading up to the dedication and especially during the days of the ceremony. One of those volunteers was Agnes Zaiontz. I was so impressed with her capabilities and work ethic that I later hired her as the authority's accountant. She became one of the authority's most dedicated and dependable employees for nearly 35 years, most of that time serving as office manager. She was largely responsible for creating the waterway's museum, which today bears her name.

The cities and communities along the waterway and the connecting Tennessee River were encouraged to have their own celebrations leading up to the Columbus event, and many did so. In Paducah, a large crowd gathered at its waterfront to hear their governor, congressman, and other dignitaries extoll the benefits of the Tenn-Tom to that region by providing a new access to the eastern Gulf of Mexico for water-borne commerce. Similar celebrations were held in Guntersville and Decatur, Alabama, as well as in other communities along the Tenn-Tom.

Owners of large pleasure boats were encouraged to join a flotilla that would start in Paducah, at Knoxville on the upper Tennessee River, and from the panhandle of Florida, all converging in Columbus in time for the celebration. Dean White, a former towboat captain who ran a deckhand training program for the towing industry at a local community college, organized the flotilla. It, too, was successful. Columbus Lake was full of transient boaters from all over the South. The flotilla was led by the Corps' massive M/V *Mississippi* with Congressman Whitten and other dignitaries aboard. The highlight of the Friday afternoon activities was when Governor Martha Layne

Collins of Kentucky, and the authority's first chairwoman, presided in the preparation of a time capsule that would be opened on the waterway's 25th anniversary. All of the towns and cities within the waterway corridor were encouraged to bring mementoes, newspaper articles, or other memories they wanted included in the time capsule. Many communities participated, and each one's mementoes were placed in individual containers and stored inside a large replica of an old paddle-wheeled steamboat. The time capsule was opened at the Tenn-Tom office in June 2010 with representatives of most of the communities present to retrieve their remembrances.

One of the critically important unknowns when planning for an event of this kind is expected attendance. Estimates for the June 1 event in Columbus ranged as high as 100,000. I believed that estimate was somewhat high, but to be on the safe side, the Corps insisted we plan for that large an attendance. There is very limited parking space along the access roads to the east and west side of the lock and dam, which dictated the need for satellite parking areas and shuttle buses. We designated these areas and publicized their availably. The authority also leased several dozens of school buses and drivers from nearby school districts.

As June 1 approached, I felt we had planned every minute detail of the two events. Two military transport planes with a large delegation of members of Congress would leave Washington early that Saturday morning, land at the nearby Columbus Air Force Base, and the dignitaries be brought directly to the ceremony. When the ceremony ended, the dignitaries would return to the base, where the authority would provide lunch before departure. One plane would return to Washington, while the other would leave for Mobile with those who wanted to attend that event. The authority also chartered a commercial passenger jet to transport authority members and special guests to Mobile.

We booked the Depot, the largest restaurant in Columbus, to feed about 200 special guests, who arrived early to participate in the Friday afternoon activities. Turns out we fed many of the restaurant's regular customers, who were not told that the entire restaurant was booked for a private party. At least that's the story they told.

The anticipated arrival of a very special guest greatly complicated all the plans. We received notice a couple of weeks before the ceremony that President Reagan had accepted the authority's invitation to attend the ceremony at Columbus. We were soon spending an inordinate amount of time with the White House's advance team and secret service agents, going over every minute detail of the ceremony. The President's participation also dictated a complete reshuffling of the program. We hurriedly got a large crystal bowl with proper etchings prepared to be presented to him at the ceremony. Then, about three days before the ceremony, the White House called to apologize and to say that something had come up that would prevent the President from attending. Understandably, everyone was very disappointed he was not coming and that all the many hours spent in preparation for his visit were for naught. With so much planning needed and false starts preparing for just a few hours of events, I knew how General Eisenhower must have felt in planning D-Day or the Normandy Invasion. Incidentally, the Reagan vase adorned my office for 20 years, and it is now in the authority's front office.

While planning the dedication's program we were confronted with what I would call a meeting planner's dream — too many dignitaries to choose from to be speakers. Most of the waterway's champions in Congress were attending and expected to speak. Then there was secretary of Army John Marsh, the highest-level official of the Reagan Administration and the Corps' representative on the dais, along with Lieutenant General E.R. "Vald" Heiberg, the commanding general. Also, Governor Martha Layne Collins, the authority's chairperson, and Bill Allain the host governor for the event, were expected to speak. I was also determined to include Glover Wilkins in the program, but he recognized my dilemma and volunteered to give the invocation instead of speaking. We made the difficult decision to eliminate from the program most of those who had spoken at the earlier ceremony for the Divide Section. Congressman Tom Bevill was chosen to preside, and other members of Congress, as well as governors from the compact states, were either recognized or asked to make some brief remarks. The other 40 or more dignitaries who came from Washington were recognized, including a couple of members of Congress who had voted against the waterway's funding. Governor Wallace chose not to attend. I hoped that he was not boycotting the Columbus ceremony since he was so opposed to having the waterway's celebration anywhere but in Mobile. I gave him the benefit of the doubt, believing that he chose not to attend two ceremonies in the same day.

Governor Martha Layne Collins of Kentucky, as chairperson of the waterway compact, presided at the dedication ceremonies. She is the only woman to have ever served as governor of the Commonwealth, and she and Governor Kay Ivey (Alabama) are the only two women to ever chair the waterway authority. By state law, the lieutenant governor of Kentucky serves as a member of the waterway compact along with the governor and four other members appointed by the governor. Therefore, Governor Collins was also actively involved with the waterway while serving as Governor Julian Carroll's lieutenant governor. Steve Beshear served as her lieutenant governor. He was later elected governor, and his son, Andy Beshear, also was elected to two terms as the Commonwealth's chief executive. All these Kentucky leaders have actively supported the waterway. Shown here with Governor Collins and me are authority staff members, William "Chubby" Ellis and Pat Broocks Ross.

The evening before the ceremony, after having dinner with all the distinguished guests, I decided to drive to the dedication site for one final check before retiring after a very long day. We'd contracted to have several thousand balloons filled with helium and stored inside a barge parked behind the speaker stand. The balloons were to be released at the end of the ceremony. I decided to check to see what progress the contractor was making to inflate all the balloons. I was shocked when I saw that he, his wife, and two children were inflating the balloons and had made very little progress. He assured me that they were working all night and would have them inflated in time for the ceremony. I learned a lesson: Do not necessarily always accept the lowest bid. I dismissed the release of balloons as a lost cause and went home.

The next morning, we were greeted with one of the hottest days ever recorded on June 1 in Columbus. Temps were in the mid-90s by the time the ceremony began. Despite the heat and an early start of 9 a.m., several thousand people had arrived for the ceremony. About as many people or more were on the east side enjoying the exhibits, vendors, and other attractions. The number was far from the attendance projections of 100,000, but it was still a very respectable crowd, considering the conditions. The large number of other celebrations that occurred throughout the waterway region prior to the main event likely affected the attendance. With the arrival of the dignitaries from Washington and the other special guests, the dedication began with an impressive demonstration of skills by the Army's Golden Knights paratrooper team. Eight members jumped from several thousand feet high, and all, carrying an American flag, landed on a bullseye in a very small area between the dais and the seated spectators. Each member carried a small container of water from one of the 23 states that now had access to the Tenn-Tom via connecting waterways. It was a spectacular event by the Golden Knights and certainly one of the highlights of the ceremony.

One of the highlights of the Columbus ceremony, which was sponsored by the waterway authority and the Corps of Engineers, was Army's Golden Knights. The eight-member parachutist team landed on a small square between the dais and the audience. Each team member carried vials of water from the 23 states that now have access to the Tenn-Tom. The water, collected by the Corps, was poured into a large basin that John Marsh, secretary of the Army, and Congressman Tom Bevill symbolically released into the Tenn-Tom by turning a large valve as shown in an earlier photograph.

Secretary of the Army Marsh, the top official from Washington, read a message from President Reagan, who congratulated all the waterway supporters for their "foresight, perseverance, and patience." The President concluded, "This truly resembles an achievement of environmentally sensitive engineering and cooperation between private citizens and their government and is a model for the rest of the nation." Such platitudes from the President certainly set a positive tone for the dedication and for the waterway's future.

All the speakers showed mercy on those sitting and standing in the torrid heat by making their remarks very brief. The ceremony concluded by mixing waters from the 23 states with the waters of the Tenn-Tom. Secretary Marsh and Congressman Bevill turned a large wheel resembling a valve while the decanters of water "mixed" in a basin that emptied into the waterway. It was certainly a vivid demonstration of the ceremony's theme, "Mixing of the Waters." While that was going on, the balloons were supposed to be released. Seeing none, I rushed to the barge where they had been inflated and stored during the night. Much to my dismay if not horror, I saw the contractor and his family scooping up balloons and tossing them over the side of the barge. Apparently, with the hot, humid weather and with the helium in the balloons several hours old, only a few of the balloons rose as intended. Thank goodness the balloon release was not written in the program. Few ever knew of the disaster. It just so happened that a couple hundred or so that made it over the side of the barge floated together in a slight current toward the lock, just like little ducks. Several who saw them facetiously complimented me for my ability to get all those balloons to float together toward the lock and dam.

After lunch, those of us who were going to the waterway festivities in Mobile flew there on charter flights from Columbus Air Force Base and arrived just in time as that celebration was getting underway. During the flight, I met Louie Nunn, a former governor of Kentucky. He had been instrumental in getting President Nixon to initially fund the waterway's construction. I was impressed that he had enough interest to return to participate in the dedication after being off the waterway authority for more than a decade. I knew he was my kind of guy when he took off his suit coat to reveal he was packing a pistol on his belt. I was also impressed that Mississippi Governor Allain, the authority's incoming chairman, had chosen to join us in Mobile. I had heard that he did not like to fly, and for that reason his office had initially said he most likely would not participate in the Mobile ceremony. In Mobile, the city had arranged for two buses to transport us, one to the hotel and the other to the stage for the ceremony. The buses were late arriving, and everyone had to stand on the tarmac in temperatures that seemed even hotter than in Columbus. After several sweaty minutes with some of us huddling underneath the wings of the two planes for shade, the buses finally arrived. I noticed that Governor Allain was not getting onto the bus for the dignitaries going directly to the ceremony. When I started to direct him to that bus, he asked, "Where is this bus going?" I answered, "The hotel," and he smiled and quickly said, "Then that's where I'm going." He, like all of us, had enjoyed as much celebration as he wanted that day, and his room at the hotel was beckoning him. We had reserved rooms at the Riverview Plaza Hotel, which was near the ceremony at the State Docks and was located on the parade route. When we arrived, the hotel lobby was jammed with bystanders who had come inside to escape the oppressive heat. They had overtaxed the hotel's cooling system, and all the elevators were malfunctioning. After a long delay, everyone, including Governor Allain, was able to retreat to their rooms using the stairs. It was not a pleasant way to end a very long day.

The Mobile Chamber and others had planned the program and the ceremony, including a Mardi Gras-style parade downtown. Speakers included Senators Heflin and Denton, Governor Wallace, Alabama Congressman Sonny Callahan, former Congressman Jack Edwards, and others. Callahan would later rise in seniority and become chairman of the House Energy and Water Development Appropriations Subcommittee that Bevill had chaired. His influence would prove to be invaluable in funding the operation and maintenance of the waterway. That evening, the authority hosted a dinner for about 400 at the Riverview Plaza where there were more speeches. Dinner that

Saturday evening finally ended two hectic days of celebrations, all of which helped memorialize the long-awaited culmination of a dream shared by many generations. The Tennessee-Tombigbee Waterway was now a reality.

The Tenn-Tom Authority held a dinner in Columbus, Mississippi, in August 1987 to honor Congressmen Jamie Whitten (Mississippi), Tom Bevill (Alabama), and Sonny Montgomery (Mississippi) for their leadership and support of the waterway. All three had participated in an inspection trip of the waterway aboard the Corps' flagship, M/V *Mississippi*. Having these three waterway champions together afforded a rare opportunity to honor them at an event on the waterway. Several hundred of their constituents attended the dinner. Shown here at the dinner are, from left: David Landreth (Tennessee), the authority's vice chairman; Congressman Whitten; Congressman Bevill; Congressman Montgomery, and me.

JOURNEY TO THE RIVER 247

This map shows the completed Tennessee-Tombigbee Waterway in relation to existing river systems, the states that the Tenn-Tom impacts, and the mileage savings created by the waterway.

Chapter XXII
Setting New, Higher Standards

As mentioned earlier, the Tenn-Tom Waterway established several precedents or set new standards for the design, construction, and operation of future water resources development projects, including waterways. For example, projects are no longer planned and designed for achieving the maximum level of national economic income. Equal consideration must now be given to minimizing impacts on environmental quality as well as for its enhancement.

New Spoil Disposal Techniques

Before Tenn-Tom, the common practice of dredging a navigation channel was to dispose of the dredged material along the banks of the waterway or stream. This process was not only unsightly, but also much of the material eventually made its way back into the channel, which caused turbidity and other water quality issues. The Mobile District developed a new process by depositing over 84 million cubic yards of material dredged from the so-called River Section into upland diked disposal areas. They were designed as a two-tier system that enabled the water pumped into the system to return to the river once all the sand, gravel, and other solids had settled out. The spoil areas were located out of sight of the waterway with a buffer area of trees and other vegetation. They were located where dredging was needed to establish the navigation but also had enough capacity to accommodate future dredging during the 50-year economic life of the project. This new process not only reduced overall costs but was also a big plus for the environment. The method is now commonplace along most waterways, as well as at ports that require dredging.

The Nashville District faced an even greater challenge to find an economical and environmentally friendly way to dispose of some 150 million cubic yards of earth excavated during the construction of the channel through the 29-mile Divide Cut at the northern end of the waterway. The enormous amount of excavation, nearly rivaling that removed in building the Panama Canal, was not accomplished by using hydraulic dredges but with conventional earth-moving equipment. Therefore, hauling costs dictated the need to find nearby disposal areas. The solution was to deposit the material in the valleys between hills in what is known to be highest elevations in Mississippi. These deposits were contoured and landscaped in a manner to avoid an unnatural setting. Topsoil was saved and used to finish these areas with native grasses. It is difficult now to distinguish these areas from the natural terrain except for the small ponds that were built to accommodate waterfowl and other wildlife.

Recreation Development

Recreation is generally a congressionally authorized purpose of most multi-purpose water projects, including waterways. However, it is typically viewed as a lower priority need, and its development usually follows navigation, or the primary purpose of a project, long after the project has been completed and operating. The time lag of finally completing the congressionally approved recreation facilities can be years if not decades. That was not the case with the Tenn-Tom. About $50 million of these facilities were designed and built during the waterway's construction, and most were open for the enjoyment of the public when the navigation feature was completed. These first-class facilities include seven class-AAA campgrounds, one located on each of the main lakes that provide a total of nearly 750 modern campsites with all the amenities that campers expect. There are 69 additional recreation areas that offer picnic tables and similar attractions, as well as numerous boat-launching areas. For the first time ever for a waterway project, two environmental education centers and two visitor centers were built as important components of the Tenn-Tom.

One of the visitor centers was planned to be built where U.S. Highway 82 crosses the waterway at Columbus, Mississippi. Columbus was selected since it is about the midpoint on the waterway and would offer more to visitors than most other highway crossings. Senator Stennis supported that location as did the authority — until it became a political issue. We learned that Congressman Bevill had decided to build the center in Pickens County, the only county in his congressional district that is on the waterway. Senator Stennis chose to demur, and the center was built next to Bevill Lock and Dam. It is a beautiful replica of an antebellum home, but because of its remote location, it attracts few visitors.

The Corps, wanting to help the congressman justify building the facility in Pickensville, called it the Corps' Southeast Regional Visitors Center. That moniker did not last long, and it's now referred to simply as the Bevill Visitors Center. The Corps also chose that location to moor the decommissioned M/V *Montgomery*, the snag boat once used to clear debris and other obstructions from waterways within the Mobile District. The boat was initially open to the public, but its hull and structure deteriorated, making the *Montgomery* in dire need of dry docking for some costly repairs. Visitation dramatically declined after a few years. The Corps offered to give the boat free of charge to the city of Montgomery, its namesake, and the city expressed an interest in acquiring it as an added riverfront attraction. Al Wise, the waterway operations manager, and I requested time at a Pickens County Commission meeting to explain the deteriorating conditions of the snag boat and to say that the Corps was entertaining an offer to transfer the boat to the city of Montgomery. Attending the meeting was an elderly lady who chaired the county's historical association, along with several of her disciples. She lambasted Al and me and told us in no uncertain terms "that Mr. Bevill had given them that boat," and we had no right to move it or give it to anyone. After we'd endured much scolding from the county's "little old ladies in tennis shoes," it was obvious to everyone that our proposal had just been shot down in flames. I told Al that meeting was the closest he and I would ever come to being "tarred, feathered, and run out of town on a rail." After considerable expense to lift the boat out of the river and make repairs, the M/V *Montgomery* now sits on the riverbank of Aliceville Lake next to the Bevill Center.

These modern and well-maintained recreation facilities became an immediate draw for campers, boaters, fishermen, and outdoor enthusiasts. Nearly 40 years later, they continue to attract nearly 2 million visitors each year, generating over $60 million in economic impacts and greatly benefiting the communities along the waterway.

Wildlife Mitigation

One of the Tenn-Tom's most acclaimed successes was the early planning and expedited execution of a plan to address adverse effects of its construction on wildlife. The Fish and Wildlife Coordination Act of 1934 was enacted "to promote the conservation of wildlife, fish, and game and for other purposes." The law was later amended in 1946, 1948, and in 1958, during the so-called big dam-building era as Congress recognized the possible adverse impacts these projects could have on natural resources. These amendments helped guarantee that fish and wildlife conservation had equal consideration with the other purposes of a water project, whether that be flood control, hydropower, or navigation. Later, the Clean Water Act (Section 404 became the primary vehicle for protecting wetlands), the National Environmental Policy Act, the Endangered Species Act, and other similar statues gave the U.S. Fish and Wildlife Service (FWS) a seat at the table with the Corps during the planning and construction phases of a project and in formulating a plan to mitigate losses of wildlife habitat.

The Mobile District began working with FWS and the two state wildlife agencies as early as 1975 to assess and monitor the damage the waterway's construction might have on affected lands and to start preparing a mitigation plan. The Nashville District was responsible for the Divide Section of the waterway. More than 85,000 acres had been purchased in fee and some 25,000 acres of easements acquired for construction and operation of the waterway, of which 44,000 acres were inundated. Studies determined that 60,000 acres of wildlife habitat would be adversely affected, of which 34,000 acres were forested wetlands, the most productive of all habitats.

Mitigation plans for water resource projects that involve the acquisition of land must be specifically approved by the Congress to be eligible for federal funding. There was a wide disparity between the Corps' findings and those of the FWS concerning the amount of compensation needed to mitigate losses caused by the Tenn-Tom. Compensation included the acquisition of habitat lands by a federal agency such as the Corps to ensure their preservation as prime habitat by removing them from private ownership. FWS recommended the acquisition and management of 95,500 acres of new habitat, while the Corps concluded that 48,700 acres would be adequate to mitigate the losses. The agencies' different methodologies and professional judgements caused the wide disparity. Biological assessments of this kind are not hard science.

The authority supported expediting the mitigation while the waterway still enjoyed strong bipartisan congressional leadership who could help fund the project in a timely manner. Although we supported a wildlife mitigation plan, we had some concerns that had to be addressed. We were opposed to acquiring any additional lands in counties along the waterway. The Corps, unlike TVA, does not pay ad valorem taxes for land it acquires, and the waterway counties were already burdened by tax losses from nearly 86,000 acres of project lands taken off the tax rolls. The authority also recommended that no additional land be acquired by condemnation. We wanted all the mitigation land to be acquired from willing sellers. The Corps initially objected, contending that it likely could not acquire tracts large enough to manage without the use of eminent domain. The authority also recommended that the mitigation project funds not be comingled with those appropriated for the operation and maintenance of the waterway. We wanted those funds to be included in a separate line item in the appropriations bill.

After undergoing several months of interagency reviews and considering public comments, Congress authorized the mitigation project as Section 601 of the Water Resources Development Act of 1986. The law authorized that 72,500 acres of land already acquired for the waterway be managed as wildlife habitat, as well as 20,000 acres of federal lands along Okatibbee Lake in east Mississippi and along the Black Warrior-Tombigbee and Alabama River waterways. In addition, it authorized the purchase of 88,000 acres of additional land from willing sellers with priority given to purchasing forested wetlands or prime wildlife habitat. The law further specified that not less than 20,000 acres be acquired in the Mobile-Tensaw River Delta and not less than 25,000 acres from the Pascagoula River, the Pearl River, and the Mississippi River deltas, with the remaining land purchased from anywhere within the two states, subject to the review and consent of the two state wildlife agencies.

The Congress quickly approved the project for funding, and the acquisition of the 88,000 so-called separable lands was completed in less than a decade at a total cost of about $66 million, all from willing sellers. Soon after the enactment, it became obvious that it was a mistake to have designated all the waterway's property as wildlife habitat. Doing so not only hampered the operation and maintenance of the waterway but also precluded future economic development, including ports and other infrastructure needed to support navigation. To remedy the problem, Congress amended the 1986 Act by removing 3,000 acres of project land by purchasing the equivalent amount of acreage deemed prime habitat. A lot of the project lands included in the mitigation project had limited habitat value. The amendment also allowed the Corps to continue using some 6,500 acres of disposal areas for dredging. Senator Trent Lott, by then the Senate majority leader, was instrumental in getting these much-needed changes enacted. Congruent to the authority's wishes, Congress agreed to include appropriations to the two states for managing about 126,000 acres of the mitigation lands as a separate line item in the budget for the Corps. Those annual appropriations are transferred directly to the two state agencies for their use. Recently, those designated funds have averaged about $2 million annually. The lands managed by the states were consolidated into several wildlife management areas that are open to the public for hunting, bird watching, and other activities.

The Tennessee-Tombigbee Mitigation Project set a high standard for future mitigation projects because of its inclusiveness and its expeditious approval and execution. Its accomplishments are not only recognized by the Corps but also by FWS and other conservation groups, since many mitigation projects are never completed. Much of the credit for the Tenn-Tom Mitigation Project can be attributed to N.D. "Skeeter" McClure, chief of the Mobile District's Planning and Environmental Division, and his interdisciplinary team, including Mike Eubanks, Glenn Coffee, Brian Peck, and others. The continued unwavering support of the waterway's congressional delegation, even after its completion, helped secure the $66 million needed to expeditiously complete the project. It is certainly one of the waterway's legacies.

Endangered Species

Federal protection of threatened and endangered species has killed many needed and meritorious economic development projects. The Congress enacted the Federal Endangered Species Act in 1973 (ESA) to conserve and protect from extinction the bald eagle, the California condor, the American alligator, the black-footed ferret, and other species that can be identified as part of our national heritage. During the past 50 years, the federal list of threatened or endangered species, both plants and animals, has grown to more than 1,300 species located in all 50 states. Federal protection of these species could adversely affect any proposed plans for economic growth. The listings were based solely on biological considerations and without considering any negative economic impacts or social costs, including the diminution of higher valued uses of those properties being included in a protected species-designated critical habitat. However, the Congress temporarily broadened the ESA's decision-making process in 1978, albeit briefly, to include consideration of the externalities associated with protecting a species.

The Tennessee Valley Authority (TVA) started construction of the so-called Tellico Dam in 1967 on the Hiwassee River near Ft. Louden in East Tennessee. The project was envisaged not as a typical water resources project but more of a land development enterprise that would attract new industrial development, add new recreation opportunities, and build from scratch a new modern community. It immediately drew strong opposition, especially from landowners of the 38,000 acres TVA acquired for the project. Much of it was taken by eminent domain. They saw the project as an endeavor not "for the public good," and some had to be forcibly removed from their homes, which garnered national media coverage. The state's fish and game agency were against it because the 14,000-acre lake would decimate the trout fishery in the Little Tennessee River. The Tennessee Farm Bureau as well as the Cherokee Nation strongly objected to building the dam. TVA ignored all these objections, which included a letter from Governor Winfield Dunn opposing its construction, until some college students nearly torpedoed the project. In 1973, while on a field trip to the dam site, a group of University of Tennessee (UT) students with their biology professor discovered the snail darter, a rare minnow allegedly found only in the Little Tennessee River. Coincidently, that was the same year ESA was enacted. Two years later in 1975, the U.S. Fish and Wildlife Service complied with a request to list the fish for protection. At that time, the dam was more than 50 percent complete.

TVA continued to ignore the conflict with the tiny fish and kept building until a UT law student filed a lawsuit to stop the project, citing that its construction was in violation of ESA. The district court's decision rendered in May 1976 not to enjoin construction was immediately appealed to the Sixth Circuit Court of Appeals, which ruled in January 1977 that Tellico was in direct violation of ESA. The Sixth Circuit enjoined TVA to cease its construction. After the U.S. Supreme Court affirmed the Appeals Court's ruling by a 6 to 3 vote in January 1978, TVA petitioned FWS to delist the fish, which it denied. Although the Tellico Dam was 90 percent complete, the project was dead in the water, thanks to some energetic college students and a small minnow.

The Tenn-Tom was facing similar possible conflicts with ESA. Alabama ranks fourth in the nation in its diversity of flora and fauna. For example, it has 180 different species of mussels, 60 percent of those found in the nation. It ranks third with 117 endangered or threatened species, following only California and Hawaii. About half of those are mussels. Mississippi also has an abundance of mussels, nearly 25 different species, of which eight species found in the Tombigbee River and its tributaries are considered rare and endangered.

I was surprised and certainly relieved that the plaintiffs for the two landmark federal lawsuits filed to stop Tenn-Tom focused little attention on the waterway's impact on these mussels. Had they done so, they might have been more successful. Construction of the Tenn-Tom, especially its channelization and impoundment, drastically altered the habitat of mussels residing in the main stem of the Tombigbee River. To better prepare for any possible legal issues with ESA and the mussels, the authority hired one of the nation's leading malacologists, Dr. Henry Van der Schalie of the University of Michigan, as a consultant. While his research and analyses did not disclose any hard evidence to oppose the listing of the mussels in question, he was invaluable in preparing our attorney, Hunter Gholson, and the other members of the defense team, to better represent our case if this issue came up during the two trials. We all learned more about mussels from Dr. Van der Schalie than we ever needed or wanted to know.

Mussels need free-flowing streams with little suspended or deposited sediments and are sensitive to water quality and water temperatures. Most all mussels also need a host, usually a small fish, to enable propagation. These hosts might also be harmed by drastic changes in a mussel's habitat. Three species of mussels found in the Tombigbee were likely extirpated by the waterway's impoundments and dredging of its channels, but they and five other species are located and now protected in tributary streams. The federal designation of these streams, including the upper east fork of the Tombigbee, the Buttahatchee River, and the Luxapallila Creek, as critical habitat for these protected mussels would likely preclude any future changes for flood control, drainage, or streambank stabilization measures. I dreaded the day a mussel would be found within the dredged material deposited in one of the spoil areas, knowing that discovery would undoubtedly shut down any further work in that area for untold time, pending exhaustive surveys searching for more mussels. Fortunately, that never happened.

As more and more species were listed for federal protection, more conflicts arose between both small and large economic development plans and ESA. A notable example was a major real estate development project in the Birmingham area. Two small fish, the Cahaba shiner and goldline darter, both found in the Cahaba River, had been proposed for federal protection as endangered species. That designation threatened an estimated $1 billion proposed commercial and residential development along the river in the Birmingham metropolitan area of Jefferson and Shelby counties. Those plans included a 3,000-acre multiple use Riverchase land development project by Harbert Construction Corporation, an international firm headquartered in Birmingham. Facing such dire economic consequences, Harbert employed Dr. John Moeller, a law professor in the School of Business and Commerce at the University of Alabama, to work with William Satterfield, the company's legal counsel, to challenge the listing of the two fish and to begin working with Congress to reform ESA.

They were successful in generating enough scientific evidence that questioned the justification for listing the two fish, resulting in FWS withdrawing both proposals. The Cahaba shiner was eventually listed as an endangered species in 1990, by which time it no longer posed a threat to the development. A large population of this two-inch, silver-colored minnow was also found in the upper Locust Fork of the Black Warrior River, a nearby but different river basin. The goldline darter was eventually listed as a threatened species in 1992. It has also now been discovered outside of the Cahaba River in some tributaries of the Coosawattee River, a tributary to the Coosa River in Georgia.

Satterfield and Moeller were quick to find allies to amend ESA, including the Tenn-Tom Authority. We were not only concerned about the implications of the protected mussels on the construction and operation of the waterway but also the possibility of the freckle belly madtom being listed. Its name would be amusing if its threats to economic development were not so serious. Although considered by some as endangered, the small catfish could be found throughout the Mobile River Basin, including the Tombigbee River, and in the Pearl River basin in Mississippi and Louisiana. It nevertheless posed a serious threat to the waterway's continued progress, but it was not listed until more than 45 years later. In 2023, FWS, after being petitioned by an Arizona-based group called the Center for Biological Diversity, added 134 miles of the upper Coosa River in Georgia and Tennessee as critical habitat for the fish, which it declared to be a threatened species. That ruling for protecting the fish was limited to only that reach and did not include the Tombigbee River and, therefore, posed no threat to Tenn-Tom.

The U.S. Supreme Court ruling in January 1978 that TVA's building of Tellico Dam was in direct violation of ESA reaffirmed that Congress was explicit in drafting the ESA law that said only biological considerations and not economic ones are relevant in any decision to protect a species. The national controversy about a small minnow stopping construction of Tellico Dam, a nearly completed major public works project, added more impetus for Congress to reform ESA by making the program more flexible. Even some members of the congress whose constituents had not yet been affected by the law were calling for changes. There was a growing consensus that the endangered species program as written in the law and rigidly administered by FWS was too restrictive and should be modified.

The right person to help accomplish that task was Congressman David Bowen of Mississippi, who at the time was a senior member of the U.S. House Merchant Marine and Fisheries Committee, which had jurisdiction over ESA. Bowen was one of Tenn-Tom's most ardent supporters in the House, and he was most willing to use his influence as a committee member to address any changes needed in the ESA program. After a lot of door-to-door lobbying by Satterfield, Moeller, Wilkins, and others associated with the Tenn-Tom Authority, like Barrett Shelton, a newspaper publisher in Decatur, Alabama, who elicited the support of the Cotton Council and other agricultural groups, Congress made some major changes to the ESA law. The 1978 amendments, for example, directed FWS to designate critical habitat concurrently with the listing and to describe the economic costs and other impacts of the designation. These externalities were to be considered in deciding whether to protect the species and at what costs.

The 1978 ESA amendments also established a committee to weigh the economic impacts and social costs to determine whether these implications are significant enough to outweigh the protection of the species or if modifications should be made to the critical habitat to lessen these impacts. The committee, labeled the "God Squad" by environmental groups, was composed of members representing seven federal agencies and a member from the state that would be affected by the listing. One of its first deliberations involved the snail darter versus TVA's Tellico Dam. The committee concluded by a split vote that the economic costs associated with not completing the dam were not sufficient to warrant possible extinction of the fish. The snail darter won that round of this epic battle, but TVA was the ultimate victor when Senator Howard Baker and other members of the Tennessee congressional delegation had enough political muscle to include a rider in an appropriations bill to exempt Tellico Dam from all federal laws, including ESA. President Carter reluctantly signed the bill, and the dam was completed in late 1979. As it seems to be the case involving many of these kinds of species, the snail darter was later found in several streams throughout East Tennessee, and those that were transplanted into the Hiwassee River above the dam site continued to thrive. In 1984, FWS downgraded the darter's federal protection status from endangered to threatened, thanks to TVA's successful recovery program for the minnow and its "discovery" in other streams throughout East Tennessee. In 2022, the Interior Department removed the fish entirely from the ESA program, citing its full recovery. The delisting was the fifth for a fish species since 1973 when the ESA was first established and the first for a fish in the Eastern United States. There are some who point to the controversial if not disreputable history of the snail darter as an example of the economic and societal costs of protecting a species of questionable justification under the auspices of ESA.

Despite the God Squad's surprising decision to write off over $100 million already spent on Tellico Dam for the full protection of a somewhat dubious ESA decision, environmental interests were hell bent to rescind the 1978 amendments. They launched a stealth attack while those of us who worked hard to reform this controversial federal program frankly went to sleep at the wheel. Much to our surprise and disappointment, they were successful in 1982 in having Congress eliminate any consideration of the economic impacts of a listing by limiting ESA decisions to only biological considerations. This serious setback came before we were faced with the most potentially consequential confrontation with the endangered species program — the protection of the Alabama sturgeon.

There were once thousands of shovel-nosed sturgeons in the Mobile River Basin. However, they were over harvested by commercial fishermen until only nine had been caught since 1989. The fish is now called the Alabama sturgeon, although DNA tests determined it is genetically the same species as the shovelnose sturgeon found throughout the vast Mississippi River Basin. Its historic habitat was throughout the Mobile River Basin, including the Tombigbee and Black Warrior rivers, but it appears to be now confined to the Alabama River. All nine were caught in the lower reach of the Alabama River, and none have been found elsewhere, despite more than 4,000 hours of exhaustive searches in the lower Tombigbee River and other streams.

FWS first classified the Alabama sturgeon as a separate species in 1976 based on taxonomy of a few museum specimens of fish caught in the 1960s. However, DNA tests conducted in 1999 by ESA's own scientist concluded that, genetically, the fish was the same species as the common shovelnose sturgeon. Nevertheless, both FWS and the Interior Department flagrantly ignored these findings and were caught trying to suppress the DNA evidence to prevail in the listing process. Those who would be affected by the listing knew they had an uphill battle with FWS. However, they chose to fight this unwarranted if not unconscionable action by the federal government to protect a fish of dubious species classification and whose continuing existence is highly questionable.

To do so, they formed the Alabama-Tombigbee Rivers Coalition (Coalition), a non-profit association composed of waterway associations like the authority, state agencies, and 16 businesses that rely on waterway transportation as an integral part of their businesses. Sheldon Morgan, then head of the Warrior-Tombigbee Waterway Association, was elected chairman of the Coalition, and I was its vice chair. The Coalition hired Bill Satterfield and his team of capable environmental attorneys at Balch and Bingham LLP as their legal counsel. Satterfield, since his earlier involvement with the Cahaba shiner and the 1978 ESA amendments, had acquired a reputation for being one of the most capable environmental attorneys in the Southeast. Dr. Mike Howell, a professor of biology at Samford University and a well-known ichthyologist, was also hired to research the sturgeon and especially critique the science FWS used in its deliberations.

FWS announced in June 1993 its proposal to list the fish as an endangered species. FWS scheduled a public hearing at Mobile College the following October. The Coalition advised the agency that the auditorium at the college was limited to 400 people and that it would not be able to accommodate the crowd likely to attend. FWS dismissed our concerns, stating that the most it had ever seen at a hearing on an endangered species was fewer than 50 people. The Coalition stressed the importance of having a large turnout, and we were confident there would be an overflow crowd. Ray Vaughn, one of the principal advocates for protecting the fish, was quoted as saying the attendance included about 500 attendees against the proposed listing, while 80 supported the listing. If he is accurate, there were nearly 200 concerned citizens who were unable to attend the hearing and had to stand outside the auditorium and listen to the proceeding from a speaker or watch through its windows. Those attending included members of Congress, state legislators, and other state and local officials, all of whom spoke in opposition to the listing. FWS officials were embarrassed that so many were unable to participate. Later, in June 1999, when FWS announced its final proposal to list the fish, it held another public hearing in Montgomery. More than 800 people attended to express their opposition to the proposal. That hearing did not end until the wee hours of the following morning. These two events made it very clear that the vast majority of the public was opposed to the proposal to protect the sturgeon, given its impact on jobs and the economy of the affected area.

Satterfield and his legal team filed two federal lawsuits against FWS and the secretary of Interior, which resulted in favorable rulings for the Coalition. One of those cases charged the Interior secretary with violating the Federal Advisory Committee Act (FACA). The Court ruled that Interior's violations of FACA were so egregious that it forbade it from using the results of its unlawfully constituted sturgeon review committee. The Coalition also sued FWS for not designating critical habitat, including its costs to the public, concurrently with the proposed listing of the sturgeon, which was a violation of ESA. It was rumored that FWS might use the fish's historic range as the designated critical habitat, which would include not only the Alabama River but also the Black Warrior and Tombigbee rivers. Such an expansive area would have huge economic costs and is likely why FWS refused to comply with that provision of the law. A study done by the University of South Alabama and Troy University predicted a potential $11.3 billion adverse economic impact and a loss of almost 20,000 jobs over a 10-year period because of the large critical habitat designation for the protection of the fish.

The Coalition offered a new proposal as an alternative to listing the fish, which in the long run could be more beneficial to the beleaguered fish's existence. After intense negotiations among all the involved parties, including FWS, a Conservation Agreement (CA) was approved to help supplement an ongoing voluntary conservation plan by the Alabama Department of Conservation and Natural Resources for improving the fish's chance of survival. A total of $2 million had been appropriated to develop ways to capture and propagate more fish in a state-run hatchery. All parties supported this five-year, multi-million-dollar plan. The CA would also provide additional funding for more ecological and biological research, including conducting more aggressive searches to find and capture more fish for propagation and learning more about the fish's habitat needs. FWS was a reluctant participant in the CA, knowing that one of the agreed-upon conditions was that the CA would immediately terminate if or when FWS ever listed the fish as an endangered species.

That day came on May 2, 2000, after nine years of strident meetings, costly court battles, and the expenditure of funds and time, when FMS listed the Alabama sturgeon as an endangered species. Contrary to law, it did not designate critical habitat for the fish until eight years later, in 2008. The designation included 81 miles of the southern end of the Cahaba River, starting from its mouth with the Alabama River, and another 245 miles of the Alabama River from its junction with the Tombigbee River to the R.F. Henry Lock and Dam, including the majority of the navigable portion of the river. Both FWS and the Corps of Engineers are on record stating that the protection of the Alabama sturgeon will never interfere with future dredging of the Alabama River's navigation channel. However, time will tell if that commitment holds.

While I was very disappointed that we lost the battle opposing the listing of the sturgeon, I believe we did win the war. The protection of the fish and its habitat does not affect the Tombigbee River and, therefore, has no adverse impacts on the Tenn-Tom or the Warrior-Tombigbee Waterway. Ironically, in more than two decades of the fish's designation as an endangered species and subsequent actions by FWS, nothing has actually been done for the fish. Sadly, the Conservation Plan and the Conservation Agreement, both of which were terminated at the time of the endangered species listing, had offered the sturgeon its best chance of surviving and increasing its population.

The only way to legitimately defeat an endangered species proposal is legally through the judicial process by challenging the credibility of the scientific data used to justify the listing. If the federal agency is preordained to list the species and not use the best available science, including genetics, or fails to conduct an honest peer review of its findings, one is, nevertheless, doomed to failure. That was illustrated by the case of the Alabama sturgeon.

Major Change in Maintaining Tenn-Tom

The Corps of Engineers had traditionally operated and maintained its waterways and other large water resource projects by using federal employees, commonly referred to as hired labor. However, Tenn-Tom changed this long-held policy when the project's features (locks and dams) transitioned from the construction stage to operations (O&M).

The Mobile District's commander, Major General Pat Kelly (a colonel at that time) faced a perplexing conundrum as the waterway approached completion. His aggressive management style and leadership abilities helped to complete the project nearly two years ahead of schedule, resulting in substantial cost savings. The project was completed under budget at less than $2 billion. By comparison, construction of a single lock like the one being built at Kentucky Lock and Dam on the Tennessee River now costs nearly that much. With the Tenn-Tom nearing completion, the enigma confronting Kelly was how to allocate the necessary personnel to operate the 234-mile waterway with its ten locks and dams, even though Corps headquarters had not approved any additional hires for the Mobile District.

The President, through the Office of Management and Budget (OMB), sets yearly ceilings on the number of full-time employees each federal agency can hire. Restrictions on full-time employment could adversely affect program execution as much as funding constraints could. Agencies frequently appeal OMB's annual employment ceilings. The Tennessee Valley Authority was one of the federal agencies assigned to me when I was a principal budget examiner at OMB. Aubrey "Red" Wagner, TVA's chairman from 1962 to 1978, felt that the public utility was an independent agency and not beholden even to the U.S. Congress and certainly not to some "bean counters" at OMB. With such attitude of unaccountability by its chairman, TVA flagrantly ignored OMB's limits on hirings as well as other directives for several years. While TVA's noncompliance was attributed to bureaucratic arrogance, adherence to the employment ceilings also posed a challenging management issue. TVA accomplished most of its program activities with its own employees and not with private contractors, including construction of its large public works projects. Performing these functions in-house resulted in abrupt fluctuations in its personnel needs. A more restrictive hiring ceiling could force the agency to use private contractors, sometimes a more cost-effective alternative but also an anathema to TVA's decision makers. It finally took a strongly worded letter from President Nixon to Wagner and the utility's board of directors for TVA to finally comply with its employment ceilings.

Blessed with a growing program, the 35 districts of the Corps were forced to fiercely compete for additional hires while staying within the employment ceilings set by OMB. The Mobile District apparently lost in that competition with its sister districts and faced the dire prospect of operating and maintaining the Tenn-Tom with no increase in personnel. Prior to becoming commander of the Mobile District, Kelly was charged with constructing missile sites for the U.S. Air Force. He was also responsible for building airfields in Israel and developing a new missile system for the U.S. Army. He learned while in charge of those military construction projects that in some cases it was not practical to operate and maintain some of those facilities using Corps personnel. Thus, he had turned to private contractors to provide some services. Based on his experience, he concluded that contracting the Tenn-Tom's maintenance services was the best option not only for the project but also for mitigating any adverse impacts on the district's other workload.

Ed Slana, a contract specialist who became the chief of contracting for the Mobile District, helped Kelly navigate the myriad governmental rules and procedures related to federal contracts to formulate what is referred to as a cost-plus award fee (CPAF) contract.

The proposed contract included all the operation and maintenance needs of the waterway, except for the lock operators needed at the ten locks, who would remain as Corps employees. The decision to contract these waterway-related services to the private sector was not universally supported. Those currently employed to maintain other projects saw the Tenn-Tom precedent as a potential threat to their livelihood. That fear was accentuated when Kelly decided to privatize the Corps' large maintenance shop in Tuscaloosa. Those federal employees were responsible for major repairs of the eight locks and dams on the Black Warrior-Tombigbee Waterway and those on the Alabama River. Those jobs were abolished, and their work was privatized to enable those positions to be transferred to hire lock operators on the Tenn-Tom. The employees at the maintenance shop were given three options: buyouts with severance pay; voluntary retirement or separation; or reassignment to other positions within the Mobile District, including positions as lock operators for the Tenn-Tom. The affected employees did not embrace these options. There were also some throughout the Corps hierarchy, including some senior military officers at headquarters, who were not in favor of private contracting. None, though, formally protested or opposed Kelly's decision to privatize Tenn-Tom O&M. Norman Connell, who had just been promoted to become the waterway's first operations manager, did a superb job of justifying if not defending the technical and financial aspects of the private contract.

The contract was advertised and awarded to R&D Maintenance Services Inc. (R&DM) of Hennessy, Oklahoma. The CPAF contract gave the Corps the flexibility to fulfill the maintenance needs of the waterway while eliminating the need to award a plethora of small business contracts, such as for grass mowing. This contractual arrangement also enabled the Corps to more quickly respond to emergency repairs or unforeseen breakdowns. That flexibility was never more evident than on the morning of July 28, 1994, when a potential disaster occurred at Coffeeville Lock on the lower Black Warrior-Tombigbee Waterway.

Navigation locks, like other structures that include heavy machinery, require scheduled inspections and periodic repairs. To do so, stoplogs (composed of welded sheets of steel) are installed outside the two gates of the lock. This forms a water barrier, which allows the lock chamber to be emptied, facilitating inspections and repairs, if needed, to the lock, including the gates. If a lock is taken out of service for an extended time, it completely disrupts transportation on the waterway, especially if there are no duplicate locks, which is the case for Tenn-Tom and the Black Warrior-Tombigbee projects. Closures can last one month or longer. To help minimize the adverse effects on shipping, the Corps works closely with the towing industry and shippers concerning the time and duration of a closure, which is announced well in advance.

In the summer of 1994, the Mobile District had scheduled concurrent closures of six locks, two on the Tenn-Tom and four on the BWT, including the Coffeeville Lock. It is unusual to close that many locks at the same time, which challenged the district's capabilities, including those of its contractor, R&DM. The closures were mostly for inspection of the lock, with little, if any, repairs needed. Taking such a large number of locks out of operation at the same time can eliminate some future closures, especially for those locks that might have been originally scheduled for closing the following year or later.

Coffeeville Lock's outage was scheduled for July 6 to August 5, 1994, and adherence to that schedule was critical since much of the barge traffic on both waterways passes through that lock. Commerce on the system was effectively halted until Coffeeville reopened for business. The lock had been down for nearly one month when, on the morning of July 28, the stoplog structure at the downstream end of the lock failed, causing a flooding of the lock chamber and extensive damage to the miter gates at that end of the lock. R&DM was responsible for inspecting and repairing the lock. Joel Smith, the contractor's employee, now its Tenn-Tom O&M project manager, was at the lock at that time, and said, "The failure occurred at 6 a.m. at the time of a shift change when painters and other workers were not inside the lock. As a result, there were no fatalities or serious injuries to the workers."

I first learned of the failure when Colonel Robert Griffin, the Mobile District commander, called, shortly after it happened. He reported the extent of damage and asked that I not contact the South Atlantic Division or anyone in Washington about the problem. He was not trying to keep it a secret but did not want him or his staff to be distracted from devoting their complete attention to addressing the problem by having to respond to a flood of inquiries from those "up the line." He said he was making a similar request to Sheldon Morgan, my counterpart with BWT Waterway Association. We both agreed to comply with his request. Wynne Fuller, a former chief of the operations division of Mobile District, said when the colonel first witnessed the extensive damages to the lock, he asked Ed Varner, who was operations manager for the BWT, what his best estimate was for how long it would take to get the lock back in operation. Griffin was expecting Varner to say it would take at least a couple of months. Fuller said, "Ed took a draw on his pipe, slowly looked around, and said, 'We'll have it back in operation in a couple of weeks,' and they did." The lock reopened on August 19 by manually operating the downstream miter gates with "come a-longs," a winching device, until the damaged machinery could be replaced. This amazing turnaround can be attributed to the hard work and resourcefulness of the Corps team, like Ed Varner and Pat Langan, and those with R&DM, such as Joel Smith and Brooks Ferguson. The contractor was able to immediately secure the services needed and procure replacement parts, instead of the Corps having to secure those through its more time-consuming contract procedures. Operation and use of the lock, including its gates, was fully restored on October 25, less than three months after the failure.

R&DM has been the successful bidder for every subsequent maintenance services contract for the Tenn-Tom and is currently the maintenance contractor for the Black Warrior-Tombigbee and the Alabama River systems. This impressive record of performance is a testament to the outstanding work by R&DM during nearly four decades of service. Its success in winning contract renewals has been challenged by its competitors with no success. One company challenged one of the renewals by filing a federal lawsuit against the Corps and R&DM. The trial was held in the Federal District Court of North Alabama in Huntsville. I was summoned as a witness for the defense. It was the first time I had ever been that personally involved in a federal case. After I'd prepared and spent a couple of days nervously sitting in the courtroom waiting to be called to the stand, the judge dismissed the case before I had to testify. Although I agreed to be a witness, I questioned what I could offer for the defense since I had not been directly involved in the contract award process. I was there merely as a third-party witness who could speak about the prior performance of the contractor. The judge's dismissal and not having to testify were as pleasing to me as I'm sure they must have been to R&DM and the Corps.

There have been some who have, as a cost-cutting measure, proposed eliminating lock staff by operating the facilities remotely. I would oppose not having a person present at the locks because of safety concerns, especially for recreational boaters who might transit the locks. In the case of Tenn-Tom and the other waterways R&DM maintains, I would propose that the positions of the lock operators be incorporated into the maintenance contracts, thus eliminating them as government positions. That would likely result in cost savings while also maintaining safe operations. It has always been a mystery to me why the Corps has never transferred the maintenance of other waterways to private contractors, based on the successful experience of Tenn-Tom's use of private contracting. I believe that transition would result in cost savings and certainly would facilitate more timely responses to emergencies.

Robert Griffin, after leaving the Mobile District, had an outstanding career with the Corps of Engineers. He attained the rank of major general and was the deputy commander of the Corps when he retired. He kept a piece of the failed stop log on his desk throughout his career. He often mentioned that the success of responding to the failure at Coffeeville Lock in such a timely way played a role in his later achievements with the Corps.

Regrettably, neither the Corps of Engineers nor Congress has shown interest in using private contractors for maintenance of other water projects. However, Congress has shown little compunction to put the Corps out of the dredging business. At the urging of private dredging companies, Congress has systematically reduced the Corps' dredging capabilities, although it has the responsibility to maintain congressionally authorized navigation channels at 400 ports and on some 12,000 miles of waterways. Since the late 1970s, the Corps has had to rely on private contractors to meet these dredging needs because of Congress's refusal to authorize it to acquire any new dredges or replacements for its aging fleet.

Private dredging interests celebrated a resounding victory in 1978 when it persuaded Congress to enact legislation directing the Corps to maintain only a minimum fleet of dredges for the sole purpose of performing emergency dredging. The upshot of this congressional directive was that private contractors would enjoy the spoils (no pun intended) of all the nation's dredging needs, whether the industry had the capability to meet that growing demand or not. A later general accounting office study found that such dependence on private contracting had increased the costs for dredging performed at federal projects, while the total amount of dredged material had actually decreased. We were having similar bad experiences with fulfilling Tenn-Tom's annual dredging needs.

Dredging is the major component of the waterway's annual maintenance needs. Each year, hydrographic surveys identify shoaling areas that need to be dredged. These needs are included in a bid that is advertised the following year. In the 1990s the response from the dredging companies was less than satisfactory for advertised maintenance work for both Tenn-Tom as well as the Black Warrior-Tombigbee. Sometimes only one company submitted a bid, and its price was above the government cost estimate. A couple of advertisements produced not one bidder. At that time, there was a considerable amount of dredging work available along the Gulf Coast, which was more attractive to the dredging companies than work on the inland waterways. For example, mobilization and demobilization costs were less for coastal dredging, and much of the dredged material along the

Gulf Coast is discharged into open water. Material dredged along the Tenn-Tom must be discharged into upland disposal areas, which adds to the unit cost of dredging.

During one of my frequent meetings with Alabama Congressman Sonny Callahan, I informed him of the Mobile District's difficulties in getting private contractors to respond to the dredging needs of its inland waterways. Callahan succeeded Jack Edwards, one of the Tenn-Tom's champions, and had acquired enough seniority to chair the Energy and Water Development Appropriations Subcommittee from 2001 to 2003. He, like Tom Bevill of Alabama and John Myers of Indiana, who had chaired the subcommittee, was a strong advocate for the Corps of Engineers and its projects, including the Tenn-Tom. I explained to him that the Congress had created this problem of fulfilling the dredging needs by purposely getting the Corps out of the dredging business as a favor to private interests. He was noncommittal during our meeting, and I was surprised when his subcommittee's report on the appropriations bill was released. It contained language directing the Corps to study the feasibility of the Mobile District acquiring a hydraulic cutterhead dredge for use on the Tenn-Tom and its other inland waterways. I was ecstatic. The directive, if nothing else, was a shot across the bow of the dredging industry, and I was convinced it would result in some changes.

The ink of the subcommittee's report had hardly dried when I received a telephone call from Robert Dawson, president of Dawson and Associates, a Washington-based governmental affairs firm that specializes in federal water resources and environmental matters. Dawson, an Alabamian and a friend, was assistant secretary of the Army for civil works, the top political position for the Corps, during the Reagan Administration. He was also an assistant director of OMB before starting his consulting business. I was honored to join his group after I retired from the Tenn-Tom Waterway Authority. He was calling on behalf of a client, one of the larger dredging companies, that was concerned about the directive in the subcommittee's report. I explained to Dawson that what led to Chairman Callahan's directive was private industry's inability to timely and cost effectively respond to the Tenn-Tom's dredging needs.

Callahan retired soon after, and his directive did not result in the Mobile District getting a dredge, but it certainly got the attention of the dredging contractors. Not by happenstance, when the Corps advertised for the Tenn-Tom's maintenance dredging the following year, it received three bids, all competitive within the government cost estimate. Earlier bid advertisements generated at best one bidder at a "take it or leave it" price, well above the government estimate. I retired a couple of years later, but I believe the dredging industry continues to be responsive to the Corps' annual bid requests. Hopefully, that will continue. The Corps recently acquired a small dredge for emergency dredging needs on the Tennessee-Tombigbee. That will be of enormous benefit to the waterway. It was acquired with no objections from private industry, and its acquisition was likely not as a result of the so-called Callahan directive. Rather, the acquisition was in accordance with the 1970 congressional legislation allowing the Corps to have a small fleet of dredges for emergency uses only.

The locks on the Tenn-Tom can accommodate eight conventional-sized hopper barges and a tow boat. That single movement of commerce amounts to 12,000 tons or 500 semi-trucks, loaded with 24 tons, that relieve congestion on the highways. Barges are also more economical, more fuel efficient, and safer than truck or rail for shipping commerce for long distances. The availability of the Tenn-Tom as an alternative to the lower Mississippi River barge route during a prolonged drought during the summer of 1988 saved shippers millions of dollars. That unexpected, sudden increase in commercial use also demonstrated that the waterway has the capacity to efficiently handle more than 30 million tons each year and that it could accommodate larger sizes and tows through double lockages as shown here.

Chapter XXIII
If You Build It, Will They Come?

There are some 25,000 miles of navigable waterways serving the United States, of which 12,000 miles are operated and maintained by the U.S. Army Corps of Engineers. That now includes the 234-mile Tennessee-Tombigbee Waterway. These waterways provide economical transportation to 38 states and hundreds of counties, many of which have as many or more assets to attract private investments and economic growth as those areas served by Tenn-Tom. Colleagues associated with more developed waterways warned us the Tenn-Tom would not develop itself. It would require planning, marketing, and promotions, as well as attendant land-based infrastructure, if the waterway were ever to achieve its potential for stimulating economic growth. Infrastructure needs include ports and terminals, waterfront industrial sites with the necessary appurtenances to support heavy industry, and reliable and efficient rail and highway connections. Very little of those needs existed along the waterway when it opened for commercial use.

As soon as the Tenn-Tom's construction began, the Waterway Authority began preparing for its completion. It secured a Section 107 planning grant from the U.S. Department of Housing and Urban

Development and hired a consultant to work with Bruce Hanson, a staff member, to begin a planning process. The consultant, Dr. Nick Thomas, was a professor of Urban Planning at Akron University. Hanson had a similar background in planning. Both were making progress when those activities were preempted by the 1972 lawsuit and other more pressing issues crucial to the waterway's fate. In the mid-1970s, Congress, through the efforts of the waterway's delegation, provided funding to the Corps of Engineers to conduct a comprehensive study to help the entire waterway region better prepare for growth. Joe Birindelli of the Mobile District's Planning Division managed the study. The so-called Tennessee-Tombigbee Waterway Corridor Study encompassed 51 counties in four states located along or near the Tenn-Tom and the Tennessee River. The study compiled information about each county's resources, both natural and labor; and important demographic data. Studies also assessed the waterway corridor's potential impacts on industrial development, tourism, and agriculture weighed against needs such as education, skilled workers, and other impediments. Voluminous amounts of data were collected on a county-by-county basis and assembled in two computerized programs called an Economic Impact Assessment Model and an Integrated Data Analysis System. The latter program was designed to help local officials and economic developers to better determine the types of industries likely to locate in the county and the most suitable locations to accommodate industrial development. Unfortunately, these programs were so technologically advanced that many of the anticipated users did not have the computer capabilities or technical knowhow to take full advantage of these highly sophisticated programs. Intensive training failed to overcome this technological gap.

One of Mobile's deputy district engineers, an Army major who had a master's degree in planning, took a personal interest in the corridor study. He was insistent that a comprehensive land-use plan be developed for all the land adjacent to the waterway, similar to what TVA had done for its property along the Tennessee River. He also convinced the Corps' Board of Environmental Consultants to support him. I was strongly opposed to his notion. Unlike TVA, which purchased all the land next to its reservoirs, the Corps acquired only what it needed to construct and operate the waterway, leaving the rest in private ownership. While the towns along the waterway might have zoning ordinances and other land-use regulations, none of the counties had such stipulations on the use of private property. I knew the local officials would strongly object to such plans and would view them as the federal government's unconscionable infringement on private property rights. Without the support of the counties, which was not forthcoming, the Corps had no legal recourse to adopt land-use or zoning regulations for land it did not own. As a result, the time spent developing such a plan would be wasteful and would be nothing more than academic exercise. Nevertheless, he was determined to prevail and decided to circumvent my opposition. Instead of addressing the members of the authority during a meeting, he had learned that one of its members, Richard Manley, was an Alabama state senator. The Corps officer met with Manley in Montgomery in hopes of getting him to overrule my opposition. Little did he know that Manley was one of the most conservative members of the authority. Manley listened to the Corps officer's spiel and then politely sent him packing. Manley immediately called me and was somewhat perturbed at me for not alerting him about the intent of the Corps' visit. I told him I was not aware of his meeting and that I was upset, too, since the Corps had not given me the courtesy of alerting me to the meeting. I later admonished Birindelli and others working on the study for not informing me of the meeting. I learned then that they had been instructed by the major not to tell me about his plans. Under those circumstances, I was pleased that Manley had agreed with me that the proposal was ludicrous and wasteful. That was the end of any further efforts on the major's part. I never let the incident affect my relationship with the study's staff.

Although I worked closely with Joe Birindelli, I never knew until years later that he was a Vietnam war hero. He was a graduate of Virginia Military Institute and served two tours as an officer with the 4th Cavalry Regiment, where he received two Silver Stars and a Bronze Star with a "V" for valor. Sadly, Joe passed away in 2022.

One afternoon, I received a telephone call from Congressman Tom Bevill. He announced that he had gotten TVA to agree to give me $200,000 annually for the next 5 years to help plan for the development of the waterway. Also, TVA was transferring one of its employees, Frank Glass, to work with me on the use of these funds. This all was a complete surprise to me since I had never discussed getting such assistance from TVA. For reasons that I could never fully discern, the hierarchy within TVA was not a fan of Tenn-Tom. I suspected that some in TVA were concerned that the Tenn-Tom region would attract industrial development and other economic activities that would heretofore have located in the Tennessee Valley. If that was the case, it was a naive concern since the waterway, would benefit the TVA service area in many ways such as providing a much shorter route for transporting commerce of shippers and producers to and from the Gulf Coast and the world.

TVA had made a big issue of the power losses incurred from the water diverted from the

Tennessee River system for the lockage of barge tows at Whitten Lock and Dam. Some claimed those diversions could have passed through hydropower plants at Pickwick and Kentucky Dams and generated revenues for its rate payers. These potential power losses, although not significant, were included in the waterway's benefit-to-cost computation as an economic cost to the project. Much to TVA's disappointment, the utility was not reimbursed by the Corps or by the Congress for these perceived revenue losses. Political ramifications made it unwise for TVA to openly oppose the Tenn-Tom, but it was not inclined to help with the project. Therefore, I was confident that TVA was not providing this generous level of funding of its own volition but had had been directed by Congressman Bevill to do so.

I knew Frank Glass but had never worked much with him. I knew he was very close to Bevill and considered himself one of the congressman's unofficial assistants in his district. The hierarchy within TVA was aware of his close relationship with the congressman, and many resented it. Glass went out of his way to flaunt his ties with Bevill, and it was obvious to everyone, including Glass, that his job would likely be terminated the day after the congressman left office. That later proved to be the case. His irascible and opinionated demeanor made me wonder how we could effectively work together. As it turned out, he became not only a congenial associate but also a friend.

I thanked Chairman Bevill and told him we would make good use of the funds. Jokingly, I said that it was worth much more than $200,000 a year to have to work with Frank Glass. There was total silence on the congressman's end of the line. It was obvious he thought I was serious, so I immediately told him I was just kidding. Having the leverage of knowing Bevill's involvement in these arrangements, I was able to work out the details much to our advantage. For example, we had complete discretion on how we used the funds, provided it was waterway related, and we did not have to get TVA approval for the work plans, etc. Also, Glass would remain a TVA employee, and the agency would be responsible for his salary and benefits as well as for paying his travel expenses. They grudgingly agreed to these and other terms that were favorable the us. I also had the Tenn-Tom Waterway Development Council be the signatory entity with TVA.

The availability of these funds enabled the Council in cooperation with the four states and waterway counties to launch an aggressive promotion and marketing program. It would be the most comprehensive and far-reaching effort of its kind to help induce the economic development of a waterway or a public works project. Some of the activities carried out are briefly described below.

Waterfront Industrial Sites

Working with state and local economic developers as well as utilities, railroads, and, yes, even TVA, the Council identified the prime waterfront industrial sites. Its scope included all the counties along the Tenn-Tom as well as those served by the Tennessee River from Paducah to Knoxville and the lower Tombigbee River from Demopolis to Mobile. A prime site was mainly defined as one served by rail and an improved highway. Its property should be publicly owned or under option from willing sellers and its development not unduly inhibited by flood risks or other environmental or cultural issues.

Much to everyone's surprise, the Council identified only 42 sites along some 1,200 miles of waterways serving four states. Lack of rail service eliminated many miles of waterfront property that was suitable for development. For example, there is only one location, New Johnsonville, Tennessee, along 200 miles of the Tennessee River from Northwest Alabama, to Calvert City, Kentucky, that is served by rail. Also, the list included a handful of sites that did not fully comply with the definition of a prime site but were added since they were the only sites in some counties, and more important, were already being marketed by local interests. None of those sites were served by rail, and to my knowledge none have been developed so far.

We prepared and distributed marketing materials for each site. Three decades later, many of these sites are now developed with industries that employ highly paid, skilled workers, and they have had major impacts on the local economies. Unfortunately, some of the sites have been preempted by other land uses, such as recreation and residential development. Locations for attracting industries dependent on barge transportation that meet the specifications are truly an endangered species and becoming rarer over time. Any county fortunate enough to have such a jewel should take measures to ensure its availability for development.

We compiled the relevant information about the individual counties of interest to industrial developers and other economic interests and stored it in an innovative computerized Tenn-Tom Regional Information Center. This FAX-on-demand system was accessed by a toll-free telephone line (1-888-TENNTOM) and proved to be very successful. During its first year of operation, it received over 1,200 inquiries, more than those received by mail or other means. An example of its success as a marketing tool was that the Galbreath Group, a national site-selection firm, used the system during its initial investigation of prospectives sites, which led to the location of Trico Steel, Inc. (now Nucor Steel) on the Tennessee River at Decatur, Alabama.

The Council contracted with the Pace Group, an economic development consulting firm, to conduct workshops at the University of

West Alabama in Livingston and at Pickwick Landing State Park in Tennessee about how to achieve economic growth at the local level. The Galbreath Group held a similar workshop in Columbus. These meetings were informative and attracted representatives from most all the waterway corridor counties.

Marketing a Waterway

The Council participated in numerous regional and national trade shows pertaining to industries that typically used barge transportation, like steel, paper and pulp, plastics, and forestry. Local developers were encouraged to attend and use the Council's booth to "sell" their city or county to show attendees. Similar participation in boat shows like the Miami International Boat Show can take credit for starting what is the popular voyage of pleasure boaters called America's Great Loop. The Loop is an all-water route that encircles the eastern half of the United States. Formerly, large pleasure boats would take the Lower Mississippi River, but they soon discovered that the Tenn-Tom offered a shorter route with less dangerous waterborne obstructions compared to the Lower Mississippi River. We learned there were several hundred of these boaters who left mid-America at the end of the summer and moved their pleasure craft to warmer climates, mainly South Florida. They made a return trip the following spring. Working with Fred and Kim Hansard, Gerald and Ginger Connor, and other marina owners and operators from west Kentucky to Mobile, the Waterway Council sold these boaters on the advantages of using the Tenn-Tom. Our promotion efforts were blunted at the outset when some local yahoos along the lower Tombigbee between Demopolis and Mobile decided these out-of-state boaters offered a means to make easy money. They would allege that the wake from one of the larger pleasure boats swamped their small fishing boat and damaged its out-board motor. They had the local sheriff issue an arrest warrant that would be served on the boater when he arrived at Coffeeville Lock and Dam. The boater, who would, of course, plead innocent, was faced with two options: go to the county courthouse, post bail, and return later for a court date, or immediately pay the damages claimed by the local accuser. In all cases the boater paid the couple hundred dollars for the "damages." News of these shakedowns spread like wildfire throughout the boating community, and some trade publications published stories warning boaters not to use the Tenn-Tom, referring to that leg of the voyage as an experience like that portrayed in the movie *Deliverance*.

The local members of the Alabama Marine Police were of no help in stopping these miscreants from harassing and fleecing boaters. The local marine police's lack of cooperation was evidence that they, too, considered these out of towners intrusive. These episodes continued, and similar situations began to occur on another stretch of the waterway. After a local miscreant shot at some boaters, boaters were warned to travel armed. Fearing that someone was likely to be injured or killed, Fred Hansard and I met with Riley Boykin Smith, who was commissioner of the Alabama Department of Conservation and Natural Resources, to apprise him of this dire situation. He had overall responsibility for the Marine Police, and after our meeting he made some much-needed changes within that agency that resulted in finally stopping these shakedowns and harassment, including having some of the police officers onboard the transient boat as it made its voyage through those areas. Smith was a strong supporter of the waterway and once served as a member of the authority, appointed by Governor Don Siegelman. He quickly recognized that these incidents were giving the waterway and the state a bad national reputation. That problem evaporated overnight, and the marinas throughout the waterway corridor now enjoy the added economic benefits of this unexpected use of the waterway.

I had the pleasure of meeting some of these boaters who would call the Tenn-Tom office for reports concerning river conditions and other waterway-related information. Many were successful self-made businessmen or were people enjoying the pleasures of trust funds or inheritances. I met Mr. Doubleday, an elderly gentleman with Doubleday Publishing, who fell on his boat and broke his hip near Columbus and spent several weeks in the area. I also got to know Joe Manchin when he brought his large pleasure boat from Panama City,

Florida, to Charleston, West Virginia, when he became governor. He decided he wanted to be the captain of that long voyage, which he had to accomplish in segments because of the demands of his office. Once he started a leg of the trip, he would call my office to get a navigation report. Those calls continued even after he left the Tenn-Tom, which required us to make some quick calls to others to obtain the information he sought. A few years later, the National Waterways Conference held a meeting in Charleston, and Governor Manchin was invited to attend. He accepted and asked one of his aides if any of the attendees were affiliated with the Tenn-Tom Waterway. Although we chatted several times on the telephone, that was the first time we had met in person. He later became a U.S. Senator, and I understand he lived on his beloved boat at a marina near the Pentagon when he was in Washington.

I often told economic developers who traveled to distant corporate headquarters in hopes of meeting with executives to convince them to make investment decisions in their state or locality that some of the people they hoped to meet with were spending days in their state. I suggested they establish a network with the marina operators and get notices about when these decision makers were passing through the state. This would present an excellent opportunity to meet them and make a soft sales pitch about the advantages of making investments in the waterway corridor. I am disappointed no one ever followed up with my suggestion.

The Tenn-Tom Council provided over $300,000, through grants and partnerships, to nearly three dozen economic development entities throughout the waterway corridor. These funds, which amounted to about one-half of the total received from TVA, were spent on projects the recipients identified as their highest priority needs. Some funds were used to market off-waterway industrial parks in counties that had no prime waterfront industrial sites. These funds were very beneficial to those counties that did not have full-time chambers of commerce, a professional economic developer, or the resources needed for marketing and promotion.

Brochures promoting the waterway and its region were printed in German, Japanese, Korean, French, Portuguese, Spanish, Chinese, and English. There were several foreign delegations, mostly from China, Korea, and Japan, that toured the waterway during that first decade of its operation.

This unique and effective demonstration marketing project came to a screeching halt in 1998. The TVA, never an avid participant, actually came kicking and screaming to the party only because of Congressman Tom Bevill and his clout. After serving 30 years in the U.S. House of Representatives, the congressman retired on January 1, 1997, ending any influence he had with the utility. At about that same time, TVA's board of directors, led by its chairman, Craven Crowell, made a profound, everlasting decision not to seek any appropriations for its non-power programs after fiscal year 1998. This meant that these programs, such as flood control, resource management, economic and community development, and a sundry of other endeavors that benefited those living in the region TVA served would have to be either funded by power revenues, transferred to other federal agencies, or eliminated. Many of TVA's supporters and beneficiaries felt this decision by the utility's governance was unwise if not unconscionable. There was never a clear explanation for the decision, but some believed the utility's decision makers felt there would be less congressional oversight of the federal agency if it no longer received annual federal funding. If so, that was the epitome of naivete since the Congress continues to keep tabs on the nation's largest electric utility, including confirming its directors. The Council's marketing project for Tenn-Tom was just one of many TVA-funded programs that were terminated. Hoping to find some justification for terminating the program, TVA officials sent a team to the Council's office to conduct both program and financial audits. After one week of thorough searching, the auditors found nothing to question and were very complimentary of the financial records that Agnes Zaiontz had maintained for the Council. Frank Glass's opponents at TVA's headquarters were quick to use its termination of the programs to abolish his position and force his retirement. This reminded me that many government bureaucrats have long-lasting institutional memories and will eventually seek retribution for a past political decision foisted on them.

Port Development

Yellow Creek Port, Tom Soya Grain, Inc. (now Ray Lucas Memorial Port), Port of Amory, and Aliceville River Terminal were the only barge terminals in service when the Tennessee-Tombigbee Waterway opened for business in 1985. The Mississippi State Legislature enacted the Inland Ports Act in 1968, which enabled TVA, the Mississippi A&I Board (now Mississippi Development Authority), and the Tombigbee River Valley Water Management District to form a pact to build Yellow Creek Port. TVA agreed to fund the terminal's

Through innovation and ingenuity, Tom Soya Grain Co. of West Point, MS were the first commercial users of the waterway, more than five years before it was completed. The company shipped its first barge loads of soybeans in April 1979 from a newly constructed privately owned barge terminal on Gainesville Lake near Aliceville, AL. Although navigation was not officially open on Columbus Lake, the company lightly loaded barges at its new port facilities there and towed the barges using a towboat with a retractable pilot house to the Aliceville Port where they were fully loaded for shipment to Mobile. The company's most unique operation was utilizing the abandoned U.S. Highway 45 bridge at Aberdeen, MS for loading barges of grain and bentonite ore until the port there was completed.

facilities and a rail spur from the Corinth and Counce rail line to serve the port, all of which were completed in 1974 at a cost of $7.2 million. The state of Mississippi (A&I Board) purchased 2,000 acres at a cost of about $1.4 million for future industrial development, and the affected counties chose the Water Management District to help underwrite the project, which is located at the northernmost end of the Tenn-Tom near where it joins the Tennessee River.

One of only two state-owned ports in Mississippi (the other is the Port of Gulfport), Yellow Creek Port opened for business in late 1974. It operated successfully during the next 10 years solely on commerce shipped and received via the Tennessee River. Its first shipment in 1975 was steel coils destined for Tupelo. The port has attracted several steel processing plants and is now one of the busiest on the entire waterway, handling about 1.5 million tons of commerce each

There are 12 ports or barge terminals along the 234-mile-long waterway. One of the most successful operations is the Yellow Creek Port, located at the northern end of the waterway where it joins the Tennessee River. The port, one of two owned by the State of Mississippi, opened for business in late 1974 and relied on shipments to and from the Tennessee River until Tenn-Tom opened in 1985. Since then, it has attracted over $450 million of new and expanded industrial development, resulting in about 800 jobs for northeast Mississippi. It and Lowndes County Port at Columbus, Mississippi, are the two busiest barge facilities on the waterway, each handling about 1.5 million tons of commerce annually.

year. Its barge services help support over 800 jobs. That phenomenal growth has occurred under the direction of the port's executive directors, beginning with Neil Davis, later followed by Cliff Mitchener, Eugene Bishop, and its current manager, Robert Dexter. The leadership of the port authority's members, such as longtime member Travis Childers, who was the authority chairman in 1985, can also claim credit for the port's success.

Amory Mayor Thomas Griffith and the city council started preparing for its barge facilities in the mid-1970s. Hobdy Bryan led the effort. According to Hobdy Bryan's son, Mississippi State Senator Hob Bryan, his job title was zoning administrator, but his involvement and influence in the city's affairs went far beyond those responsibilities insinuated in that title. Working with the Corps of Engineers, Bryan was able, through trades and purchases, to secure 130 acres of waterfront property for the city. The city then used federal grant funds and a small bond issue to finance its $2.5 million facility, which opened in June 1985. It was successful in attracting one of the first industries to locate on the waterway, a $10 million wood chip mill. E.C. "Cookie" Epperson, who owned an automobile dealership and was a leader of the Amory chamber of commerce, was one of the early supporters of developing the port. Governor Ray Mabus later appointed Epperson as a Mississippi member of the Tenn-Tom Waterway Authority.

Tom Soya Grain, Inc. has the distinction of being the first company to utilize the waterway for barge service nearly six years before the project was completed. The company leased a barge slip from Aliceville River Terminal where in April 1979 it loaded four barges with soybeans using a newly constructed conveyor belt system. Warrior Gulf Navigation, Inc., of Mobile, provided the barge service. The terminal was located on the Gainesville reservoir at the crossing of U.S. Highway 17. It was privately owned and built by two Pickens County businessmen, Bob Johnson and Bill Martin. Although not an engineer and having no experience with barge transportation, Johnson designed the terminal and its loading facilities, and it is still in operation 45 years later.

At that time, there was a growing demand for soybean exports, and Tom Soya, led by Jimmy Bryan and Ray Lucas, continued to seek other ways to take advantage of the cheaper barge transportation, even though the waterway was still under construction. In 1980, the company purchased waterfront property on Columbus Lake in Clay County near the historic Waverly Plantation to build its main general cargo port facilities. The property included the bridge abutment from the remains of the old Mississippi Highway 50 bridge that was replaced with a higher elevated new bridge across the waterway. It proved to be an ideal pier for loading and unloading barges. Although the navigation channel in Columbus Lake was not yet completed, including the removal of the Columbus and Greenville Railroad bridge that was later abandoned and removed, Tom Soya began using its new port facilities in July 1981. By loading two barges only one-half full of wheat and using a towboat with a collapsible wheelhouse owned by Yazoo Towing, the tow was able to pass underneath the railroad bridge. The barges, loaded to a shallow draft, were able to negotiate the uncompleted navigation channel from there to the Aliceville River Terminal, where they were fully loaded for their final voyage to Mobile.

By far, the most innovative process Tom Soya used to offer barge service in advance of the waterway's official opening was at Aberdeen, Mississippi. The company loaded grain and locally mined bentonite ore by cutting a large hole in the floor of the old U.S. Highway 45 bridge that had been replaced by a new four-lane bridge. Trucks would dump their load through the hole into a barge positioned underneath the bridge. The use of the bridge was eventually discontinued due to lack of depth from silting and by construction of the nearby City of Aberdeen Port.

Tom Soya and its determination to make early use of the waterway was the epitome of the adage, "If there is a will, there is a way." Ray Lucas' son, Perry, now manages the company's operations. The demand for U.S.-grown soybeans has since declined, requiring the Raymond Lucas Port to diversify its business plan. It's now a busy general cargo barge facility.

Columbus, the largest city on the waterway, had not taken the steps needed to build a port by the time the waterway opened. A local businessman had assured city and county officials that he planned to build a port on waterfront property he owned. When those plans did not materialize by the time the waterway opened for commerce in January 1985, local leaders acted. T.E. "Tommy" Lott, a community leader, convened a meeting to discuss the steps needed to develop a port. Those who attended that initial meeting were Harold Blalock, president of the Lowndes County Board of Supervisors; Charleigh Ford, executive director of the Columbus/Lowndes County Economic Development Association; Bobby Harper, a local banker and civic leader; and me, representing the Waterway Authority. That meeting was productive, and it led to a larger meeting at Harper's bank. The consensus was that the county would be economically disadvantaged without a port and its appurtenant facilities to take full advantage of the transportation benefits the waterway offered. Earlier that year, the Lowndes County Board of Supervisors established a port authority, composed of five appointed members, including Henry Weiss, a local businessman, as its chairman. The group's first orders of business were to decide on the location of a possible publicly owned port and to begin identifying possible sources of funding needed to build its facilities. After studying possible sites for the port, which were very limited, the port authority chose a 160-acre tract of land on the so-called island between the waterway and the old river run of the Tombigbee. Part of the land had been used by the Corps of Engineers as a spoil disposal area for placement of materials dredged during construction of the nearby navigation channel. The port facilities, to be built along the old river run, were estimated to cost $6.2 million. A group of local leaders, including Supervisor Blalock and Birney Imes, a local newspaper publisher, traveled to Washington to meet with the Mississippi congressional delegation to seek grants and other means of funding the port. Bobby Harper, a member of the delegation, reported that Senator John Stennis commented during the meeting that he felt "the Tenn-Tom was not completed until Columbus had a port." The trip was productive, and the requested funds were soon forthcoming, including grants from the Appalachian Regional Commission and the Farmers Home Administration.

Two years later, the port opened for business, and its daily operations have been run continually by Logistic Services, Inc., a national stevedoring firm, or its predecessor companies. It is arguably the most successful of the twelve public ports served by the Tenn-Tom, much to the credit of its three port directors, Bob Reynolds, John Hardy, and the current director, Will Sanders. Several years ago, the port built a dock and other facilities on the west side of the main channel of the waterway to serve a large steel mill and other nearby users. These improvements have helped the port's commerce to grow to about 1.5 million tons each year and have helped attract over $4 billion of new and expanded industrial development to the Golden Triangle area.

Notwithstanding the early success of the ports at Yellow Creek and Amory and the novel ways Tom Soya found to benefit from barge transportation, I became concerned that most of the towns and counties along the waterway believed that a port was paramount for capitalizing on the waterway's economic potential. My concerns were valid as towns and counties scrambled to build ports next door to each other. When the waterway opened, there was a dearth of heavy industries near the waterway, especially those that used large amounts of raw materials, intermediate products in its production, or products that were amenable for shipping by barge. I discovered that the feasibility studies being conducted by the consultants for the individual counties assumed that the proposed barge terminal was the only one to be built in that market area. Thus, they assumed the port would not be competing for such a limited potential market. Some of these studies did not include what I felt was a thorough analysis of how the costs of barge transportation would compare to other modes of transportation, like truck or rail.

At that time, the state of Mississippi had a planning office that conducted studies of interest to the state. It also played an important role in the review and approval of grant requests. I expressed my concerns to those office officials and recommended it conduct a system-wide shipping survey and analysis for the waterway corridor. Based on its findings regarding locations of potential shippers or users, the state could then determine the number of ports needed to serve those shippers and strategically decide where the ports should be located. Those counties where a port was not justified could direct their efforts and resources toward building waterfront industrial parks to market and attract new industrial development. Knowing the study's findings would be controversial, with winners for some counties and losers for others, likely resulting in political fallout, the planning office declined to conduct such a study. As a result, the waterway became overbuilt with ports and terminals and had fewer waterfront industrial parks to market for prospective industries that could benefit from barge transportation.

With so much interest in developing ports along the waterway, the Tennessee-Tombigbee Waterway Development Council organized several tours of existing port facilities within the waterway region. These familiarization visits enabled the prospective developers of ports to learn from the experiences, both good and bad, in building and operating an inland commercial port. The Council organized these trips and furnished transportation, generally a large passenger bus owned by the athletic department of Mississippi State University. The participants paid for their meals and lodging, and the response for each tour was great.

The port tours included visits of all the public ports in west Kentucky, the complex of public facilities at Memphis, two trips to those facilities along the Arkansas River (the McClellan-Kerr Waterway), and a trip to South Louisiana. The tours of the ports along the McClellan-Kerr were especially enlightening. Having opened in 1971, it was America's newest waterway until the Tenn-Tom was completed. Principal public ports on the McClellan-Kerr are Pine Bluff, Little Rock, and Ft. Smith in Arkansas and Muskogee and Tulsa (Port of Catoosa) in Oklahoma. They were all open for business when the waterway became navigable. In little more than a decade, all had become vibrant and growing as commercial hubs. Although located at the head of navigation, some 445 miles from the confluence of the

Mississippi River, the Port of Catoosa's operations were especially impressive. Through the vision of its port director, Bob Portiss, and its port authority, a 2,000-acre industrial park was developed adjacent to the port facilities. Those port features have now attracted 70 companies that employ nearly 3,000 workers. Although at the head of navigation, the port had the distinction of receiving the first shipment of commerce on the waterway in 1971 — a barge load of newsprint from Tennessee. It now generates about 20 percent of all the waterway's commerce.

Most all the port officials interviewed were open and forthcoming with advice, based on their experiences. For example, they advised not to sell any port property or its facilities but to lease them. If a land sale is needed to close a deal, then they advised to include a buy-back clause in the deed. They also advised that the port be operated by a stevedoring or logistics firm and not by someone with little or no experience with commercial navigation. Last, the success of any port depended on an aggressive and well-funded marketing and promotion program.

The tour of the Louisiana ports was memorable. Bob Patterson was a long-time member of the city council for Aberdeen, Mississippi. He was a very strong supporter of the Tenn-Tom and attended many of the waterway's activities, including the port tours. He was one of the most gregarious people one would ever meet and always brought with him a large bag of snacks that he shared with everyone. He loved to talk and would move from one fellow passenger to another to share his stories. We had made several stops that day at ports along the Gulf Intracoastal Waterway and were behind schedule when we arrived at Morgan City, Louisiana. The port office was closed, but the director stayed to greet us. He gave us a short briefing, locked his office, and followed us in his car for a quick windshield tour of the port. After the tour, he followed us from the port as we left for New Orleans, where we would stay overnight and leave for home the next morning. About halfway to New Orleans, I realized that Bob was not on the bus, and no one could tell me the last time they had seen him. Some said they hadn't seen him since early that morning at breakfast. We had no recourse other than to start back-tracking until we found him. Everyone was relieved to see him sitting on the curb in front of the Port of Morgan City's office. He, of course, had no phone, and with the office closed, he had decided to stay there for a while. If we hadn't returned, he planned to walk to town and try to hire someone to take him to New Orleans. During the briefing, he had gone to the men's room, and when he came out, we were gone, and the office was empty and locked. The moral of that story is always to make a headcount at every stop to make sure everyone is present and accounted for.

There are now 12 public ports or barge terminals along the Tenn-Tom. Five are in West Alabama and the other seven in Northeast Mississippi. Some of these facilities have enjoyed great success by attracting shippers and new industrial development, creating new, higher paying jobs for the area. The availability of water transportation has helped shippers and producers enjoy lower competitive freight rates for all modes. These savings can be the determining factor for natural resources, commodities, and products to reach distant markets that likely would be foreclosed by higher freight rates. But as I had feared, some of the ports did not live up to expectations. While this lack of progress has been disappointing, I remain hopeful that all 12 facilities will bear fruit. For example, I am encouraged that despite many years of little activity at the Port of Epes in Sumter County in west Alabama, Enviva, the world's largest producer of wood pellets, is building a $375 million plant there that will produce 1.1 million tons of wood pellets for export to Asia and Europe as a renewable energy source. The 375 jobs this investment will produce will be a godsend to Sumter County and that part of West Alabama, one of the most economically depressed areas inf the nation. Sumter County's per capita income is less than one-half the national average. A third of the population lives below the poverty line. Activity at the port in Aberdeen, Mississippi, should increase now that a nearly 3-mile rail spur is being built to connect the port with the Kansas City Southern Railroad. Its dock facilities have also been upgraded. Last, I am mystified by why Itawamba Port at Fulton, Mississippi, has not been more successful. It is ideally located to serve manufacturers and other prospective shippers from the Tupelo area as well as those in Northwest Alabama.

Texas A&M Transportation Institute's Center for Ports and Waterways conducted a study for the U.S. National Waterways Foundation in 2014 and updated the study in 2022. The study found that water transportation was more fuel efficient, safer, and more environmentally friendly than truck and rail. One gallon of diesel fuel will transport a ton of commerce 675 miles by barge compared to 472 miles by rail and only 51 miles by truck. Barges are as much as three times less likely to have an accident or a spill than the other modes. The study also found that barges release some 15.1 tons of carbon dioxide for every million ton-miles of commerce it ships compared to 21.6 tons by rail and 140.7 tons (or 800 percent more) for truck. Water is by far the most preferred mode for air quality.

Continued Media Attacks

An aggressive and multi-faceted marketing program conducted for the waterway was not only crucial to help promote its development, but just as important to counter the decade or longer of negative publicity its opponents conjured up as they schemed to kill the project. Nearly every major newspaper printed stories that questioned if not condemned the economic worth of the waterway, calling it a "boondoggle" and devastatingly harmful to the environment. Most all those allegations had been spoon fed to the media by national environmental organizations and the railroads that opposed it. Most TV networks aired similar negative or "hit" stories, which did not cease once the waterway was in operation, and they continue some 30 years later. For example, the Associated Press wrote a negative story in September 2019 about the waterway not fulfilling everyone's expectations. Reporters learn early in their careers they do not have to search very long to find someone who is in opposition to anything, regardless of whether the issue has broad public support. I call those reporters the "Chicken Littles of the World." AP was able to find such a person, the mayor of the small town of Epes, Alabama, who was more than eager to share his disappointment with the waterway. Epes, again, is the epicenter of one of the most economically impoverished areas in the nation. No one should have expected that the waterway would solve the systemic socio-economic problems that have existed in that area for generations. Since the AP story ran, Epes has been successful in attracting a $375 million forestry products plant that will create 350 much-needed jobs. The company selected that location solely because of the availability of the Tenn-Tom to ship wood pellets by barge to the Gulf Coast for export. An announcement of a company creating this number of jobs in a large metropolitan area would likely go unnoticed, but in a rural area like Epes, it is headline news and greeted as a blessing.

Several of the national television networks also continued to air hit pieces about the Tenn-Tom. I have lost count of how many times I was interviewed by CNN, ABC, CBS, and other networks. None were ever pleasant. One of those interviews comes to mind. In the late 1980s and early 1990s ABC enjoyed one of the more popular prime time news shows that aired on Wednesday evenings. The show was called *Prime Time Alive* and was co-hosted by Diane Sawyer and Sam Donaldson. Donaldson had a reputation for being a very aggressive, take-no-prisoners kind of an interviewer. The show's producer called the Tenn-Tom office one morning to report that the show was airing a segment by Donaldson about the Red River Waterway, and they wanted to include an "update" about the Tenn-Tom. The ABC team planned to fly to Birmingham after filming in Louisiana and wanted to know where the best place was to meet for an interview and film some commercial activity on the waterway. I told him I would call him back shortly with an answer. I then called Norman Connell, the waterway operations manager, to alert him about the visit and to learn where barge tows were located on the waterway. He checked and reported there were two 8-barge tows near Bevill Lock and Dam, one headed south and the other north. I asked Norm to contact the lock operator at Bevill and alert him about the arrival of the TV crew and tell him to contact the boat captains of the two tows and inform them if they wanted to be on national television to anchor out of sight of the lock until we told them to proceed. I then called the TV producer back and told her to meet me at Bevill Lock and Dam and gave her directions.

    I immediately left for the lock and dam to get prepared for the ABC crew's arrival. When I turned onto the access road and approached the waterway, I realized that I had likely made an egregious error by picking Bevill for the interview. Sitting next to the lock was the magnificent Bevill Visitors Center, the newly completed replica of a large antebellum plantation home. Moored next to the center was the old paddle-wheeled snag boat, the M/V *Montgomery*. I was confident that the purpose of ABC's visit was to film a desolate Tenn-Tom with little or preferably no commercial activity as an example of what would likely be the case for the Red River Waterway once it was completed, or another "boondoggle project." I now feared that, once they saw the Bevill Center, it could become the central focus of the Tenn-Tom coverage, not only portraying the waterways as a waste of federal funds but also painting a caricature of the old South and its way of life. I was at a loss about how I would respond when questioned about the center. I decided to joke that it was my residence and say more seriously that it was the Corps' Regional Visitors Center, which ironically, the Corps later designated it to serve as such.

    Once the TV crew arrived, I signaled to the lock operator to tell the two barge tows that it was time to approach the lock. For the next one and half hours while the cameras were shooting film alongside the lock wall, there was a tow of barges inside the lock with their massive loads. Finally, the producer questioned me, suggesting that the barge traffic had been staged. My response was that she wanted to see some commercial activity on the waterway, and that I wanted to accommodate her. After they conducted nearly one hour of interviews on camera, of which probably a minute or two would likely appear on the show, they left for Birmingham for a flight to New York. I noticed that one of the staff traveling with the group appeared to have already written the script for that segment that was to be aired the next evening. I was convinced the story's content would be negative, regardless of what they filmed or heard about the waterway. Much to my amazement and utter relief, no one mentioned or seemed to recognize the visitors center or the snag boat.

I was in Atlanta on the evening the show aired, and all my family members at home tuned in to watch the show. I had already convinced myself that it was going to be a rip job and more negative publicity for the waterway. As expected, it was a very negative portrayal of the Red River Waterway, but to my family's disappointment, as well as friends who had tuned in to see me on national TV, the show did not include any footage or narrative about the Tenn-Tom. It was evident that their visit to the Tenn-Tom, with all the background of commerce that was filmed at the lock, did not fit their script. The producer and/or Donaldson decided not to include Tenn-Tom, which I felt was the best thing that could happen. That was one of the very few times I snookered or got the best of the national media, and it felt wonderful.

It is difficult to understand why the national media was so fixated on trashing the Tenn-Tom a decade or longer after its completion. I believe part of the answer was they had invested so much ink and their credibility attacking the project that they were determined to prove their long-standing opposition was warranted. Frankly, there were many other events and activities occurring daily in America or in the world that were much more newsworthy. For example, the most expensive highway project ever built, one fraught with controversy and cost overruns, was started in 1991 and was completed in 2007 at a total expense of $15 billion, including federal, state, and local costs. Its price tag was nearly eight times of what was spent on building the Tenn-Tom. The so-called Big Dig Tunnel project was built to relieve traffic congestion traveling through Boston on two interstate highways and another expressway. The project experienced serious design and building difficulties and protracted delays in construction that led to exorbitant cost overruns. It also had to overcome strong, vocal opposition from environmentalists and other groups. Yet there was little if any negative national media coverage of this enormous project at a time when the Tenn-Tom continued to be ridiculed.

The media and its other detractors had only one legitimate complaint about the Waterway's performance in terms of its generating expected benefits. Economic studies associated with the waterway, including shipper surveys and freight analyses, conducted during the 1960s and the following decade, analyzed coal and other kinds of commodities that are typically shipped by barge. Demand for coal, both here and abroad, was expected to continue growing, especially the use of steam coal to generate electricity. With the Tenn-Tom and its connecting network waterways positioned to serve two-thirds of the nation's recoverable coal reserves, coal was projected to be the dominant commodity shipped on the waterway. These lofty projections of increased coal production, especially in east Tennessee and Appalachia, are likely why L&N (CSX) Railroad spent so much of its resources trying to eliminate the waterway as a competing mode, both in the courtroom and in the Congress, only to fail. Anticipating a growing demand for coal exports, the Alabama State Port Authority expanded its McDuffie Coal Terminal in Mobile to eventually handle as much as 30 million short tons of both steam and metallurgical coal annually. Regrettably, coal production began to take a nosedive, especially within the region served by Tenn-Tom and connecting barge routes. The decline was attributed to two main factors: environmental regulations like the Clean Air Act, which restricted sulfur emissions from coal-fired powerplants; and advances in fracking technology that greatly increased supplies of natural gas that had lower, more competitive prices than coal. Coal production in the mines served by the Tenn-Tom further declined when some electric utilities began switching to lower sulfur, bituminous coal from the Powder River Basin in Wyoming. The use of the western-produced coal made it easier for utilities to comply with federal regulations to reduce sulfur from its emissions. The bleak future of coal-fired generation was further exacerbated by the crusade to address climate change by eliminating all uses of non-renewal energy sources, mainly coal and natural gas, in favor of renewal sources, such as solar and wind. Some of the shortfall in coal shipments on the Tenn-Tom have been offset by unexpected increases of other commerce like chemicals, steel, petroleum, and forestry products. The low-cost barge rates offered by the waterborne carriers are saving the waterway's commercial users an estimated $100 million each year as well as greatly expanding markets heretofore foreclosed by transportation costs. These economic benefits will continue to grow as fuel costs increase.

An aggressive marketing and promotion of the waterway has helped to fulfill one of the waterway's primary missions: to attract capital-intensive, heavy manufacturing and other kinds of industrial development that utilize skilled workers and pay above-average wages. Researchers at Troy University and the University of Tennessee conducted a study that found that the Tenn-Tom generated nearly $43 billion of total economic impacts to the four compact states and to the nation from 1996 to 2008. These impressive results do not include economic growth during the first 10 years of the waterway's operation, and those impacts that have occurred since 2008. The study, titled "Analysis of the Economic impact of the Tennessee-Tombigbee Waterway 1996–2008," dated February 17, 2009, found that the economic growth generated by the waterway had created directly over 29,000 new jobs and added a total employment of 138,000, including indirect and induced jobs. The study's principal researchers were Dr. Judson Edwards and Philip Mixon of Troy University's Center for Internationl Business and Economic Development and Dr. Mark Burton with the University of Tennessee's Center for Transportation Research.

A more recent economic impact study was conducted in 2015 on the waterway's 30th anniversary of its operation. The conclusions of that research by Mississippi State University, in collaboration with five other universities in the waterway region, were equally impressive. Dr. Domenici Parisi, executive director of the National Strategic Planning and Analysis research center, led the study. It found that the waterway had helped create nearly 25,000 new full-time jobs in the four-state waterway corridor, equating to nearly $2 billion of additional annual personal income. The availability of more economical barge services helped generate more than $8 billion of added annual economic impact and nearly $390 million of new tax revenues each year, nearly one-half of that accruing to state and local governments. Any fair-minded, unbiased person would conclude that the public investment in the Tennessee-Tombigbee Waterway has paid off in multiple dividends and will continue to do so for many decades to come. Other federal programs and projects would be hard-pressed to measure up to the Tenn-Tom's economic worth and its contributions toward improving the quality of life for many.

The waterway authority, as part of its marketing and promotion program, established an International Sister Waterway association with the Rhine-Main-Danube waterway in Europe because of that waterway's similarities to Tenn-Tom. Its system of 13 locks provides a connecting water transportation route between the North Sea and the Atlantic Ocean with the Black Sea. Its cost, environmental issues, and political opposition were some other similarities it shared with Tenn-Tom. Hans Peter Siedel, Germany's executive director for the project, attended the Tenn-Tom Waterway Development Conference in 1989 where he spoke and presented a proclamation from Germany's transportation agency. Shown here are some authority members who joined me to present a similar resolution that the the compact governors signed. From left: me; Don Hines (Alabama); Bill Lang (Alabama); Bob Cornman (Kentucky); Siedel accepting the proclamation from Z.C. Enix (Kentucky), the authority's vice chairman; Cookie Epperson (Mississippi); Clatus Junkin (Alabama); and Bill Thrash (Alabama). Authority administrators Mike Tagert and Mitch Mays established similar formal relationships with the Panamá Canal Company.

Europe has made significant advancements in the use of its waterways for transporting containers and other higher valued goods by barge than what now occurs on U.S. waterways. About 2 million TEUS (20-foot equivalent units) of containers are shipped on the Rhine River on barges each year. Most of the barges are motorized or self-propelled like the one shown here, and many are family-owned and operated with family members living on board. With more than 70 million tons of commerce each year, the Rhine is the busiest waterway in Europe.

It is common practice in Europe to ship cars on river barges as shown here to distant domestic markets or to seaports for export. The Tenn-Tom is in the center of automobile manufacturing in the South. About 3.5 million cars, SUVs, and light trucks are produced each year in the four waterway compact states. The manufacturers rely on truck or rail to transport these vehicles to markets, although a cheaper water mode may be available., According to Business Alabama, Alabama is the leading U.S. exporter of autos, exporting more than $11 billion of vehicles in 2023. None reached seaports by water.

Chapter XXIV
The Authority, One of a Kind

The Tennessee-Tombigbee Waterway's completion and its subsequent development can be largely attributed to the work of the Tennessee-Tombigbee Waterway Development Authority. It has now been over 65 years since the authority was enacted by the U.S. Congress and ratified by President Dwight D. Eisenhower as a federal interstate compact. It was the first interstate compact approved for the primary purpose of promoting the development of a waterway. It is quite astonishing that Neil Metcalf, an Alabama state senator, with no precedent to follow, had the foresight and ability to craft the original legislation. The provisions he included in the original legislation, which were overwhelmingly approved by the Alabama State Legislature and later replicated by the other member states, has enabled the compact to carry out its mission and program functions for nearly seven decades without the need for amendments or changes to its organic authorization.

I was employed by the authority for 30 years, 21 of those years as its administrator. Since retirement, I was appointed by Alabama Governor Robert Bentley to serve as a member of the Waterway Authority. I have continued to serve as one of Alabama's five members, having been reappointed to another 4-year term in 2023 by Governor Kay Ivey. Having spent such a large part of my life associated with the Waterway Authority, I am admittedly biased, but I firmly believe the waterway would have never been built had it not been for the work of the authority. There are many references contained in this narrative, which spans over six decades or longer, that more than adequately demonstrate the crucial role the authority played to overcome the myriad obstacles and challenges that threatened the waterway's completion. Since the waterway's completion, the compact, working closely with its member states, has played a crucial role in promoting its economic development, as described earlier.

Contrary to some beliefs, the authority has never received any federal funding. It is financed solely from the contributions of the member states. Historically, the majority of its funding has come from the states of Alabama and Mississippi, but Kentucky and Tennessee have also been generous financial supporters since joining the compact. Florida's financial contributions during the time it was a member were mainly limited to reimbursements for the expenses of its members.

Because of the waterway's widely recognized success, other waterway-related groups have tried to replicate the Tenn-Tom Authority to aid their waterway development plans, but all have failed so far. Those working to form a multi-billion-dollar plan to modernize the Ohio River's navigation system held discussions to formally organize the affected basin states similar to the way the authority formed the Tenn-Tom compact. Those efforts failed mainly because of lack of political will by the affected states' elected officials.

The states of Oklahoma and Arkansas established a similar organization, albeit not a federal interstate compact, to help facilitate the completion of the McClellan-Kerr Waterway. Once the waterway was completed, the two-state organization was disbanded on the premise that its mission was accomplished. Later, waterway interests realized the importance of such an organization to help promote the development of the waterway, but attempts to reinstitute the two states' original partnership were not successful. The Tenn-Tom Authority remains the only multi-state compact ratified by the U.S. Congress with the primary purpose of promoting development of a waterway.

The law establishing the Tenn-Tom Authority stipulates that legislation must be passed by the affected state legislature and approved by the governor for a state to become a member of the compact. Similar legislation is required for a state to formally withdraw as a member. Florida was the last state to become a member in 1967. Although the potential economic impact of the Tenn-Tom was mainly limited to the panhandle or the northwestern part of that state, Glover Wilkins and other members of the Waterway Authority were able to convince the Florida State Legislature to approve the state's membership. With the strong support of Governor Claude Kirk, the legislation passed unanimously in both the House and Senate, but a companion bill authorizing an annual appropriation of $15,000 was never enacted. Florida's participation broadened the compact's political influence, which was helpful in overcoming opposition within Congress concerning the waterway's funding.

Political and public support for water resources development in Florida took a nosedive during the years after the state joined the Tenn-Tom Authority. The majority of the members of the State Legislature are from south Florida, and they never met a waterway they liked. President Nixon knew there would be little political fallout in that part of the state when he stopped construction of the Cross Florida Barge Canal in 1972. South Florida then and still is that state's political power base, and many of those legislators questioned why the state should support the Tenn-Tom while opposing the Cross Florida Barge Canal. Knowing that Governor Bob Martinez supported the Waterway Authority, as had his predecessors, and would likely veto any legislation withdrawing the state from the compact, those opposing the state's participation included such language in an omnibus bill the governor was forced to sign. That strategy worked, and the governor reluctantly signed the bill in June 1990, thus ending Florida's membership in the compact. Ironically, Martinez had agreed to serve as the authority's chairman for that year, the first Florida governor to do so. By signing the bill, he not only formally withdrew his state from the compact, but he also fired himself as its leader.

Losing Florida's participation also meant the loss of some of the authority's most influential members, such as Doyle Connor, the state's agriculture commissioner for more than 30 years, and James Loudermilk, an influential businessman from Pensacola. Loudermilk had been elected vice chairman to serve with Chairman Martinez that year, but soon thereafter he was tragically killed in a plane crash. He was a veteran pilot, and shortly after taking off on a duck hunting trip to South Louisiana with a fellow hunter and his beloved dogs, he experienced engine trouble. He tried to return to the Pensacola airport but crashed before reaching the runway, killing all aboard.

The authority lost another influential member earlier in 1985 in a similar accident. Jack Paxton was editor/publisher of the *Paducah Sun*, one of several media companies owned by the Paxton family. He was traveling the world as a foreign correspondent for NBC News when his father, Ed Paxton, called to ask him to come home. The newspaper had a long-standing policy that mandated the retirement of its employees at a certain age, and while he owned the newspaper and could have ignored the company policy, he announced to Jack that he was retiring and wanted Jack to succeed him. Jack abided by his father's wishes and returned to Paducah, where he quickly became one of its influential civic leaders. Governor John Y. Brown appointed Paxton as a member of the authority, and he succeeded his father, who was one of the original members when Kentucky joined the compact in 1962. Ed Paxton had served continually since then. Jack was one of my earliest and most loyal champions, and I credit his support for my being selected as administrator of the compact. He was a man of few words and seldom engaged in colloquies with other members during meetings, but when he did speak, it reminded me of a popular TV ad for a brokerage firm at the time, "When E.F. Hutton Talks, People Listen." He was an avid pilot and owned two airplanes, one of which was a Pitts stunt biplane. Having flown with him several times in his fast two-seater, Mooney plane, called the sports car of the skies, I found him to be an excellent pilot, but he pushed the envelope of safety while performing acrobats and other similar maneuvers in his stunt plane. One afternoon after work while flying the Pitts that he had built from a kit, he crashed into a soybean field next to town. Paducah, the Tenn-Tom Authority, and anyone who knew him grieved his loss.

While the track record is replete with the many contributions of the authority and the leadership of its members, the compact's continued effectiveness will be paramount to ensure the waterway remains a cost-effective transportation mode and an economic engine for the region and nation. Although the Tennessee-Tombigbee is the nation's youngest inland waterway, except for the Red River Waterway, it is, nevertheless, approaching its 40th year of operation. While some locks and dams are still functioning after nearly 100 years, a waterway's economic life is conservatively fixed at 50 years. Its economic benefits and costs, including its capital investment as well as estimated annual operation and maintenance costs, are amortized over that time period to determine the project's worth. Its average annual benefits must equal or exceed its annualized costs. A conservative amortization period of 50 years, instead of a longer time based on physical life, helps ameliorate the prospects of future changes in new transportation technology or other advancements that could lessen the value of the waterway's capital investment, or at worst, make the project obsolete as a transportation mode. As the Tenn-Tom now approaches its 50 years of operation or toward the end of its economic life, it faces the prospect of becoming an antiquated if not obsolete waterway unless it is improved to comply with more modern transport standards.

For several years, the nation's waterways have been undergoing needed improvements, including deepening of navigation channels to enable barges to be loaded to 12 feet. Currently, all the mainstem waterways, such as the Mississippi River, the Ohio, and the Gulf Intracoastal Waterway, now provide 12-foot-deep channels. The Tennessee River has a natural depth of 12 feet or more, and similar improvements have been authorized by Congress for the Arkansas and Red Rivers projects, with work to deepen the Arkansas now underway. A study to determine whether such improvements of the Tenn-Tom and the Black Warrior Tombigbee Waterway (BWT) are economically feasible is several years from completion. The federal process for the Corps of Engineers to study, authorize, design, and construct waterway improvement is a protracted one that can take many years, if not decades. Until these needed improvements of the Tenn-Tom and the BWT are made, the commercial users of the two important barge routes will be economically disadvantaged relative to shippers on other waterways that have deeper channels. According to the Corps of Engineers, a standard hopper barge loaded to a 12-foot depth can transport about 43 percent more cargo with little if any additional shipping costs, resulting in significant savings to shippers. Until they are deepened, the Tenn-Tom and the BWT could lose barge traffic that originates or terminates on connecting waterways that provide a 12-foot channel. Moreover, those industries, producers and other shippers located along that system will have a competitive disadvantage with those being served by a 12-foot waterway. It is imperative that the stakeholders of these two waterways, especially the shippers and carriers, become much more aggressive in urging the Congress to accelerate the needed improvements to these two transportation arteries that are so important to the region they serve and to the nation. If not, the commercial use of both waterways as an efficient transportation artery could digress and become another Erie Canal or the Atlantic Intracoastal Waterway with not enough commerce to justify the federal funds needed to operate and maintain them.

The Corps of Engineers' programs, especially navigation, have been flush with funding since President Barack Obama's American Recovery and Reinvestment Act was passed in 2009. The Corps estimates that its funding averaged about $4.9 billion a year from 1992 to 2004. Stimulus funding, however, has increased the agency's civil works program to an average of $6.4 billion annually since 2005. It received $6.8 billion in the fiscal year 2022. Those heady days of little funding constraints may be ending because of growing concerns over the out-of-control federal deficit, which exceeded $34 trillion at the end of 2023 and is still growing. In 2022, the national debt was the equivalent of nearly $93,000 for each American. Most of that debt has occurred during the past 40 years. For example, it reached $1 trillion for the first time in 1982 largely because of President Reagan's tax cut and has been spiraling out of control ever since.

There are two solutions to address the growing deficit: raise taxes or reduce federal spending. Any efforts to control federal spending will greatly affect the Corps' programs, including those funds needed to operate and maintain the Tenn-Tom Waterway. According to the Cato Institute, only about 25 percent of all federal spending is discretionary and considered to be controlled by the Congress, pertaining mainly to domestic programs, like water resources development. The remaining three-fourths of federal spending is considered mandatory based on prior congressionally approved acts, such as defense spending, Social Security payments, Medicare, and the biggest elephant of all in the room, interest on the growing national debt. Therefore, any serious efforts by the Congress to address the budget deficit by reducing spending will put the Corps' appropriations in the crosshairs for cutbacks. If so, the Tenn-Tom's funding and that for other tributary waterways could suffer with other waterways like the Mississippi River or the Ohio River systems, with more barge traffic enjoying a higher budget priority. Metrics, such as tons of commerce or ton-miles of shipments, were used in the past for establishing relative priorities for funding waterways and resulted in less-than-adequate funding for the operation and maintenance of the Tenn-Tom. These budget cuts over time would greatly degrade the waterway's ability to effectively serve barge transportation. The authority's only recourse is to convince the Congress to offset any cuts in funding proposed by a President's administration. That process became routine for most of the annual budget cycles until 2010 when funds became more plentiful. Future budget belt-tightening by the leadership of the Congress and prohibition of "earmarks" of additional funding for a specific project by its congressional supporters would preclude such a budget "fix" for the Tenn-Tom.

Modernization of the Tennessee-Tombigbee Waterway, such as

providing a 12-foot-deep channel and ensuring adequate operation and maintenance funding to enable it to serve its users are just two challenges, albeit important ones, that the authority will face in the future. I hope it will have the support, willingness, and the resources to do so. The states, working in unison, certainly helped to lay the golden egg, and that cooperative manner will be needed in the future.

Waterway stakeholders' work in Washington is not over once a project is built. Continued relations with members of Congress and with executive branch officials, including those at the Corps of Engineers' headquarters are crucial to ensure that the project's operation and maintenance needs are adequately funded, and issues that may adversely affect its development are properly addressed. One such group that has maintained such a close working relationship is the Coalition of Alabama Waterway Associations. Some members of that group and their affiliation are shown here during one of its congressional meetingsin March 2010. They are, from left: Larry Merrihew, Warrior-Tombigbee; Jerry Sailors, Coosa-Alabama; Cline Jones, Tennessee River; Ralph Clemens, Coosa-Alabama; Terah Huckabee, Parker Towing; Tom Littlepage, Alabama Department of Economic and Community Affairs; U.S. Senator Jeff Sessions (Alabama); Billy Houston Tri-Rivers; Bill Satterfield, Balch and Bingham LLP ; me; and, Bob Dawson, Dawson and Associates.

Epilogue

I never planned to spend most of my adult life working for or having a connection to the Tennessee-Tombigbee Waterway. Whether it was by happenstance or divine providence, the 60 years and counting of my involvement with the waterway have been one of the most rewarding personal experiences of my life. This endeavor has afforded me opportunities to meet and know many interesting people, from national leaders in government, governors, business and civic leaders, economic developers, and those who designed, built, and managed this engineering wonder. Over the years, many of these contacts and associates became lifelong friends.

As I have tried to describe, it was a miracle that the waterway was able to overcome myriad impediments and challenges, all of which drove up the costs to build the project and delayed its completion by more than two years. Although effective, some of the attacks or allegations by the waterway's opponents were disingenuous. Many of the members of Congress from the so-called Rust Belt section of the nation, who opposed the waterway, were concerned it would induce more industrial development in the South at their region's expense. At that time, there was a flood of industries and corporations leaving the Midwest and Northeast and relocating to the Sunbelt. They were afraid the Tenn-Tom would exacerbate this migration of investments and jobs.

Of all the national environmental organizations that tried to kill the waterway in the federal courts and in Congress, I can't recall any of their representatives ever visiting the waterway area. Their lack of interest or willingness to spend the time to see firsthand the waterway's construction and the steps taken by the Corps of Engineers to minimize its environmental impacts made me question the sincerity of their concerns. The waterway became the poster child for groups that opposed large public works projects. I do not want to disparage all the waterway's opponents and their opposition to the waterway, but I believe that some groups who allied with national news media to further their cause had hidden agendas. Brent Blackwelder was the principal strategist who organized and coordinated those national environmental organizations to oppose the Tenn-Tom. In response to the symbolic value of getting the Congress to stop construction of the Tenn-Tom Waterway, he was quoted as saying, "If you could eliminate the biggest project and beat the chairman of the Appropriations Committee (Jamie Whitten of Mississippi) ... you could win a devastating blow to pork barrel." Blackwelder and other environmentalists felt that if they could kill the Tenn-Tom, any water project would be fair game.

It was personally annoying that I, as well as other Tenn-Tom supporters, had to continue spending time revisiting the oft-repeated allegations about the waterway's worth and its environmental harm, even years after it was completed. The following is a quote by me in response to a similar query about the waterway. *The Clarion Ledger*, Mississippi's leading newspaper, published my remark in March 1989, nearly five years after the waterway's completion: "Debate on major public policy issues, such as the Tenn-Tom, evoke honest differences of opinions on the pros and cons of these kinds of projects. With the exception of some interests outside the Tenn-Tom region, the vast majority of those affected by this waterway are strong supporters of the project. Tenn-Tom has always enjoyed bipartisan support of the region's elected officials. Not one governor from the five-state region of the waterway has ever opposed the waterway. Every congressman and senator from the waterway corridor have always supported the project, primarily because of the strong grassroots support it has always enjoyed. Can all these people be wrong? I doubt it."

Federal District Judge William C. Keady, in his order on May 9, 1983, that finally ended litigation against the waterway, made the following astute statement: "We must leave to the verdict of history, which may probably not represent an informed judgment until the next century, whether the Tennessee-Tombigbee Waterway will prove to be the great economic boon and national treasure which its supporters, in and out of Congress, have both vigorously and consistently claimed, or whether, as predicted by its foes, it will be a colossal injury to the area environment brought about by wasteful expenditure of public funds. Disclaiming any power of clairvoyance as to what may be TTW's destiny, this court expresses understandable relief that the litigation has come to an end." Now that we are in the third decade of that century, I believe the judge and the waterway's supporters, who tirelessly labored on its behalf, would be pleased with the economic growth it has helped generate and its compatibility with the environment.

To end more on a personal note, the highlight of my career without question occurred in 2014 when the U.S. Congress enacted a law that said, "It is the sense of the Congress that at the appropriate time in accordance with the rules of the Senate and House of Representatives … that the lock and dam located at Mile 357.5 on the Tennessee-Tombigbee Waterway should be known and designated as the Donald G. Waldon Lock and Dam." The designated lock and dam are at Aberdeen, Mississippi, and is one of 10 such structures along the 234-mile-long waterway. To have my name permanently associated with the waterway and to be included with some of the Tenn-Tom's greatest champions who were similarly honored in the designation of the other locks on the system is without question one of my greatest honors. The Congress has a rule that a federal facility cannot be officially named in honor of a private citizen until after his or her death. The rule does not apply to members of Congress, but in my case, the name change will not be official until after my passing, which I hope is some time in the distant future.

One of the highlights of my career occurred in 2014 when the U.S. Congress passed a law naming the lock and dam at Aberdeen, Mississippi, shown here, as the Donald G. Waldon Lock and Dam. I am indebted to U.S. Senators Roger Wicker (Mississippi), Thad Cochran (Mississippi) and Jeff Sessions (Alabama) and U.S. Representative Robert Aderholt for sponsoring the legislation and to other members of Congress as well as President Barack Obama, who approved the legislation, for such an honor.

According to congressional rules, changing the name of the lock and dam cannot officially occur until my passing. Nevertheless, the Tenn-Tom Waterway Authority and the Corps of Engineers held a ceremony at the lock and dam to enable me to celebrate this personal honor with my friends, associates, and family members. Some who attended are shown here. They are, from left: Martha Stokes, Tenn-Tom Waterway Authority (TTWDA); Bud Phillips , TTWDA; partially hidden, Major General Robert Griffin, Dawson and Associates of Washington, D.C.; Brian Roy, TTWDA vice chairman; Dale Pierce, TTWDA; Wynne Fuller, chief, Operations Division of Mobile District Corps; April Bushorn, daughter; Laura Bushorn, granddaughter; Jeremy Sprinkle, son; Jackie Waldon, wife; partially hidden, Yogi Waldon, son; and Angie Barder, daughter.

Agnes Zaiontz, my longtime colleague, and the members of the Tenn-Tom Authority, with support from the Corps of Engineers, held a ceremony at the lock and dam in October 2015 to celebrate the name change. I especially enjoyed this event since I will be deceased when the name change becomes official. Therefore, I will not be able to attend that event, but I hope some of my friends and family members will show up.

During my remarks at the ceremony, I reminded the crowd that there are many who have made lasting contributions to the waterway during its long and storied history, dating back to 1946 when it was first authorized. The project faced many challenges from then until it was completed nearly four decades later. It seemed there was always someone in the right place at the right time to enable the waterway to overcome its many obstacles. While some of those champions have been memorialized by locks and other features being named in their honor, the contributions made by many others have been lost in the passage of time. I facetiously told those in attendance that, while I was humbled and somewhat embarrassed to have my name associated with the waterway since there are so many others whom I felt were more deserving of that honor, those others would have to find their own lock and dam, because this one is mine!

In writing these recollections of my many years associated with the Tenn-Tom, I wanted to recognize some individuals whose important contributions have heretofore gone unnoticed. I regret that I did not undertake this task years earlier, since many of these waterway champions are now deceased. Hopefully, their friends and family members will enjoy my mentioning the roles they played. I apologize for inadvertently failing to mention others who made important contributions to this engineering marvel. Hopefully, their notable involvement will come to light in future endeavors by researchers or authors. Regardless, they are forever part of the waterway's history and legacy.

Understandably, each passing generation of the waterway's beneficiaries has a lesser appreciation of the many struggles that occurred during the waterway's history. I hope this memoir will remind them that the waterway did not occur by happenstance, but because of the dedication, leadership, and untiring efforts of a legion of its past supporters. They, individually and collectively, are largely responsible for this vitally important asset that has improved the economic well-being and quality of life of those who have enjoyed its benefits. Fortunately, for them and for future generations, the Tennessee-Tombigbee Waterway had more champions than it had enemies. It is now a permanent fixture of the nation's geographic landscape.

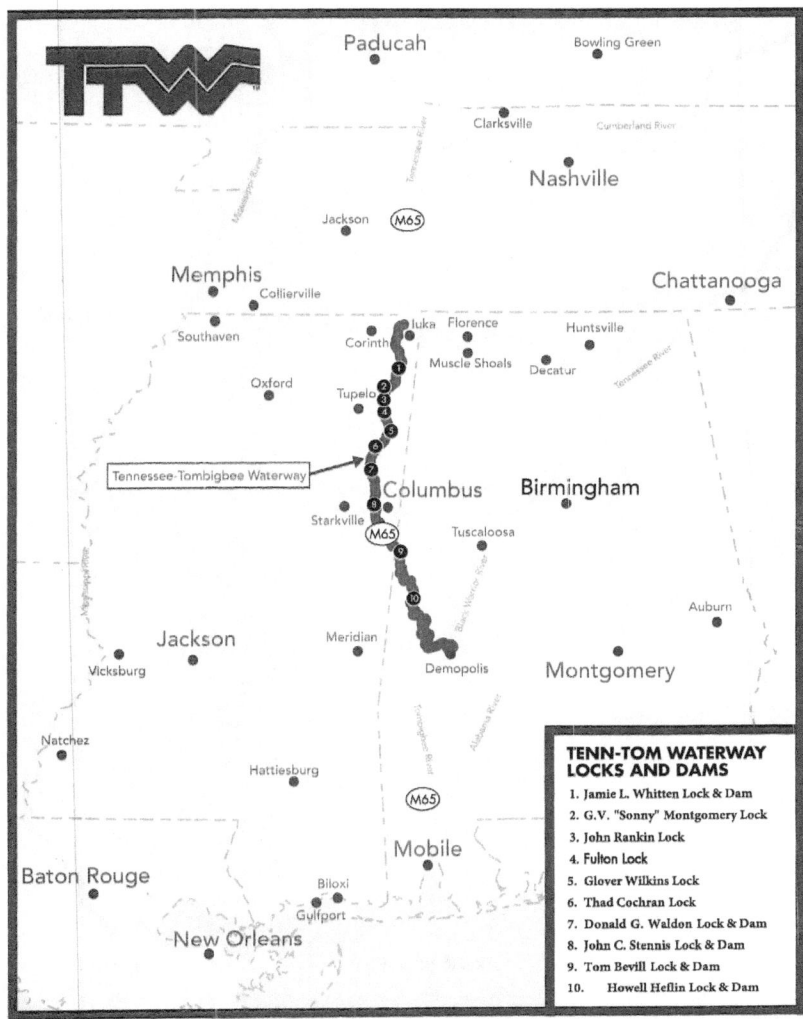

The Tenn-Tom and its locks and dams

APPENDIX A

Tennessee-Tombigbee Waterway
Facts
First Studied: 1874 during President Grant's Administration
Authorized for Construction: 1946 Rivers and Harbors Act
Preconstruction planning funded: President L.B. Johnson in FY 1967
Construction first budgeted: President Richard Nixon in FY 1972
Project dedication: May 25,1971, President Nixon in Mobile, AL
Construction starts: December 12, 1972, Gainesville, AL
First Commercial Shipment: April 1979, Aliceville River Term. (Tom Soya)
Construction Completed: December 12, 1984 at Amory, MS
First Transit Tow of Commerce: The Eddie Waxler in January 1985
Grand Opening Ceremonies: June 1, 1985, Columbus, MS, and Mobile, AL

General Information
Length of waterway: 234 miles
River section, 149 miles
Canal Section, 46 miles
Divide Section, 39 miles
Number of locks: 10
4 in River Section
5 in Canal Section
1 in Divide Section
Total lift of 10 locks: 341 feet
Lock dimensions: 110 feet by 600 feet
Lock capacity: 8 hopper barges and tow boat
Project dimensions: 9 feet by 300 feet, except 12 feet by 280 feet in Divide Section
Total project cost: $1.991 billion
$1.838 billion federal cost
$153 million non-federal cost
Project lands acquired: 110, 779 total acres
85,579 acres fee title

25,200 acres easements

Number of bridge relocations: 13 highways and 6 railroad bridges

Bridge clearances: 52 feet high and 300 feet wide

Total water surface area: 43,942 acres

Deepest cut or excavation: 175 feet in Divide Section near Paden, MS

Total material excavated: 307 million cubic yards, more than Panama Canal

Labor to build project: 25 million manhours.

Construction materials: 2.2 million cubic yards of concrete, 33,000 tons of reinforcing steel

Number of contractors: 125 prime and 1,200 subcontractors

Number of recreation areas: 37 including boat launches

Land designated for recreation: 13,000 acres.

Wildlife mitigation land: 72,500 acres of federal project land.

88,000 acres purchased from willing sellers.

Waterway's project components

Segment between Demopolis and Heflin L/D

Length of waterway channel: 52.5 miles

Commercial activities: Demopolis Yacht Basin (216 River Miles (RM) 1_/, Kingfisher Marina (216 RM), Rattlesnake Bend Fleeting (223 RM), Port Epes (247 RM), Crossroads of America Portand Industrial Park (249.5 RM)

Recreation development: City of Demopolis Access (215.5 RM), Belmont (219.1 RM), Confluence of the Tombigbee and Warrior Rivers (217 RM)

All river miles noted are measured from the foot of Government Street in Mobile via the Mobile and Tombigbee rivers.

Howell Heflin Lock and Dam

Location: Greene County, AL near Gainesville: 267.9 RM

Construction start: December 1972

Open for navigation: October 1978

Lock Lift: 36 feet

Construction cost: $32.3 million

Prime contractors: Al Johnson Co. of Minnesota, Guy James Co. of Oklahoma

Corps' project engineers: Harold Mullins, John Bennett, and George Baker

Lake impoundment: 6,400 acres

Bridge relocations: AL Hwy 39 (RM 266.3), AL Hwy 17 (RM 292.8)

Commercial activities: Bevill-Hook Port (292.4 RM), Aliceville River Terminal (292.7 RM)

Recreation development: Gainesville (267.9 RM), Sumter (270.0 RM), Riverside (271.8 RM), S.E. Taylor (274.0 RM), Vienna (283.4 RM), Cochrane (294.4 RM), Memphis (300.4 RM), Ring Bluff (303.2 RM)

Tom Bevill Lock and Dam

Location: Pickens Co., AL, near Pickensville(306.8 RM)

Construction start: March 1974

Open for navigation: December 1979

Lock Lift: 27 feet

Construction cost: $45 million

Prime contractor: Al Johnson Const. Co. of MN

Corps' project engineers: L.E. Bridges, Norman Connell and Terry Jangula

Lake impoundment: 8,300 acres

Bridge relocations: AL Hwy 86/MS Hwy 388 (308 RM), ICG Railroad (330.9 RM, U.S. Hwy 82 (331.9 RM)

Commercial activities: Pickens County Port (308 RM), Tom Soya Grain (310.2 RM), Luxapalila Fleeting 329 RM), Lowndes Co., MS, Port (330 RM)

Recreation Development: Bevill Visitors Center (306.8 RM), U.S. Snagboat M/V *Montgomery*, Pickensville (308 RM), Bigbee Valley (309.3 RM), James Creek (316 RM), Luxapalila Creek (328.9 RM), Columbus (LeRoy's Landing) (331 RM), Plymouth Bluff Env. Ctr (334 RM)

John C. Stennis Lock and Dam

Location: Lowndes Co., near Columbus, MS (334.7 RM)

Construction start: April 1975

Open for navigation: January 1981

Lock lift: 27 feet

Construction cost: $44.7 million

Prime contractor: Arundel Corp of MD, Albert Lee and Alan Bugg

Lake impoundment: 8,910 acres

Bridge relocations: MS Hwy 50 (339.4 RM), U.S. Hwy 45 (356.6 RM), BNSF Railroad (357.1 RM)

Commercial activities: Columbus Marina (334.5 RM), Ray Lucas Mem. Port (338.6 RM), Aberdeen Port (356.5 RM)

Recreation development: Columbus East (335 RM), Waverly Ferry (338 RM), Dewayne Hays (340 RM), Town Creek (341.5 RM), Barton's Ferry (343.7 RM), McKinley Creek (349.5 RM), Morgan's Landing (355.5 RM)

Aberdeen Lock and Dam

(Proposed Donald G. Waldon L/D)

Location: Monroe Co. Aberdeen, Mississippi (357.5 RM)

Construction start: April 1975

Open for navigation: January 1985

Lock lift: 27 feet

Construction cost: $44.7 million

Prime contractors: Granite Const. Co. of CA, S.J. Graves & Sons Co. of IL

Corps' project engineers: John Bennett, George Baker, Al Wise, and Paul Perkins

Lake impoundment: 8,910 acres

Bridge relocations: U.S. Hwy 278 (368.4 RM), BNSF Railroad (369.9 RM), MS Hwy 6 (370.1 RM)

Commercial activity: Amory Port/ Ind. Park (369-370 RM)

Recreation development: Blue Bluff (359 RM), Aberdeen Marina (359 RM), Acker Lake (361. RM), Becker Bottom (364.0 RM)

Thad Cochran Lock

Location: Monroe Co., Amory, MS (371 RM)

Construction start: March 1977

Open for navigation: January 1985

Lock lift: 30 feet

Construction cost: $23.3 million

Prime contractor: Al Johnson Const, Co. of MN

Corps' project engineers: Billy Parks and Leo Phillps

Lake impoundment: 914 acres

Bridge relocations: None

Commercial activities: None

Recreation development: Amory (371.5 RM)

Glover Wilkins Lock
Location: Monroe Co. near Smithville, MS (376 RM)
Construction start: January 1978
Open for navigation: January 1985
Lock lift: 25 feet
Construction cost: $33.5 million
Prime contractor: Arundel Corp. of Maryland
Corps' project engineers: Billy Parks and Leo Phillips
Lake impoundment: 718 acres
Bridge relocations: I-22 (U.S. Hwy 78) (389.6 RM), Mississippi Railroad (only trackage)
Commercial activities: Smithville Marina, Port Itawamba
Recreation development: Smithville (376.3 RM), Bean Ferry (387 RM)

Fulton Lock
Location: Itawamba Co., Fulton, MS (391 RM)
Construction start: October 1978
Open for navigation: January 1985
Lock lift: 25 feet
Construction cost: $28.3 million
Prime contractor: Blount International of AL
Corps' project engineers: Albert Lee and Jerry Bruce
Lake impoundment: 1,643 acres
Bridge relocations: none
Commercial activities: Midway Marina (393.8 RM)
Recreation development: Old U.S. Hwy 78 (392 RM), Whitten Historical Center (393 RM), Fulton Campground (393 RM)

John Rankin Lock
Location: Itawamba Co., MS (398.4 RM)
Construction start: December 1980
Open for navigation: January 1985
Lock lift: 30 feet
Construction cost: $43.9 million
Prime contractor: Blount International Ltd. of AL
Corps' project engineers: John Bennett, Barney Davis, and Harry Stone
Lake Impoundment: 1,992 acres

Bridge relocations: None
Commercial activities: None
Recreation development: Beaver Lake (399.9 RM), Walker's Bridge (403.2 RM)

G.V. "Sonny" Montgomery Lock
Location: Itawamba Co., MS (406.7 RM)
Construction start: April 1981
Open for navigation: January 1985
Lock lift: 30 feet
Construction cost: $47.3 million
Prime contractor: Granite Const. Co. of CA
Corps' project engineers: John Bennett and Barney Davis
Lake impoundment: 851 acres
Bridge relocations: Natchez Trace (410.8), MS Hwy 4 (411.8 RM)
Commercial activity: Cooper terminal (411 RM)
Recreation development: Saucer Creek (407.2 RM)

Jamie Whitten Lock and Dam
Location: Tishomingo Co., MS
Construction start: April 1979
Open for navigation: January 1985
Lock lift: 84 feet
Construction cost: $74.4 million
Prime contractor: Al Johnson Const. Co of MN
Corps' project engineers: (See Divide Cut List)
Lake impoundment: 6,600 acres
Bridge relocations: None
Commercial activities: Bay Springs Marina (413 RM)
Recreation development: Bay Springs Visitor Center, Cotton Springs, Old Bridge Beach. West Damsite, Gin Branch, Bayberry Access, Piney Grove, McDougal Branch, Crows Neck Environmental Education Center, Crow's Neck Access, Paden Access

Divide Cut
Location: Tishomingo Co., MS
Description: 29-mile canal from Bay Springs Lake (Hwy 30) to Pickwick Lake, created by excavating 150 million cubic yards of material, more

than that dug for the Suez Canal.

Dimensions: Navigation channel: 12 feet deep by 280 feet wide

Construction start: April 1974

Open for navigation: January 1985

Construction cost: $486 million

Prime contractors: Martin K. Eby Co. of Kansas, Peter Kiewit and Sons, Inc. of NE, Harbert Const. Co. of AL, Universal Construction Co. of GA, Tenn-Tom Contractors (joint venture, Brown & Root, Martin K. Eby, and Morrison-Knudson Inc.)

Corps' project engineers: Dan Hall, Bill McGraw, Jerry Rainer, J.C. McDaniels, George Brunner, Clyde Orr, Tommy Haskins, Joe Orr, Josie Buckner, Hoyt Holder, Tony Crow, Odie Curtis, Danny, Enoch Knight, Frank Cope, John Hart, Carl Mallow, Neil Schilling, and Johnny Wilmore

Bridge relocations: MS Hwy 30 (421.9 RM), ICG Railroad (424.8 RM), U.S. Hwy 72 (435.3 RM), MS Hwy 25 (443.4 RM)

Commercial activities: N.E. Mississippi Industrial Park (434 RM), Yellow Creek Port (448.3 RM), Barge fleeting (447.6 RM), Goat Island Marina, Aqua Boat Harbor, Grand Harbor

Recreation development: Divide Overlook, Holcut Memorial Park, Burnsville Access Area, Little Yellow Ck Fishing Area, Doskie Fishing Area, Robinson Creek, Scrugg's Bridge

Compiled with assistance of the Tennessee-Tombigbee Waterway Development Authority

APPENDIX B

Tennessee-Tombigbee Waterway Development Authority

The authority is a four-state, interstate compact enacted by the U.S. Congress and ratified by President Eisenhower in 1958 to promote the development of the waterway and its economic and trade potential. Its membership is composed of the governors of the states of Alabama, Kentucky, Mississippi, and Tennessee and five appointees from each state. Funded entirely by the member states, the authority devotes its resources to address any impediments that might affect the waterway's ability to generate its expected benefits to the region and nation. Florida was a member of the waterway compact from 1967 until 1990.

Officers (Listed First is Chairman, Followed by Vice Chairman)
    1958: Gov. Jim Folsom (AL); Louis Wise (MS)
    1959: Gov. John Patterson (AL); Louis Wise (MS)
    1960: Gov. John Patterson (AL); Louis Wise (MS)
    1961: Colonel Gil Dorland (TN); Louis Wise (MS)
    1962: Gov. John Patterson (AL); Louis Wise (MS)
    1963: Gov. Ross Barnett (MS); Col. Gil Dorland (TN)
    1964: Gov. Frank Clement (TN); Gov. Bert Combs (KY)
    1965: Ed Paxton (KY); Rankin Fite (AL)
    1966: Rankin Fite (AL); Dr. Frank Davis (MS)
    1967: Gov. Paul Johnson; Kenneth Woods (TN)
    1968: Gov. Buford Ellington (TN); Kenneth Woods (TN)
    1969: Gov. Louie B. Nunn (KY); Walter Reichert (KY)
    1970: Gov. Louie Nunn (KY): Albert Brewer (AL)
    1971: Gov. George Wallace (AL); Doyle Connor (FL)
    1972: Gov. George Wallace (AL); Doyle Connor (FL)
    1973: Gov. Winfield Dunn (TN); Jack Draper (TN)
    1974: Gov. Bill Waller (MS); Thomas Keenum (MS)
    1975: Gov. George Wallace (AL); Thomas Keenum (MS)
    1976: Gov. Ray Blanton (TN); Thomas Keenum (MS)
    1977: Gov. George Wallace (AL); Gene Blanton (TN)
    1978: Gov. Julian Carroll (KY); Z.C. Enix (KY)

1979: Gov. Cliff Finch (MS); David Shelton (MS)
1980: Gov. Lamar Alexander (TN); James A. Skinner (TN)
1981: Gov. Fob James (AL); Richard S. Manley (AL)
1982: Gov. John Y. Brown; Redwood Taylor (KY)
1983: Gov. William Winter (MS); James Loudermilk (FL)
1984: Gov. George Wallace (AL); Fuller Kimbrell (AL)
1985: Gov. Martha Layne Collins; Z.C. Enix (KY)
1986: Gov. Bill Allain (MS); Bennie Turner (MS)
1987: Gov. Ned McWherter (TN); David Landreth (TN)
1988: Gov. Guy Hunt (AL); Richard Manley (AL)
1989: Gov. Wallace Wilkinson (KY); Z.C. Enix (KY)
1990: Gov. Bob Martinez (FL); Jim Loudermilk/D. Connor (FL)
1991: Gov. Ray Mabus (MS); Z. Enix (KY)/C. Epperson (MS)
1992: Gov. Ned McWherter (TN); Richard Holcombe (TN)
1993: Gov. Guy Hunt (AL); Allen Layson (AL)
1994: Gov. Kirk Fordice (MS); Ray Gore (MS)
1995: Gov. Brereton Jones (KY); Brian Roy (KY)
1996: Gov. Don Sundquist (TN); David Long (TN)
1997: Gov. Fob James (AL); W.H. Borders (AL)
1998: Gov. Kirk Fordice (MS); T.L. Phillips (MS)
1999: Gov. Paul Patton (KY); Will Shadoan (KY)
2000: Gov. Don Sundquist (TN); John Bennett (TN)
2001: Gov. Don Siegelman (AL); Bruce Windham (AL)
2002: Gov. Ronnie Musgrove (MS); Bill Renick (MS)
2003: Gov. Paul Patton (KY); Mike Miller (KY)
2004: Gov. Phil Bredesen (TN); David Dickey (TN)
2005: Gov. Bob Riley (AL); Bruce Windham (AL)
2006: Gov. Haley Barbour (MS); Nick Ardillo (MS)
2007: Gov. Earnest Fletcher (KY); Ken Wheeler (KY)
2008: Gov. Phil Bredesen (TN); Joe Barker (TN)
2009: Gov. Bob Riley (AL); Robert Barnett (AL)
2010: Gov. Haley Barbour (MS); Charlie Williams (MS)
2011: Gov. Steve Beshear (KY); Mike Miller (KY)
2012: Gov. Bill Haslam (TN); Jason Rich (TN)
2013: Gov. Robert Bentley (AL); Ross Gunnells (AL)

2014: Gov. Phil Bryant (MS); Nick Ardillo (MS)
2015: Gov. Steve Beshear (KY); Brian Roy (KY)
2016: Gov. Bill Haslam (TN); Jason Rich (TN)
2017: Gov. Robert Bentley (AL); Horace Horn (AL)
2018: Gov. Phil Bryant (MS); Dale Pierce (MS)
2019: Gov. Matt Bevin (KY); Kenny Imes (KY)
2020: Gov. Bill Lee (TN); Dan Pallme (KY)
2021: Gov. Kay Ivey (AL); Martha Stokes (AL)
2022: Gov. Tate Reeves (MS); Mike Armour (MS)
2023: Gov. Andy Beshear (KY); John McConnell (KY)
2024: Gov. Bill Lee (TN); Dan Pallme (TN)
2025: Gov. Kay Ivey (AL); Horace Horn (AL)

Administrator/ Secretary
W.H. Drinkard (September 1958–January 1962)
Glover Wilkins (November 1062–June 1984)
Donald G. Waldon (July 1984-June 2005)
Bobby "Doc" Roberson (July–August 2005)
Thomas Griffith (March 2006–November 2007)
Mike Tagert (January 2008–January 2011)
Bruce Windham (March 2011–October 2014)
Craig Stephan (February 2015–March 2016)
Mitchell Mays (June 2016–current)

APPENDIX C

Tennessee-Tombigbee Waterway Development Council

The Council was established in 1984 as a non-profit 501(c)3 trade association to serve as the medium for public and private interests concerned with the operation and development of the waterway. Although chartered by the Tenn-Tom Waterway Authority, the council is autonomous and is governed by a board of directors and officers duly elected from its membership. The council complements the authority as a forum for the wide range of interests in the waterway and its impacts, including commercial navigation, trade and commerce, industrial development, recreation, and tourism. To help ensure closer cooperation between the two groups, the authority's administrator serves as the council's president.

Officers

1985–1986: President: Don Waldon; Charman: T.L. "Bud" Phillips, Phillips Contracting, Inc., Columbus, MS

1987–1988: President: Don Waldon; Chairman: Tim Parker, Jr., Parker Towing, Inc., Tuscaloosa, AL

1989–1990: President: Don Waldon; Chairman: W.R. "Ron" Coles, W.R. Coles & Associates, Nashville, TN

1991–1992: President: Don Walton; Chairman: Dovell Haley, Monsanto Chemical Co., Decatur, AL

1993–1994: President: Don Waldon; Chairman: Walter Stevenson, Alabama Department of Economicand Community Affairs, Montgomery, AL

1995–1996: President: Don Waldon; Chairman: Hon. Thomas Griffith, Mayor of Amory, MS

1997–1998: President: Don Waldon; Chairman: Wayne Meunier, McCracken Co. Port Authority, Paducah KY

1999–2000: President: Don Waldon; Chairman: Ken Stacy, International Paper Co., Prattville, AL

2001–2002: President: Don Waldon; Chairman: Dr. Don Hines, Alabama Department of Economic and Community Affairs, Montgomery, AL

2003-2004: President: Don Waldon; Chairman: Dean White, Foss Maritime, Inc., Seattle, WA

2005–2006: President: Don Waldon; Chairman: Eugene Bishop, Yellow Creek Port Authority, Iuka, MS

2007–2008: President: Thomas Griffith; Chairman: Steve Alley, Ingram Barge Co., Nashville, TN

2009–2010: President; Thomas Griffith; Chairman: Tim Weston, Tennessee Valley Authority, Tupelo, MS

2011–2012: President: Bruce Windham; Chairman: Fred Hansard, Demopolis Yacht Basin, Demopolis, AL

2013–2014: President: Bruce Windham; Chairman: Ken Canter, McCracken Co. Port Authority, Paducah, KY

2015–2016: President: Mitch Mays; Chairman: Lucian Lott, Parker Towing Co., Tuscaloosa, AL

2017–2018: President: Mitch Mays; Chairman: Stephen Surles, TVA, Nashville, TN

2019–2020: President: Mitch Mays; Chairman: Kevin Stafford, Neel Schaffer, Inc., Columbus, MS

2021–2022: President: Mitch Mays; Chairman: Josh Tubbs, Kentucky Lake Economic Development, Benton, KY

2023–2024: President: Mitch Mays; Chairman: Mike Williams, Westervelt Renewable Energy, Tuscaloosa, AL

2025: President: Mitch Mays; Chairman: Will Sanders, Lowndes Co. Port Authority, Columbus, MS

APPENDIX D

U.S. Army Corps of Engineers
Mobile District

Employees Who Contributed Much To Tenn-Tom's Success
District Office
District Engineers: Brigadier General Harry Griffith; Colonel Drake Wilson; Colonel Charlie Blalock; Colonel Robert Ryan; and Colonel Patrick Kelly. Cathy Rees and Les Currie.

Engineering Division
Frank Deming, Fred Thompson, Gus Baer, Harry Lawson, Leon Cromartie, Harvey Blakeney, Ray Gustin, Mike McKown, Trent Toland, Hal Gates, Jim Gibson, Mike Nettles, Jack Granade, George Poiroux, Fred Robeson, Fred Lewter, Jack Ward, Tom Groce, Gene Wyatt, Carvel Deese, Frank Sigler, George Rogers, Rudy Danis, Jim Jordan, John Drago, Ed Burkett, Don Graham, Kenny Underwood, Bud Cronenberg, Jack Bryan, Sid Bufkin, Richard Bonner, Howard Whittington, George Atkins, Alan Kerr, Janie Wood, Mike Thompson, Joseph Lamar, Brad Flott, Wendell Mears, Joe Ellsworth , John Mc Fayden, Ed McLaurin, George Rogers, Wayne Odom; Bill Gwin; and, Dick Kimbrough

Planning Division
Larry Green, N.D. McClure, John Rushing, Joe Birrindelli, Glen Coffee, Curtis Flakes, Emanual Drago, Florence Southall, Bill Ruland, Don Conlon, Hugh McClellan, Tommy Lightcap, David Luckie, Brian Peck, Don Chatelain, Betty Vickery, Dot Joseph, Mike Eubanks, Ken Sims, Jack Mallory, Jerry Nielsen, Charles Moorehead, Bob Watson, Kenneth Pope, Keith Graham, John Bowen, James Harris, Dottie Gibbens, Lynn Bradford, Glenda Smith, Ernie Seckinger, Bruce Thornton, Charles Owen, Neil Robinson, Sissy Scott, Stephen Carter, Bill Greenlee, Henry Malec, Chamaigne Bell, Diane Findley, Phyllis Bruce, Dewayne Imsand, Roger Burke.

Construction Division
On-site
Area Engineers: Freddie Jones and Nick Moon; Assistant Area Engineer Jack Alford
Heflin Lock and Dam
Harold Mullins, John Bennett, George Baker
Bevill Lock and Dam
L.E. Bridges, Norman Connell, Terry Jangula
Stennis Lock and Dam
Albert Lee, Alan Bugg, and Army Captain Carl Strock, who later advanced to the rank of Lt. General and Commander of the Corps
Aberdeen Lock and Dam
John Bennett, George Baker, Al Wise, Paul Perkins
Cochran Lock
Billy Parks, Leo Phillips, Dennis Newell
Wilkins Lock
Billy Parks, Leo Phillips
Fulton Lock
Albert Lee, Jerry Bruce, and James Hannon, who later became head of Operations Division at Corps headquarters
Rankin Lock
John Bennett, Barney Davis, Harry Stone
Montgomery Lock
John Bennett, Barney Davis
District Office
Cleon Moore, Dan Burns, Joe Smith

Real Estate Division
Melvin Dovith, Herman Weiss, Joe Hewell, Tommie Pierce, Joe Wilson, Larry Beale, Joe Abbot, Lex Lawrence, Bo Lewis, John Croley, Don Burchett, Jimmy Ratcliff, Joe Givhan, Ashford Kettler

Programs
Vernon Holmes, Jeff Tidmore, Ted Love

Contracting
Jim Campbell, Leo Hickman, Ed Slana, Jimmy Smith, Patsy Newell

Counsel
Alfred Holmes, David Webb, Joe Gonzalez, Tom Burt, Debbie Shoemake

Operations Division
Norman Connell, Erwin Topper, Doug Blount, Rick Saucer, Roger Gerth, Nelson Sanchez, John Anderson, Jim Meredith, Al Wise

Public Affairs
Sam Green, Doris Green, Pat Robbins

Litigation Support Unit
Norma Sue Beech, Sharon Ali

Operations Project Managers
Justin Murphree (2018–Present)
Rick Saucer (2006–2018)
Al Wise (1997–2006)
Norman Connell (1979–1997)

List compiled with assistance from N.D. "Skeeter" McClure, Al Wise, and Wynne Fuller

APPENDIX E

Nashville District Corps of Engineers
Employees Who Contributed Much to Tenn-Tom's Success*
District Engineers
Colonel William Brandes, Colonel Henry "Hank" Hatch, Colonel Robert Tener, Colonel Lee Tucker, Colonel William Kirkpatrick, and Colonel Edward Starbird

Deputy District Engineers
Major Ralph Danielson, Major David Dean and Major Scott Graves

Engineering
E.C. Moore, Jimmy Bates, Mike Wilson, Herman Gray, Jack Hoffmeister, Rick Connor, Dennis Williams, Hank Phillips, Bob Sneed, Tom Porter, Tommy Allen, Will Forte, Jim McClellan, Steve Eli, Brad Hoot, Jesse Perry, Mickey Sullivan, Jerry Brown, Bert England, Moe Powell, Buddy Abbott, John Hall, Connie Flatt, Ken Ingram, Ben Couch, Jim Paris, Mike Zoccola, Tim McCleskey, Marvin Simmons, Joe Melnyk, Emily Carr, Paul Bluhm, Wayne Swartz, Jody Stanton, Tom Lerner, Andy Guinn, Doug Webb, Ruben Buttery, Kenneth Whitley, Don Reddick, Taylor Cooper, Tony Chapman, Preston (Putt) Smith, A.W. Bess, Wayne Thompson, Doug Jackson, Dalton McCrary, Elva Soapes, Larry Lampley, Don Kranz, Steve Duncan, Harold Dyer, Bill Odom, Bill Hund, Phil Mitchell, Bill Fisher, Jim Deal, Gary Stinson, Bob Bowles, Bill Vecchione, Bill Gray, Guy Rochelle, Barney Johnson, Walter Green, Gordon McClellan, Jim Caulder, James Gunnels, Ed Lockett, Joe Serena, Charlie Anderson, Carl Durrett, Foster Hudson, Tim Rochelle, Tom McGee, Gene Short, Henry Dahlinger, Bobby Ezell, Harold Seymour, Carl Nelms, Hugh Lowe, Don Kranz, Jimmy Morrissey, Mary Robillard, Bill Tuggle, Niles Peterson, Jack Baker, Tong Haw, Francis "Hammer" Haynes, Hoyt Burge, Ron Utley, Chuck Hallford, Terry Collins, Joe Cathey, Danny Olinger, Cathy Ganzel, Ray Hedrick, Rob Karwedsky, Jeff Linkinhoker, Vechere' Lampley, O.B. Meadors, "Digger" Drake, James Simmons, Albert Regg, Garland Cash, and Frank Tacker

Planning
Cliff Reinert, Gene Ottinger, Harry Blazek, Bob Byington, Bob Bailey, Doug Radley, Cynthia Drew, Mitch Overend, Ira Blankenship, Judy Kenyon, Brent Smith, Jack Kepler, and Phil Pierce

Construction
On-site: Bill McGraw, Dan Hall, J.C. McDaniels, Jerry Rainer, George Brunner, Clyde Orr, Tommy Haskins, Josie Buckner, Hoyt Holder, Odie Curtis, Tony Crow, Danny Crow, Enoch A. (Snag) Knight, Frank Cope, John Hart, Neil Schilling, and Carl Mallow, Dan Riggs, John Mindock, George Laughlin

District Office: A.C. Bogaty, Dick Russell, Bob Thomas, Bob Hampton, Johnny Wilmore, Tom Pirkle, Ces Dodson, Wiley Sam Isom, Joe Orr, Oneida Orr, Royce Collins, Jim Baber, Ben Hawkins, Winford Daniels, John Guyton, and Tommy McReynolds

Real Estate
On-site: Bob Baker, Bill Christian, Harry Short, D. Ray Ammonette, Bill Stahl, Pete Jones, and Homer McKay

District Office: Jordan Antle, Charlie Hooper, Charlie Hayes, A. J. Reed, Perry Sweet, Bill Barnes, John Miller, Janie Billingsley, Jay Neely, Shirley Overby, Johnny Rice, John Coleman, David Wilburn, Ron Frazier, Don Burchett, Jeanette Mandigo, Diane Clark Siburt, Bess Bryan, Sam Roark, and Robert Strobe

Programs
Bill Eastland, Tom Cayce, Jim Goad, and Mary Jane Connor

Contracting
Lacy Campbell, Hobart Parrish, and Marie Gish

Counsel
Robert Smyth, Bob Miller, and Fred Shelton

ADP
Sam Bradley, John Lambrecht, Wayne Abernathy, and J.D. Eden

Operations
Jackie Vied and Stephan Hurst

Public Affairs Office
Darrell Armstrong, Donna Willett, and Stony Merriman

Audio/Visual Support
George Green, Lynn Bowden, Janis Clark, and Sherrie Overton
Administrative – EEO Office
Melvin Evans

List compiled with the assistance of Tom Cayce and Mike Wilson

Index

Symbols

1-888-TENNTOM 280

Aberdeen Lock and Dam 130–131, 131
Aberdeen, Mississippi 84, 229, 288, 292, 293, 313–314
Abernathy, Thomas 41, 44, 234
AFL-CIO 193, 216, 218
Alabama Department of Conservation and Natural Resources 282
Alabama-Tombigbee Rivers Coalition 262–263
Alaska Natives Claims Settlement Act 112
Álvarez, Luis Escheverria 96
Alyeska Pipeline Service Company 112
America's Great Loop 281
Andrus, Cecil 172–173
Arkansas River 224, 291
Arkansas River Navigation Project 186
Association of American Railroads (AAR) 175, 192
Association of General Contractors (AGC) 193
Atlantic-Pacific Interoceanic Canal Commission 61
Atomic Energy Commission (AEC) 60, 61, 61–64

Bay Springs Lake 135–136
Bay Springs Lock and Dam 233. See also Jamie Whitten Lock and Dam
Bear Creek 10, 43, 63
benefit-to-cost ratio (BCR) 43, 181, 181–183
Bevill, Tom 197, 201, 201–207, 210, 219–220, 241, 244, 245–247, 251, 272, 278–279, 284
Birindelli, Joe 276–277
Black Warrior River 10, 258
Black Warrior-Tombigbee Waterway (BWT) 183, 188, 206, 217, 230, 267, 267–269, 308
Blackwelder, Brent 192, 198, 312
Bowen, David 155, 259
Brown and Root, Inc. 136
Brownell, Herbert 93, 96–97
Bureau of Indian Affairs 119

Bureau of Land Management (BLM) 107, 107–108, 110, 115–116
Bureau of Reclamation (BuRec) 15, 42, 58, 87–88, 93, 101, 116–118, 162
Bureau of the Budget (BOB) 28–38, 41, 56, 57–60, 66–67, 69–70. See also Office of Management and Budget (OMB)
Burgin, Bill 43, 46, 82, 168
Butcher, Jake 169–171
Buttahatchee River 208, 258

Callahan, Sonny 246, 272–273
Carroll, Julian 170–171, 173, 242
Carter, Jimmy 60, 106, 159–174, 176, 186, 191–192, 260
Center for Biological Diversity 259
Chain of Lakes (Canal) Section 133–135, 189
Cherokee Nation 256
Cheyenne River Sioux 118–120
Clean Air Act 298
Clean Water Act 194, 252
Coalition of Alabama Waterway Associations 310
Cochran, Thad 154–157, 199, 214, 234, 314
Coleman, J.P. 42–46, 234
Colorado River 15, 87, 89, 92–93, 96–97
Columbus Lock and Dam 236. See also John C. Stennis Lock and Dam
Committee for Leaving the Environment Natural (CLEAN) 81–82, 175
Congressional Budget and Impoundment Control Act 70
Connor, Doyle 51, 306
Copeland, Al 113–114
Corinth, Mississippi 46, 176, 286
Council on Environmental Quality 71, 76, 162
Crabill, Don 95
Cross Florida Barge Canal 50, 55, 72–73, 75, 81–82, 218, 305
CSX Railroad 76, 163, 175, 187, 192, 298. See also Louisville and Nashville (L&N) Railroad

Dakota Access Pipeline 120
Dawson, Robert K. 34, 272, 310, 315
Department of Energy 60, 61, 64, 100, 186

JOURNEY TO THE RIVER 337

Development Opportunities Conference 225–229
Divide Cut 63–64, 135–136, 141–142, 250
Divide Section 186, 233, 241, 253
Dolive, Bill 22, 28, 32, 38
Donald G. Waldon Lock and Dam 313–314

Eastland, John 44, 83–84, 155, 176–178
E&D. See also engineering and design
Edelman, Les 180–181
Edwards, Jack 74, 77, 199, 211, 234, 246, 272
endangered species 255–265
Endangered Species Act 71, 155, 252, 255
Energy and Water Development Appropriations Bill 194, 216
Energy and Water Development Appropriations Subcommittee 195, 212, 246, 272
engineering and design 56, 74
Environmental Defense Fund (EDF) 72, 81–82, 175–176, 187, 192, 194–195, 198
Environmental Impact Statement (EIS) 72, 76, 84, 112, 169, 178, 188–189
Environmental Policy Center (EPC) 192, 198, 213
Environmental Protection Agency (EPA) 71, 101
Epperson, E.C. "Cookie" 287, 300

Federal Advisory Committee Act (FACA) 263
Federal Aid Highway Act 156
Finch, Cliff 163–167, 170–171
Flint River 161
Ford, Gerald 100, 106, 116, 120, 156, 159–160
Fordice, Kirk 193
Fort Tombecbe 9
Fuller, Wynne 11, 269, 315

Gholson, Hunter 82, 176, 178, 180–181, 189, 257
Gillham Dam 81–82
Glass, Frank 278–279, 284
Glover Wilkins Lock (B) 134
"God Squad" 260–261
Golden Knights 243–244
Grant, Ulysses S. 9, 30
Griffin, Robert 269–270, 315
Gulf Coast 9, 271–272, 278
Gulf Intracoastal Waterway 50, 292, 307
Gulf of Mexico 27, 110, 239

Haley, Alex 225
Harrison, Esther 148

Hathaway, Stanley 120–121
Hayes, Dewayne 237
Heflin, Howell 85, 198, 204, 213–214, 217, 246
Heiberg, Elvin "Vlad" 186–187, 189, 241
Holmes, Vernon 129–130
Hoover Dam 88–89
Horton, Jack 102, 105–107, 118, 121–122, 123–125, 127
Howell Heflin Lock and Dam (L/D) 130

Inland Ports Act 285
Intergovernmental Personnel Act (IPA) 124, 160
International Boundary Water Commission (IBWC) 58

Jamie Whitten Lock and Dam 135, 135–138, 278. See also Bay Springs Lock and Dam
John C. Stennis Lock and Dam 130–131. See also Columbus Lock and Dam
John Rankin Lock (D) 134
Johnson, Lyndon 31, 34, 36–37, 50, 53, 55–56, 66, 72, 74, 105, 146, 152, 182
Jordan, James 214, 216

Keady, William 84, 176–179, 182–189, 313
Kelly, Pat 221, 265–267
Kennedy, John F. 22, 50, 55, 72–73, 215
Kissinger, Henry 69, 93, 95–96
Kroh, Egil 95–96

Lance, Bert 170–171
League of Women Voters 192, 213
LeTellier, Carroll 129, 153
Levin Amendment 217
Limited Test Ban Treaty 62
Logistic Services, Inc. 290
Lott, Trent 154–155, 155, 199, 202, 211, 219, 236, 254
Loudermilk, James 51, 306
Louisville and Nashville (L&N) Railroad 49, 76, 163, 175–177, 192–193, 195, 198, 298. See also CSX Railroad

Mabus, Ray 287
Manchin, Joe 282–283
Margorie Harris Carr Cross Florida Greenway 73
Martin K. Eby Construction Company 136
Mays, Mitch 11, 12, 228, 300
McClellan-Kerr Waterway 186, 291, 304
media attacks 294–297

Merchant Marine and Fisheries Committee 155, 259
Metcalf, Neil 42–43, 43, 45–47, 303
Miami International Boat Show 281
Michener, James A. 226
Minority Peoples Council (MPC) 147
Mississippi River 64, 201, 224, 274, 292, 307
Mississippi State University (MSU) 14–15, 81–83, 291, 299
Mississippi University for Women 82, 168
Missouri River 42, 116–118, 117, 118
Mobile, Alabama 7, 13, 77, 79, 237
Mobile District (MDO) 15–17, 27–28, 76, 83, 129–133, 149, 167, 189, 217, 235, 249, 251–252, 255, 265–270, 272–273, 276, 315
Montgomery, Sonny 155, 247
Morgan, Sheldon 262, 269
Morris, Jack 162, 186–187
Morrison-Knudson Corporation 136
Morton, Rogers 101, 106
M/V Mississippi 233, 239, 247
M/V Montgomery 251–252, 296
Myers, John 207, 234, 272

Nashville District (NDO) 47, 129–130, 135–136, 139–140, 142, 149, 186, 233, 250, 253
National Campaign to Stop the Tenn-Tom 183
National Environmental Policy Act (NEPA) 71–72, 75–76, 81–82, 84–85, 101, 116, 186, 252
National Waterways Conference Inc. (NWC) 214–215
Navaho 119
Nelson, Gaylord 194–196
Nevada Test Site (NTS) 61–63
Nixon, Richard M. 10, 59, 67, 69–79, 93, 96–97, 100–102, 103, 105, 108, 112, 124, 146, 155–156, 159–160, 182, 191–192, 194, 235, 245, 266, 305
Norfolk Southern Railroad (NSR) 193

Oahe Dam 119–120
Obama, Barack 120, 308, 314
Office of Management and Budget (OMB) 29, 70, 74–76, 87, 89–92, 95–96, 99–103, 105–106, 109, 117, 121, 123–124, 162, 170, 265–266, 272. See also Bureau of the Budget (BOB)
Office of Saline Water (OSW) 94
Ohio River Division 129, 186

OMB 70
operation and maintenance (O&M) 20, 134, 246, 265
Oppenheimer, J. Robert 63

perched canal 133
Philadelphia Plan 146
Pick, Lewis 42, 117
Pickwick Lake 135–136, 200
Planning, Programing, and Budgeting System 69
Plowshare 61–64
Prime Time Alive 295
"Project Independence" 108–110
Public Works and Transportation Committee 155–156

Quantum Fund 227

Rankin, John 23, 41, 134
R&D Maintenance Services Inc. (R&DM) 267–270
Reagan, Ronald 34, 59–60, 101, 159, 174, 199–201, 218, 241, 245, 272, 309
Red River Waterway 34, 148, 162, 295–297, 307
R.F. Henry Lock and Dam 264
River Section 130–132, 189, 249
Rogers, Jim 37, 101, 227–228
Roose, John "Jack" 29, 31, 33–34, 57, 67

Sasaki, Wes 72, 99–100
Satterfield, Bill 11, 258–260, 262–263, 310
Sawhill, John 60, 100
Schultze, Charles 59–60
Sonny Montgomery Lock 134
South Atlantic Division (SAD) 129, 153, 179, 186, 235, 269
Sprewell Bluff 161
Standing Rock 119–120
Stennis, John 35, 41, 44, 74, 155, 196–197, 207, 210, 212–216, 218, 220, 234, 251, 289
Stine, Jeffrey K. 11
Swartz, Carl 36, 62

Teller, Edward 63–64
Tellico Dam 256–257, 259–261
Tennessee-Tombigbee Affirmative Action Committee (TTAAC) 147–148
Tennessee-Tombigbee Waterway Development Council 228–229, 283, 291
Tenn-Tom Constructors 136, 139

Thad Cochran Lock (A) 134
Tofani, Joe 29–30
Tom Bevill Lock and Dam 130–131, 251,
    295–296
  Visitors Center 296
Tom Soya Grain 285, 287–288, 290
Tozzi, Jim 34–35
Trans-Alaskan Pipeline 111–112
Trico Steel, Inc. (now Nucor Steel) 280
Trinity River 34–37, 152
Trump, Donald 120
TRVWMD 176, 185

U.S. Fish and Wildlife Service (FWS) 252–253,
    255–264

Wallace, George 45, 55, 73–74, 77–79, 160,
    170–171, 234–236, 242, 246
Warrior-Tombigbee Waterway 130, 183, 217,
    230, 262, 264
Water Resources Council 102
Water Resources Development Act of 1986 147,
    254
Water Resources Subcommittee 197, 200
Waverly Plantation 288
Waxler Towing, Inc. 230
Whitaker, John 71, 100–103, 106, 160
Whitten, Jamie 41, 74, 135, 154, 156–157,
    191, 196–197, 200, 211, 219,
    233–234, 239, 247, 312
Wicker, Roger 134, 202, 211, 314
Wild Horses and Burros Act 115
Wilkins, Glover 44–48, 51, 58–59, 82, 82–83,
    123–127, 142, 169, 172, 180, 191,
    208, 214–215, 221, 234, 241, 260, 305
Williams, Jason D. 227
Winter, William 208, 234
WRDA Bill 196

Yellow Creek 64, 139, 285–286, 290, 330

Zaiontz, Agnes 239, 284, 316

About The Author

Donald G. Waldon was employed by the Tennessee-Tombigbee Waterway Development Authority for 30 years, 21 years as its administrator. Since retirement, he has continued to serve as one of the gubernatorial appointed members of the authority, representing the State of Alabama. Prior to joining the four-state interstate compact, he was a deputy assistant secretary of the U.S. Department of Interior during the Ford Administration and was a principal budget examiner in the Office of Management and Budget of the Executive Office of the President during the Johnson and Nixon Administrations. A registered civil engineer, he began his career as a water resources planner with the U.S. Army Corps of Engineers. He led some important state and national organizations that promote the nation's water transportation system, including being elected as U.S. Commissioner to the Permanent International Association of Navigation Congresses, headquartered in Belgium. After retirement, he was awarded the Department of the Army's Outstanding Civilian Service Medal and the Army Engineer Association's prestigious Silver Order of the de Fleury Medal. In 2014, the U.S. Congress designated the lock and dam on the Tenn-Tom at Aberdeen, MS as the Donald G. Waldon Lock and Dam in appreciation of his contributions.

www.ingramcontent.com/pod-product-compliance
Lightning Source LLC
Chambersburg PA
CBHW020048170426
43199CB00009B/208